EXPAND YOUR SPANISH

LINDA HALL DE GONZÁLEZ

SANTANA BOOKS

EXPAND YOUR SPANISH
Is published by
Ediciones Santana S.L.,
Apartado 422, Fuengirola 29640 (Málaga), Spain.
Tel. 952 485 838. Fax 952 485 367.
E-mail: info@santanabooks.com
www.santanabooks.com

First published 1994
Reprinted 1996
Second Edition 2004

Copyright © 2004 Linda Hall de Gonzalez
Illustrations by Maggy Young
Design by Chris Fajardo

Printed and bound in Spain by
Gráficas San Pancracio S.L.
Polígono Industrial San Luis, Málaga.

Depósito Legal: MA-579/2004
ISBN: 84-89954-31-3

ABOUT THE AUTHOR

Linda Hall was born on Canvey Island, Essex, in 1944. She received a typically average education and later, she says, worked at typically average jobs she was thus suited for. In 1968, she came to Spain where she met and married Andrés González, a painter. For the past 16 years she has been a regular contributor to newspapers and magazines in Spain. The first edition of *Expand your Spanish* was based on a popular weekly column she wrote for a Costa Blanca newspaper. Her interests include cats, English and Spanish literature, music, cats, good food and wine, cats, art and cats. She has a grown-up daughter and now lives on the Costa Blanca with her husband and four cats.

CONTENTS

PART TWO
WATCH YOUR STEP ... 115

PART THREE
THERE'S NO PLACE LIKE IT ... 207

FILLING IN THE GAPS

If you have got as far as picking up this book, it's only fair to warn you straight away that it won't teach you Spanish. With a little luck it might help you learn it, though.

Someone asked me the other day why couldn't I write a book for absolute beginners? The answer, of course, is that teaching anything from scratch is a tremendous responsibility – rather like being an infants' teacher. I'm happier and more interested in helping to fill in some of the gaps.

If you have some grounding in the language – however ill-absorbed and poorly understood – so much the better. If you haven't but intend to learn Spanish, don't put this book down too quickly, because you should find that it anticipates queries and clears up points you're not too clear on. And if you haven't the slightest desire to learn Spanish, reading about some of the gaps could whet your appetite to find out about the bricks and mortar of the language, too.

How you go about learning once your formal education is completed must be your choice. Principally, it should be enjoyable and adapted to suit your needs, interests and temperament. Personally I believe that at some stage it's advisable to put your elbows on the table and get your nose in a book but not everyone learns or absorbs the same things in the same way. Some people play the piano by ear and others can learn a language by ear. The former might not be up to concert standard and the latter will never find employment as a simultaneous translator but that's not what they're after anyway – both simply want to make some sort of music or some sort of sense.

If you learnt a language or languages at school, particularly French and Latin, then you will have a head start, but if you didn't, that needn't be a drawback. Wanting to do something is halfway to getting there and if you are living in Spain then you already have a twenty-four-hour a day language tape playing in the background.

In the first edition of Expand Your Spanish I said that a Spanish partner was the best shortcut imaginable and I still don't think this can be improved on. Having small children at Spanish schools is equally effective, though, and once you entertain their friends and help with homework, you will find yourself learning without even trying.

... take a Spanish lover

The classic advice of watching Spanish television and videos, or reading Spanish books and magazines specialising in your interests continues to make sense. Read the Spanish press as well as an English-language daily: apart from the linguistic advantages you'll also profit from the different standpoint. And to that the computer-friendly can add Spanish websites and all the Spanish-language doors that Internet can open for you.

The best advice for anyone wanting to do something is simply to do it. Dive in and immerse yourself in Spanish. Without isolating yourself from your fellow-countrymen, mix with and speak to the Spanish as often as possible (although sometimes they will hinder you by wanting to practise their English).

A minimum investment in the Spanish language achieves maximum growth without your realising it, however modest your aspirations. Apart from anything else, another language is the key to understanding another people and another culture. Spanish, like Spain, is fascinating. It reflects the country's history just as much as its people, architecture and food – including *cocido madrileño* which I pretend to scorn but secretly love. Admitted, *cocido* might not be everyone's cup of tea but I promise you that a taste for the Spanish language is more satisfying to acquire and far easier to digest.

ESPAÑOL VERSUS CASTELLANO

It used to be argued that referring to Spanish as **castellano** was as inaccurate as describing Italian as Tuscan because modern Italian is based on what was spoken in Tuscany. Formerly, few saw any good reason for questioning the use of the word **español** to describe the Spanish language, but in my local bookshop I recently heard a Spanish customer remark, **"Lo quiero en español,"** only to be rebuked most amiably by the bookseller, **"En castellano, querrá decir."** The customer hastily admitted the error of his ways and amended his request to a chastened **"Claro, en castellano."** My own hissed and uninvited **"Español,"** was either unheard or ignored by both purchaser and vendor.

In the words of the old song, everybody's doing it and foreigners are especially fond of describing themselves as **castellano-parlantes** although thankfully few of them refer to **castellano** as **Castilian** in English.

Generally, the more widely-spoken and understood a bilingual Spanish region's second language – or principal language, it depends on your point of view – the easier it is to detect a desire to label Spanish as **castellano**.

Gallego, spoken in Galicia, is catching up fast on Spanish despite initial reluctance to speak it on the part of the middle and professional classes who formerly associated it with rural illiteracy and poverty. The Basques suffer fewer inhibitions. They are justly proud of their mysterious language although, until the transition to democracy after Franco's death in 1975, few understood it and fewer spoke it.

The languages spoken elsewhere in Iberia either allowed Latin to be superimposed upon them or can be directly traced to Latin. The end product of mutant Latin, plus contributions from later invaders and traders were, and still are, **castellano, catalán** and **gallego**. Some English-speakers, cheesed off at having learnt Spanish only to be confronted by something else, condescendingly refer to these other languages as dialects. This is also inaccurate because in Spain dialects are corruptions of the three basic languages, with a special mention for **leonés** and **aragonés** which didn't quite make the first division.

Once a language reaches other areas it tends to be recognised by name rather than identified by its birthplace. Whether it is identified as **Spanish, español** or **castellano,** an undeniable feature of Spain's language is that, like some wines, it has travelled well and far. It is only now, since arriving in the United States via Latin and Central America, that terms are getting out of line.

There have always been differences between the Spanish of Europe and Latin America, as there are between the English spoken in Britain, America, Australia or Africa. Sometimes variations have been a matter of vocabulary and shifting definitions or pronunciation, but what emerged was always intelligible and correct.

Formerly unacceptable transatlantic deviations are now accepted, so that **honesto,** whose principal definition was always accepted as **decent, decorous, chaste** increasingly replaces the more correct **honrado** for **honest**. The words and phrases that often catch European students of Spanish on the hop have metamorphosed into what they sound like but aren't, so **una carpeta is** now agreed to be a **carpet** instead of **a folder**.

Te llamo atrás is understood in the United States to mean **I'll call you back** and **una secuela** is **a sequel** instead of **a consequence, result**. Some modern Spanish-English dictionaries do give **sequel** as a secondary translation for **secuela** but even so, any **sequel** or **part II** sounds better as **una continuación** or **segunda parte**.

If you have your suspicions about the legitimacy of some of the words you hear, and if you like to get to the bottom of things and to know where to draw the bottom line, it's worth looking up doubtful words in a Spanish dictionary. This is as good a reason as any to invest in the Spanish Royal Academy's *Diccionario de la Lengua Española*. What's more, if you feel like being contentious and taking sides in the *español* versus *castellano* issue, you need do no more than point silently but eloquently to its title and the word *Española*.

21

PART ONE
LANGUAGE! LANGUAGE!

Is it just coincidence that *grammar* and *groan* both start with something that looks and sounds like *grrr*? Grammar's not the beast it's supposed to be, though, but let's put it at the beginning and get it over and done with. In any case, what follows doesn't deal exclusively with grammar although it does touch on grammatical points. I'm aware that I tend to nag in the following chapters, particularly about adjectives, adverbs, pronouns, prepositions and the subjunctive. These are the things that seem to be the most common obstacles that an English-speaker learning Spanish comes up against, but there's nothing like nagging coupled with brisk encouragement for getting results.

Don't want even to look at it? Don't be a coward: give it a try.

FIRST THINGS FIRST

The old jokes and generalisations about the Spanish and their sense of time belong to the past, but it's undeniable that Spanish handling of dates and dating (chronology, not fraternisation) is different from ours.

Date is **fecha** but the question we ask at least once a day can be put two ways: **¿qué es la fecha hoy?** and **¿qué día es hoy?** Nothing particularly world-shattering about that of course, but there's more difference in the reply because ordinal numbers aren't used for dates. **Hoy es lunes, el día dos de mayo** means **today is Monday 2nd May,** but you are actually saying **today is Monday, day two of May** although many now prefer the shorter **es el dos de mayo,** literally **it's the two of May.**

Ordinal numbers appear in other circumstances, of course,

and like all self-respecting numbers they stretch from here to infinity although in everyday talk they are restricted from **first to tenth:**

first –	primero
second –	segundo
third	tercero
fourth –	cuarto
fifth –	quinto
sixth –	sexto
seventh –	séptimo
eighth –	octavo
ninth –	noveno
tenth –	décimo

On reaching **tenth** it's usual to revert to cardinals, although many people go up to **undécimo – eleventh.** The erudite are prone to trot out ordinals as far as twenty or even further if they are ostentatious with it. However, most would agree that saying **fifty-second** is one thing, but dragging out **quincuagésimosegundo** hardly compensates the effort involved. Contrariwise, while English-speakers are happy with high-value ordinal numbers, if a Spaniard refers to **the fortieth page** he is certain to say **la página cuarenta.**

Centuries aren't expressed in ordinals, so the **ninth century** is **el siglo nueve.** As in English, the Spanish write centuries with Roman numerals: **siglo IX.** Ordinal numbers designate the chronological appearance of royalty but, again, only up to **tenth** so the Spanish say **el Rey Juan Carlos Primero – King Juan Carlos the First** but **Alfonso XIII** is always **Alfonso Trece – Alfonso the Thirteenth.**

Where you do find ordinal numbers above ten is in the number of apartment storeys and as buildings rise ever higher it is not unusual to hear the least erudite announce **vivo en el piso décimocuarto – I live on the fourteenth floor.**

Abbreviations are less intricate than in English and consist of the written number followed by a minute, frequently underlined ° or ª, depending on the ordinal's gender.

Because they are adjectives, ordinal numbers agree with the nouns they accompany: **primera semana – first week; Segunda Guerra Mundial – Second World War; Tercer**

Mundo – Third World; cuarto campeonato – fourth championship; quinta columna – fifth column; sexto sentido – sixth sense; séptimo velo – seventh veil; octavo mes – eighth month; Ninth Symphony – la Novena Sinfonía; décimo aniversario – tenth anniversary. When an ordinal ending in –ero immediately precedes a masculine noun, the final –o is dropped, as it is with adjectives like bueno, malo or ciento. As always, feminine adjectives before feminine nouns behave as expected: la tercera vez – the third time.

Ordinals can be used as nouns as well as adjectives, so el primero is the first whether a firstborn child or the winner of a race or competition. Un segundo is a straight translation of a second that is the sixtieth part of a minute as well as the person who comes second or is a stand-in or deputy: el segundo maitre – the second head waiter.

A la tercera va la vencida is Spain's version of third time lucky. Spanish is more decimalised than English but a fractional third is still referred to as un tercio, a word that also means an army regiment, a division of the Guardia Civil, a third of a litre (usually beer), a phase of a bullfight and a section of the bullring itself.

Una cuarta is a measure approximate to a hand's breadth while the masculine un cuarto is a fractional quarter and needed for time-telling: son las tres menos cuarto – it's a quarter to three. Una cuartilla is a sheet of cuarto-sized paper.

Una quinta describes a group of boys called up for military service in one particular year and an adult will say somos de la misma quinta of a contemporary who shares his or her generation. Un quinto is another fraction – a fifth – as well as another measure, this time a fifth of a litre (beer again). With the verbal laziness of our time, many now refer to this as un botellín – a little bottle.

Una octavilla is a pamphlet or leaflet which, logically enough is octavo-sized, and una novena is a Catholic English-speaker's Novena or nine-day cycle of prayers. Un décimo is a tenth and although some kind of state draw or lottery is now held every day, Saturday is the day of the original national lottery – lotería nacional which those of modest means continue to buy in décimos – tenths of a ticket.

UFOs

Not every UFO is a flying saucer and a more earthbound interpretation of this acronym might be Unnerving Formidable Object, because a lot of people get their grammatical underwear in an uncomfortable twist over direct and indirect objects as well as the pronouns **le, la** and **lo** that sometimes replace them.

Where's my dog? I heard him in the garden

First of all it helps to have an unmuddled notion of what constitutes a direct and an indirect object. Take **I'm going to write a letter** and **I'm going to write a letter to Elena**. In the first sentence, ask *what* are you going to write? **A letter,** of course – and that's a direct object for you. In the second, ask the same question and you are still going to write... *what?* **A letter** – but hold on: *to whom?* To Elena - and hey presto! Elena has entered your life as an indirect object.

In Spanish these two sentences are **voy a escribir una carta** and **voy a escribir una carta a Elena,** all of which is plain and simple enough. However, when you use the pronouns **le, la** and **lo** to substitute the nouns **carta** and **Elena** you might feel that things are less plain and far less simple on seeing that **I'm going to write it** and **I'm going to write to her** are **la voy a escribir** and **le voy a escribir** respectively.

A direct object that has feminine gender is substituted by la/las: **Where's my** (female) **cat? I saw her on the windowsill – ¿Dónde está mi gata? La ví encima del alféizar; I can't find my glasses, I think I've lost them – No encuentro mis gafas, creo que las he perdido.**

As we saw with Elena and the letter, an indirect object of feminine gender is substituted by **le** and **les.** You imply, but do not mention, **to** when substituting indirect objects with pronouns and although gender is so important and so apparent in Spanish, **to her** is always translated as **le. I made the skirt for her** is translated as **I made the skirt to her: le cosí la falda** with **le** referring to the indirect object **her**.

Masculine direct objects that are human, inhuman or inanimate – which doesn't automatically rule out all men – are translated as **lo** or **los** depending on whether they are singular or plural. So you say, **Where's my dog? I heard him in the garden – ¿Dónde está mi perro? Lo oí en el jardín** or **I like these gloves, may I try them on? Me gustan estos guantes ¿los puedo probar?**

Masculine indirect objects are also **le** and **les,** so in the extremely unlikely event that I were able to, I would say **le he cosido un pantalón a mi marido – I have made a pair of trousers for my husband.** Were I to make fish pie and give some to Cato (less unlikely than my making trousers) I would also say **le he dado pastel de pescado – I've given him fish**

pie. Spanish-speakers abhor **leísmo, laísmo** and **loísmo** – not obscure ailments but grammatical pitfalls awaiting the lazy or unwary. Strictly speaking **I saw him** and **I invited him** should both be translated as **lo ví** and **lo invite** respectively, but most people seem to say **le ví** and **le invité;** this is **leísmo,** considered the most forgivable of the reprehensible trio. Less forgivable is the **laísmo** present in **la hablé** (instead of **le hablé**) for **I spoke to her** as well as the inelegant **loísmo** in phrases like **lo dí una invitación – I gave him an invitation.**

There are more pronouns to replace indirect objects – **me, te, se, nos, vos** and, again, **se.** They correspond to the first, second and third person in both singular and plural but, unlike **le, lo** and **la** they do not induce headaches because they are one-size fits all with no agonising over number or gender: **nos habló – he spoke to us; te escribió – she wrote to you. Se** appears in sentences like **she sent it to him** where an indirect object immediately precedes a direct object: **se lo mandó.** This sounds trickier in theory than it actually is in practice, especially if you hear a lot of Spanish and speak as it much as you can. Then you reach the reassuring stage where your ear tells you something sounds right – and you find you get it right, too.

If direct and indirect objects are as far beyond your orbit as UFOs, don't forget that many Spaniards ignore basic grammar and few will look askance when you get it wrong, too. And although it has nothing to do with the matter in hand, you might like to know that by joining **le, lo** and **la** you produce two delightful words meaning **soppy: lelo** and **lela.**

TO BE OR TO BE...

For want of anything more pressing to do the other day I asked my husband to explain concisely and pithily why and when he uses **ser** and when and why he uses **estar.** He was eating at the time and sighed as he laid down his knife and fork. He looked wistfully at the whiting on his plate, aware that any explanation would take some time, that we might not see eye to eye and that the cats would probably steal his lunch from under his nose.

Bueno, he began. **Bueno,** he repeated. **Bueno...** he tailed off.

He gazed at the ceiling and waited for inspiration, then said none too gently: **estoy comiendo y quien come soy yo y no esos tres caraduras**. Given the peculiar natures of **ser** and **estar** this statement is best translated ungrammatically and idiomatically as **I'm eating and it's me who's eating, not those three hardcases**. With which he removed Billy from his plate, extracted Bessy's paw from the mayonnaise, disengaged Spats – who does everything the hard way – from his trouser leg and renewed his acquaintance with what was left of the whiting before I could get a word in edgeways.

I hadn't expected an illuminating reply, in any case. On hearing us whine about our uncertainty concerning **ser** and **estar**, any Spaniard will tell you that it is our own fault for using one verb – **to be** – to translate two totally different concepts like **ser** and **estar**. When a Spaniard says **soy** the circumstances are totally different from when he says **estoy** and generally speaking **ser** is used for what is permanent, inherent, unchangeable, continuing or abstract.

This means you say **Londres es la capital de Inglaterra – London is the capital of England; los bígaros son caros en este momento – winkles are dear at the moment; somos seres humanos – we are human beings; algunos gatos son grises – some cats are grey; es una persona fría – he is a cold person; es cojo el lotero – the lottery seller is lame; era esquizofrénica – she was schizophrenic; ¡eso es! – that's it!**

Estar is used when **to be** appears as an auxiliary verb with the present participle: **estoy escribiendo – I am writing; estaréis leyendo – you will be reading,** all of which is pleasantly straightforward and requires neither analysis nor soul-searching.

But **estar** also indicates physical position or physical occupation of space as well as what is impermanent, acquired, changeable and tangible and this means you will say: **Londres está en Inglaterra – London is in England; el precio de bígaros está en alza – the price of winkles is going up; el ser humano está en crisis – the human race is in a critical situation; hoy está gris el mar – the sea is grey today; sus manos están frias – his hands are cold; está cojo el lotero – the lottery seller is lame; estaba loca – she was crazy; ¡ya está! – that's that done!**

It helps to remember that **estar** is used whenever you can substitute **to be** with **to stay: will you be there?** could be reworded with **will you be staying there?** and both would be translated as **¡estarás allí?** Neither is this a coincidence, since both **stay** and **estar** developed from the Latin verb, **stare** which means **to stay, to stand** amongst other things.

Neither is it a bad idea to bear in mind that **state** in Spanish is **estado**, the past participle of **estar**. Consequently this is always the right verb to use when describing any transient **state** of mind, body or physical location: **estoy triste – I am sad; el estaba abstraído – he was preoccupied; estaremos juntos – we shall be together.**

This is generally speaking, but ungeneral things will immediately start to occur to you. Why, for instance, can both **ser** and **estar** be used to say the lottery seller is lame? In fact, this is the beauty of **ser** and **estar**, because without knowing him and without further explanation, you would surmise from the first phrase that he was disabled, and from the second that although he was lame this was probably a temporary situation. Similarly, a grey cat is always going to be grey, although tomorrow the sea could easily be blue or even green.

Very often though, you should do what the Spanish do: try not to analyse and don't make comparisons with English. That way it comes as less of a surprise to find out that **ser** is used for telling the time, although nothing is less permanent or more transient: **¿Qué hora es? Son las cuatro y diez – What time is it? Ten past four**. If you've forgotten to keep an eye on the clock, you might exclaim: **¡qué tarde es! – how late it is!** and you will need **ser** to comment on timekeeping: **eres poco punctual – you're not very punctual.**

Although people's politics, religions, ideologies and leanings are notoriously impermanent, changeable and lacking in continuity, these are always conveyed by **ser. Era socialista – he was a socialist; son de derechas – they are right wing; era budista – she was a Buddhist. To be beautiful** and **to be ugly** need **ser – ser guapo** and **ser feo** – without taking into account their notorious inconstancy and the transforming wonders of diet, money, dress sense and cosmetic surgery.

Whether you choose **ser** or **estar** when uniting an adjective to a noun, you will still make sense if you make the wrong choice. At the same time, what you say undergoes a subtle change, so **ser rico** means **to be rich (financially)** but **estar rico** means **to be tasty** (foodwise). If, perhaps, a woman gets it wrong and tells a male millionaire **estás rico** he's not going to mind, because the combination of **estar** and **rico** can mean **you're cute.**

In the same way, **ser salado** means **to be salted: son almendras saladas – they're salted almonds but están saladas las almendras** implies **these almonds are over-salted. Ser pálido** means **to be habitually** or **naturally pale** but **estar pálido** denotes **temporary paleness** and when you say **son ciruelas verdes** you are stating **they are greengages** but **están verdes las ciruelas** is a complaint that **the plums are unripe** whatever their variety.

El café es rico is as correct as **el café está rico** because the **estar** formula means the coffee you're drinking at that moment is pretty good. Use **ser** and you're referring to the fact that coffee, all coffee, is normally pretty good. **Estar sorprendido** means **to be surprised** or **amazed** but **ser sorprendido** corresponds to the **surprise** experienced when **caught unawares,** just like Billy when he thought the whiting was his. And as my husband remarked, **Billy tendría que ser – it would have to be Billy...**

SUBJUNCTIVITIS

Many English-speaker can feel ill at the very thought of the **subjunctive**. It's simply not fair to go to the bother of learning that **he laughs** is translated as **el ríe,** only to be informed that occasionally this is allowed to turn itself into **el ría.**

That's the **subjunctive** coming the old moody again. So just what is this affliction that attacks verbs and strains nerves? The Shorter Oxford English Dictionary explains it as "designating a mood the forms of which are employed to denote an action or state as conceived (and not as a fact) and therefore used to express a wish, command, exhortation, or a contingent, hypothetical or prospective event."

This definition may not do much to contribute to your

grammatical health, but the Spanish – high and low, rich and poor, illiterate and erudite – use the subjunctive all the time and though there are linguistic giveaways to a person's class and condition in the Spanish language, use and misuse of the subjunctive is not one of them.

The subjunctive of any Spanish verb is usually similar to its indicative counterpart but with a different ending. There is a present tense, two past imperfect tenses and another that a Spanish-speaker might be prepared to identify as the future tense but which is used less often than the rest. There are also compound tenses using the present, imperfect and future tenses of **haber.**

Apart from a few token breakouts and anomalies that have more to do with verbal irregularity than the subjunctive itself, it is reassuringly reliable and Spanish obliges as usual by providing, and not breaking, dependable rules. Nevertheless, as always with verbs, the only way to learn them is parrot-fashion.

English is full of pitfalls for the socially conscious but grammatically insecure. One of these was handling the few occasions when it is necessary to use the subjunctive of the verb **to be** and although speech is changing radically, it is still more correct to say **were** and not **was** after **if.**

To be is the only English verb with the kind of subjunctive that jumps up and down and waves its arms around to make its presence felt. This isn't to say that other verbs aren't proud subjunctive possessors, but they are harder to distinguish from their indicative cousins and we tend to use them only when wishing to sound formal, legal, pompous or pedantic.

Most would agree that **I'm going to tell Fausto to be quiet** could be put as **I'm going to tell Fausto that he be quiet** but not everybody would identify the business part of the verb as a subjunctive in both cases. A little-used, rather dramatic exclamation like **may Fausto be quiet!** also conceals an English subjunctive that sheds its camouflage in translation.

Our most conspicuous English subjunctive has three Spanish translations, all of which are irritatingly verbless, so that rendering **if I were you** into Spanish means choosing between **yo en tu lugar, yo que tú** or the less-heard but still encountered **yo de ti.**

I'd like it if Fausto were nicer to my cats is translated as **me gustaría que Fausto fuera más amable con mis gatos. I'm going to tell Fausto to be quiet** and **I'm going to tell Fausto that he be quiet** both become **voy a decirle a Fausto que se calle** while an English **may he be quiet!** sounds less antiquated in Spanish: **¡qué se calle Fausto!**

You don't need to get tense as to which subjunctive tense to use, because **were** will always be translated by one of the past tenses. Sometimes you can take your lead from the first verb, because when this is in the present or future and a subjunctive follows, this too will be in the present tense. When it's anything else you can use whichever of the past tenses takes your fancy, but if two of these crop up in the same sentence, it's considered better to use one of each. You don't have to think twice about exclamations like **¡qué se calle!** as they are always subjunctive, anyway.

Were should follow **if** and **as if** in English, and so should a subjunctive follow their Spanish equivalents **si** and **como si** when preceding vague or patently impossible circumstances: **si Fausto se callara, la vida sería más fácil – if Fausto were to keep quiet, life would be easier.** Or **es como si su voz fuera un martillo – it's as if his voice were a hammer.**

On the other hand, when **si** is followed by something definite, practical or possible to carry out, it is necessary to use the indicative: **si habla Fausto, los demás tienen que callar – if Fausto speaks, everyone else has to keep quiet.**

Should this strike you as arbitrary and requiring too much analysis of what constitutes fact, fiction and fantasy, remember that you'll know the subjunctive is necessary in imaginary, non-existent or not-yet-existing situations where **if** could be substituted by **should** or expanded into **if** plus **should. Should my neighbour offend you, if** (should) **my neighbour offend you** or **if my neighbour should offend you** sound faintly biblical but unmistakably subjunctive and, what is more, each is translated as **si mi vecino te ofenda.**

Something similar happens with **aunque – although, even though** or **even if. Although my neighbour offends you and even if my neighbour should offend you** can be translated the same way: **aunque te ofenda mi vecino.**

What also tips the balance towards subjunctive or indicative is whether something happens or not. **Estaba allí, aunque no ví a Elena – I was there although I didn't see Elena –** needs the indicative because I *was* there. In contrast, **no la habría saludado aunque hubiera estado allí – I wouldn't have said hallo even if I'd been there –** is subjunctive because I *wasn't* there so my bad-manners were hypothetical..

The subjunctive is needed when **aunque** can be translated as **if I were, if you were, if he were** etc. So you say **aunque intento ser agradable, nos llevamos muy mal – although I try to be pleasant, we get on very badly** but **aunque intentara ser agradable, nos llevaríamos mal** means **if I** (were to) **try to be nice, we wouldn't get on.**

The following do no more than skim the surface of the subjunctive's fathomless depths, but are further warning that a Spanish subjunctive could be on its way: **a condición de que – on condition that; a menos que – unless; en el supuesto de que – supposing that; para que – so that/in order that; siempre que/con tal de que/con tal que/mientras que –** all of which mean **if** when substitutable with **as long as/so long as.**

Que, when it can be translated as **that** and is followed by a verb, is another indication of a subjunctive on the horizon as is the construction **querer** followed by **que** and another verb. Similarly subjunctive is **ser mejor que – to be better that** but – and this is a very big but – this can only apply when **que** means **that** and not **than.**

Removing that subjunctive-friendly **que** means you *don't* need the subjunctive, however, and can skirt the whole issue by using an infinitive: **con tal de estar en el jardín estoy feliz – as long as I'm in the garden I'm happy.** Or **en el supuesto de vender su casa, no tendrá donde vivir – supposing that he sells his house, he won't have anywhere to live.**

When translating an English infinitive, Spanish often requires **que** plus a subjunctive tense if the verbal goings-on involve more than one person: **Fausto asked me to lend him my watering can – Fausto me pidió que le dejara mi regadera** or **Esperanza says it would be nice if Nieves were to spend the summer with her – Esperanza dice que sería agradable si Nieves veranease con ella.**

If all this is beginning to sound like too much of a good thing, don't despair because what's important for the moment is to understand *why* you sometimes hear or read **el ríe** and **el ría** when it is obvious that both mean **he laughs**.

Apart from which, even though you haven't the vaguest idea about how to apply it in the ordinary way, you'll need the present subjunctive for the polite **usted** and **ustedes** versions of the imperative. And everybody at some time or other wants to beg the plumber **please mend my burst pipes** – **por favor, repáreme las tuberías rotas**.

All negative imperatives, polite or otherwise, are again formed by the present subjunctive: **don't do that** – **no hagas eso** or **don't be silly** – **no sea usted mezquino**. You'll need the first person plural of the subjunctive for **let's** too: **let's be happy** – **seamos contentos; don't let's get cross** – **no nos enfademos.** It's all simple enough, but it's all subjunctive too.

Being on nodding terms with the subjunctive starts to make sense out of **sea como sea** – **be that as it may** and decodes that most Spanish of all Spanish interjections **o sea** – lifesaver of the inarticulate, the confused, the embarrassed, the bored and the self-conscious and whose rightful place in a sentence is wherever you care to put it.

For those who neither speak, read nor hear much Spanish, the subjunctive might remain intimidatingly mysterious and take some dominating. Once you try to speak Spanish – or even if you merely read and listen to it – things change rapidly and you'll find yourself using and understanding the subjunctive without knowing quite why and without being able to explain exactly how. When that happens, you can impress everyone by being able to identify the subjunctive in English, too, and what is more, you'll use **were** and **was** in a most recognisably superior way.

GIVING YOU WHAT FOR!

With some of us it's fear of flying or spiders but what makes many an English-speaker froth at the mouth and sweat with uncomprehending apprehension is deciding when to use **por** and when to use **para**.

As with **ser** and **estar**, if you get **por** and **para** in a twist, you are still going to make sense. However, you might not be getting across the exact message you intend: **sufro por tí** – **I suffer for (because of, though) you** but **sufro para tí** – **I suffer for (instead of) you.**

Somewhat more subtle are **hablas por mí** and **hablas para mí. Hablas por mí** means **you speak for me** or **because of me**, but **hablas para mí,** which would also be translated as **you speak for me** implies **you are talking so that I can be spellbound by your pearls of wisdom.**

Much of the trouble with **por** and **para** arises because the first definition a dictionary gives for both is **for.** All the same, you will save much unnecessary suffering by taking into account the supplementary definitions for each word and although it's a fallible rule, as a rule **for** in English becomes **para** in Spanish.

Having said which, you will find **por** means **for** in **for the time being** – **por ahora** and in **I'm going for cigarettes** – **voy a por tobacco** (strictly speaking the preposition **a** does not belong here, but most people insert it). **Por** retains its **for** identity in **for how long?** – **¿por cuánto tiempo?** and also in situations when **for** involves substitution: **quiero cambiar este libro por otro** – **I want to change this book for another.** You use **por** when expressing gratitude: **gracias por todo lo que has hecho** – **thank you for everything you've done.** That unsolicited Spanish keepsake, **a fine for double parking** needs **por** as well as money: **una multa por aparcar en doble fila.**

When an English **for** implies **over** it makes little difference whether you choose **por** or **para** although **voy a Inglaterra por Semana Santa** means **I'm going to England for Easter** while **voy a Inglaterra para Semana Santa** is more vague and closer to **I'm going to England some time over Easter.**

You will find that **por** is appropriate wherever **per** appears in English: **ten per cent** – **diez por ciento; a hundred kilometres per hour** – **cien kilometros por hora; mil euros por mes** – **a thousand euros per month.**

Por generally means **because of, due to, owing to, on behalf of, on account of** and **by.** On the occasions when **for** substitutes one of these without altering the sense, then **por** is the **for** you seek. **Es por el gato** – **it's because of, due to, owing to,**

on behalf of, on account of and by the cat – which is like listening to Fausto on the subject of Gilbert.

The carefree little phrase **no me preocupo por el gato** can be translated as **I'm not worried for the cat** although there's nothing to prevent your saying **I'm not worried *about* the cat** (that tough cookie can look after himself). And few who know him would disagree with a cautious statement like **por ser tan impredecible Gilbert, es aconsejable tratarle con cuidado – because Gilbert's so unpredictable, it's advisable to handle him with care** (while wearing body armour).

You will also meet **por** as **by** in **un libro escrito por una mujer – a book written by a woman; viajamos por carretera – we travelled by car; se libró por los pelos – he escaped by the skin of his teeth** (literally **by the hairs**); **she will send the parcel by post – enviará el paquete for correo.** On occasion **por** is similar to **of: love for (of) cats – amor por los gatos.**

Sometimes a simple English adverb needs the addition of **por** in Spanish: **por desgracia – unfortunately; por suerte – luckily; por favor – please. Por** is vital when giving directions: **por aquí** and **por acá** mean **this way, along here, round here. Por allí** and **por allá** mean **that way, along there** and **round there.**

Por ahí – by or **round there** gives more than directions as it is intentionally vague and/or laconic and is eminently suitable when you don't wish to be forthcoming. When Fuensanta asks César **¿dónde has estado todo este tiempo? – where have you been all this time?** you can bet your life he'll mumble **oh, por ahí - oh, just round and about.**

Por ahí is not restricted to **whereabouts** and can be an unforthcoming **thereabouts,** so an unhelpful answer to a nosy question like **¿Cuánto te han costado esos zapatos? Cien euros? – How much did those shoes cost? A hundred euros?** might be **por ahí.**

Por joined to **que** produces **porque – because.** Exasperatingly, **¿por qué? – why?** looks pretty different but sounds much the same unless you really latch on to that accented **-é**. This creates fruitless question-and-answer-routines and to add to the confusion, the noun **el porqué** means **the motive** or **reason why.** The unaccented **por que** means **through which** or **because of which** but happily these similarities seldom have much bearing on potential **por** and **para** dilemmas.

For me, for you, for him etc. are translated by **para: es para tí, Gilbert – it's for you, Gilbert. Para** is employed when implying **to, in order to, in order that: se lo doy para hacerle contento – I'm giving it to him to make him happy.**

Make a very Spanish question out of **para** by adding **que** for a phrase that is more like **what for** than **why: Voy a ver a Nieves. ¿Para qué? – I'm going to see Nieves. What for?**

Para con is an alien-sounding construction that can be translated as **towards: hemos sido muy comprensivos para con Fausto – we've been understanding towards Fausto.**

Expect to hear something you decode as **p'acá** and **p'allá** – a slurring of **para acá** and **para allá** – in phrases like **ven p'acá – come here** and **voy p'allá – I'm going there** but nearer to **I'm on my way.** In fact it would be better to say **ven hacía acá** and **voy hacía allá** but their correctness doesn't mean you encounter them more often.

It would be unrealistic to pretend that **por** and **para** are anything other than a slippery pair of customers who need a minimum of analysis before you settle unhesitatingly for the right one. Until you do, it's always possible to chicken out and put things another way round: **voy a Inglaterra durante Semana Santa** or **voy a comprar tabaco** or **te he comprado un regalo, Fausto.** Then again, if you reach the point where you are reduced to shrieking **for pity's sake!** don't forget to use **por: ¡por piedad!**

SIMPLY TOO, TOO

You'll like **demasiado** because it corresponds to **too, too many, too much** and turns up in the same circumstances as its English counterpart. However, you will like it less if you abhor adjectives and are averse to adverbs.

We chat away without pondering on the grammatical identity of the words we use. **A cat** is a noun and **a fussy cat** is a noun preceded by an adjective although it doesn't make any difference to the cat or his nature whether you are aware of this or not. When you mention **a too-fussy cat** you are referring to a finicky feline and you scratch your head over number and gender only if there are kittens on the horizon.

But once you string together more than two Spanish words you will be required to analyse. Is that a noun? Where's the adjective? And look out – can that be an adverb? Don't lose heart though, because even if you get it wrong on all three counts your meaning should still be clear, if slightly blurred.

It's not too taxing to translate **a cat** as **un gato**. Translating **a fussy cat** is a straightforward **un gato exigente** and **a too-fussy cat** is **un gato demasiado exigente** – which in itself suggests a certain quota of exasperation that has nothing to do with translation traumas.

So far, so good. We've established that when somebody is **too** something or other, we put **demasiado** before whatever the something or other expressed as an adjective happens to be: **demasiado gordo** – **too fat, demasiado guapa** – **too beautiful, demasiado tímido** – **too shy.** This is because **demasiado** is functioning as an adverb and behaves as you'd expect. As an adjective, **demasiado** also reacts as you would expect: **demasiada atención** – **too much attention; demasiado tiempo** – **too much time, demasiados gatos** – **too many cats**

This must be the **umpteenth time** (**enésima vez** if you want it in Spanish) that I've brought up the adjective/adverb dilemma. It must sound like nagging but this is one of the things that English-speakers who give grammar little thought find hard to get their heads round. So read on if you want, but it won't be the end of the world if you skip the next bit.

When preceding a feminine adjective, **demasiado** does not change: **mi gata es demasiado gorda** – **my (female) cat is too fat; es demasiado guapa** – **she is too beautiful; demasiado tímida** – **she is too shy.** Adverbs are the part of speech that tell you more about an action and are more rapidly recognised when ending in **–mente** in Spanish or **–ly** in English: **mi gata se porta cariñosamente** – **my cat behaves affectionately.**

When not preceding an adjective, **demasiado** is still a full-blooded, full-blown adverb as you can see in a phrase like **Pushy come demasiado** – **Pushy eats too much and ternera picada cuesta demasiado** – **minced beef costs too much**.

When a noun is implied but not mentioned, **demasiado** acquires the number and gender of the unmentioned, but implicit, noun to become a pronoun: **elige unas esmeraldas – choose some emeralds.** A supremely gormless reply to this would be **no puedo, hay demasiadas – I can't, there are too many.**

Logically, when an adjective is implied but not mentioned, **demasiado** sticks to its adverbial guns: **Pushy es demasiado,** a truism you could translate as **Pushy is too much** or **Pushy is too, too** while leaving the omitted adjective to the imagination of the individual.

INDECENT PREPOSITIONS

Unless you are mega-rich, your bathroom is usually the smallest room in the house, but no less important for all that. This could easily be the longest chapter in the book but it is going to be the shortest – although, like a bathroom, no less important for all that.

Taken by and large, prepositions should be no big deal. They're small words like **a – to, at; ante – before; bajo – under; con – with; contra – against; de – of, from; desde – since, from; en – in, into; entre – between, amongst; hacía – towards; hasta – until, till, as far as; para – for, in order to; por – for, by, through; según – according to; sin – without; sobre – on, upon; tras – after, beyond.**

Despite their insignificant size, though, be prepared for prepositions to make significant nuisances of themselves. On some occasions they are mirror images in both languages but there are others when you can't even hope for a spot of lateral inversion, so although **de** does mean **of** or **from,** different speech patterns mean you will meet it in different places in Spanish. For example: **estar DE pie – to be ON foot** as well as **es hora DE hablar – it's time TO talk** or **iremos DE madrugada – we'll go IN the early hours of the morning.** Sometimes you can expect to find **de** where you wouldn't in English: **dejar DE hablar – to stop talking.**

And that's just **de...** although, to be fair, **de** is the worst of the bunch.

What is the best way to treat them? There's not much

you can do, except to give them a thorough looking-over so that you recognise them the next time you meet them. However good an English-speaker's Spanish and however good a Spanish-speaker's English, prepositions will often be a stumbling block. So don't forget: "By their prepositions shall ye know them."

IN CONJUNCTION WITH...

Once you take away the verbs, nouns and accompanying adjectives from a sentence, what you're left with are conjunctions, adverbs or prepositions. Anyone with an unquenchable desire to get to grips with Spanish conjunctions might like to learn that they can be co-ordinate, subordinate, disjunctive, distributive, adversative, explicative and copulative, too.

Conjunctions are words like **y, o, o bien, es decir, pero, entonces** and **no obstante** which correspond to **and, or,** again **or, that is to say, but, then** and **nonetheless** respectively although these are no more than a very modest selection. Their aim in life is to connect two words or phrases: **me gustan las ostras pero me conformo con mejillones** – **I like oysters but I make do with mussels.** Or **compro mejillones; no obstante lo que quiero son ostras** – **I buy mussels; nonetheless, what I want are oysters.**

Prepositions are itsy-bitsy little words like **to, before, under, against** and **above.** They metamorphose into itsy-bitsy little Spanish words like **a, ante, bajo, contra, en** and **encima** and they tend to hang out with nouns: **hay paella con mejillones** – **there's paella with mussels** or **una docena de ostras** – **a dozen (of) oysters.**

Having given conjunctions and prepositions a whirl, it's time to look at words like **rápidamente, francamente** and **horriblemente** whose **-mente** ending makes them easily recognisable as adverbs. Their English counterparts are equally easy to put the finger on because they end in **-ly: quickly, frankly** and **horribly.** You can't rely on adverbs in either language to end in **-mente** or **-ly** so you get words

Alice in Wonderland

like **bien, hoy** and **entonces – well, today** and **then.**

Entonces has already turned up as a conjunction and here it is again, calling itself an adverb – but this also happens in English: **if you don't want these mussels, then I'll give them to Cato – si no quieres estos mejillones, entonces se los daré a Cato.** In this instance **then – entonces** is a conjunction, but you could also say **I went to the market this morning but I didn't see any oysters then – fui esta mañana al mercado, pero no vi ostras entonces –** and this time it will be an adverb.

And yet… and yet… Having come so far, was our journey

really necessary? If you enjoy friendly relations with English conjunctions, prepositions and adverbs, you'll know how to treat them in Spanish. If you were under the impression that conjunctions was an eye infection you won't need to dissect the innards of a sentence in order to deal with words or phrases like **puesto que – since; fantásticamente – fantastically or contra – against.** They aren't conjugated like verbs and it's not necessary to bother about number and gender as you would with nouns and adjectives. More than anything else it's a question of knowing what they mean and using them where appropriate.

Meanwhile, for those still skulking around at the beginning, pondering the implications and possibilities of copulative conjunctions, you might as well know that they are **y** and **ni**. They mean **and** and **nor,** an ill-assorted couple at the best of times and something of an anticlimax.

LITTLE BY LITTLE

Alice nibbled one side of a mushroom to get smaller in Wonderland, but in the normal world every Spanish noun and adjective comes ready-equipped with diminishing endings. They are principally **-ito/-ita, -illo/-illa** as well as the more regional **-ico/-ica, ín/-ino/-ina** and **-iño/-iña** and provide a built-in D.I.Y. kit allowing you to cut things down to size without using **small** or **little.**

Any of these can be joined to the word of your choice, so although **a puppy** is **un cachorro** it can be made even more puppyish with **cachorrito** while a **small dog** of any age is **un perrito, un perillo** or **un perrico. Un gato – a cat** becomes a **kitten** as well as an adult but miniscule moggy when called **un gatito, gatillo, gatico, gatino** or **gatín.**

A noun or adjective that ends in **-o** or **-a** usually drops this before tacking on the suffix of your choice: **chair – silla, sillita; table – mesa, mesilla.** Words that end in **-l** need no modification: **tree – árbol, arbolito** but words ending in **-e** or **-n** acquire **-c** before the suffixes **-ito** and **-illo: car – coche, cochecito; cloud – nube, nubecito** or **nubecillo; heart –**

corazón, corazoncito, corazoncillo.

Un pájaro – a bird becomes un pajarillo – fledgling while un cuadro – a picture can be reduced to un cuadrito or un cuadrico. Spaniards from central cities regard -ico/ica and also -ín, -ino/-ina as rustic-sounding, to put it kindly. Nonetheless, you will still hear them and in Murcia it is possible to turn un poco – a little into the even smaller un poquico. City-dwellers are no better, though, and if you listen hard enough you'll catch un madrileño saying un poquitín, a double diminutive that is in danger of diminishing itself into nothingness.

-In, -ino and -ina are often used for pet names and nicknames so that Pedro can become Pedrín as well as Pedrito, and instead of shortening Margarita you can make it longer and sweeter: Margaritina. The Spanish do not use caro – dear as an endearment but instead add the suffix -iño and turn it into cariño – darling, a word that applies to males and females alike, despite ending in -o.

Chico – boy and chica – girl are often turned into chiquitín and chiquitina as well as chiquitito and chiquitita. All are suitable for anything – animal, vegetable or mineral – that is undersized but are also endearments between outsize adults, because as well as smallness a suffix frequently indicates affection. Thus love converts mi amor into mi amorcito (again, suitable for either sex) and the object of affection understands that despite being addressed as a little love, little things mean a lot.

A suffix can sometimes be ironic, so an invitation like ¿comemos una paellita? – how about a spot of paella? heralds a mammoth, marathon blow-out. The adjective gracioso – nice, appealing is not always so nice and can be less than appealing when transformed into the sarcastic graciosillo. Guapito damns faintly with diminutives because an adult thus described may still be guapo – handsome but there could be something less than beauty in the eye of the beholder.

Some people use diminutives more than others but once started, the practice can become addictive and is responsible for phrases like daos prisita instead of daos prisa for hurry up or hasta lueguito instead of hasta luego – so long. And take care when making a dimutive out of female servants –

criadas because not even the wildest imagination can turn **criadillas** into **tiny maids**.

BIG BUSINESS

Alice evened things up in Wonderland by nibbling at the other side of the toadstool when she wanted to get bigger. Similarly, Spanish words not only incorporate diminutives but take on suffixes like **–ón/ona; -azo/-aza** and **–ote/-ota** which indicate an increase in stature for nouns and adjectives when attached to the business end of a word.

The adjective **hermoso,** for example, means **fine, handsome, lovely** so that **hermosote** and **hermosota** mean **fine,   handsome, lovely** but more so. Another adjective, **triste – sad** loses its final **-e**, gains the masculine **–ón** or the feminine **–ona** to give you **tristón** and **tristona** which describe someone who is **sad to the point of depression.**

A noun like **un libro – book** gets predictably thicker and heavier after it is called **un librote**. However, more often than not suffixes imply an increase in quantity and not quality, so **un animal** bares its fangs at you and changes into the more ferocious **animalote**. When **una mujer – a woman** expands into **una mujerona** she turns into **a very large, not necessarily beautiful, but very formidable lady. Un gato** inflates into **un gatazo** or what might be termed **a heavy, hefty and probably overfed cat.**

The addition of **–azo** sometimes redefines a word. **Un pincho** is **a thorn** but **un pinchazo** is **a jab, puncture** or **stabbing pain; un látigo** means **a whip** but **un latigazo** becomes **a lash, a crack of the whip** or **a sudden pain**. When the feminine **zarpa – paw** changes gender and adds **–azo** you will be faced with **un zarpazo – a swipe** administered by a bear or feline. **Un fogón** is a **small stove, range,** but **un fogonazo** is **a flash, small explosion** which speaks volumes about the former behaviour of small stoves and ranges.

When Spanish grafts the masculine **–ón, -ote** and **-azo** to a feminine noun, the switch in gender promptly dictates a switch in meaning from **una taza – cup to un tazón – a big cup. Una**

jarra is **a jug** but **un jarrón** is an **urn** while **una caja** – **a box** loses its lid to do service as **a drawer**. **Una medalla** – **a medal** grows into **un medallón** – **a medallion** which, unlike an English medallion, can be of enormous proportions and is seen more often in plasterwork than hanging round someone's neck. **Una lámpara** is **a lamp** and the word now applies to **an electric lamp**, but would once have been **an oil lamp** and this, no doubt, is why **un lamparón** is an **oil stain, grease spot**.

When **una pared** – **wall** is converted into **un paredón** it changes into the sinister **wall that a person stands against when facing a firing squad**. **Una mano** – **a hand** takes a turn for the worse as **un manotazo** – **a slap** and although the augmented **manazas** – **butterfingers** looks like a feminine noun it describes a clumsy person of either sex, depending on whether it is preceded by **un** or **una**.

Una cabra is **a goat** but once amended to **cabrón** the family tie remains but the resulting word is what used to be the ultimate Spanish insult and not a large male goat. A newer phenomenon is **una culebra** – **adder** that lengthens into **un culebrón** or **soap opera**.

The addition of **–ón** converts an unattractive **rat** into a tolerable **ratón** or **mouse** even though the suffix might have prepared you for an increase, not a decrease, in size. Not all houses have mice these days, but if you have a computer **el ratón** sits happily on your desk as **a computer mouse**.

Last of all come the disdainful suffixes – **uza, -ajo, -rrio, ucho, -astro** and **–acho**. Thus **gente** – **people** are turned into **gentuza** – **rabble** and **hierba** – **grass** grows into **a weed** – **hierbajo**. **Una villa** – **town** becomes a place of mean streets when it is **un villorrio** where more than one unfortunate inhabitant probably lives in **una casucha** – **a horrid little house**. It doesn't seem fair that adding **–astra** to **madre** should produce **madrastra** – **stepmother** and I don't think it is at all nice to hear my **cat**, Pushy, described as **un animalacho** by Elena, especially as I am always careful to refer to her as **mi vecinita**.

SEX

Perhaps it would be more accurate and less attention-seeking to say **gender** but the magic word always makes you sit up and take notice, doesn't it?

English-speaking sailors call ships **she** but apart from this we are uninventive when it comes to nouns and all we put in front of them are the definite article **the** or the indefinite articles, **a** and **an,** regardless of whether they are masculine, feminine or neuter.

Spanish nouns are always masculine or feminine but never neuter and are preceded by the definite articles **el** and **la** respectively, or the indefinite articles **un** or **una: the man – el hombre, the woman – la mujer, a man – un hombre, a woman – una mujer**.

Now that sex has reared its head, instead of going forth and multiplying, let's pluralise instead. English nouns turn plural while their definite articles stay the same: **the tadpoles**. Spanish rarely does things by halves so it can make a plural of the definite article as well: **los renacuajos – the tadpoles** and **las ranas – the frogs.** Not only that, but Spanish – although like English it eliminates plural indefinite articles when it wants to – doesn't see the need to replace them with a different word as we do: **tadpoles/some tadpoles – renacuajos/ unos renacuajos, frogs/some frogs – ranas/unas ranas**.

You can usually take it for granted that words ending in **–s** are plural but there are exceptions like **mes – month; lunes – Monday; lejos – far** and **crisis** (a situation fraught enough not to need translating). As far as nouns are concerned, the definite articles announce whether you are dealing with a **Monday – un lunes** or **Mondays – los lunes** as well as **the crisis – la crisis** or a succession of **crises – las crisis**. In words like these that don't end in **–o** or **-a,** the article can nearly always be relied upon to indicate gender.

Nouns ending in **–a** are generally feminine and those ending in **–o** tend to be masculine. Nevertheless, others have different endings: **la nieve – snow, el lápiz – pencil, el melón – melon, la sartén – frying pan, el aparador – sideboard, el mantel – tablecloth, la pared – wall.** Don't worry, because you won't be called upon to do any guesswork since the article, definite or indefinite, should indicate whether a word is masculine or feminine.

Even when nouns do end in **–o** or **–a** there are exceptions, so you meet **la radio** – radio, **la dínamo** – dynamo, **la nao** – ship, **la seo** – church and **la mano** – hand which are feminine and **el sofá** – sofa, **el clima** – climate, **el tema** – theme, **el problema** – problem, **el drama** – drama and **el mapa** – map which are masculine. Be careful though, because despite their masculine article, **el agua** – water and **el hacha** – axe break the rules and are feminine nouns. The reason for the apparent irregularity is simply that they are easier to say than **la agua** and **la hacha**.

The names of many animals of either sex end in **-a: foca** – seal; **ardilla** – squirrel; **mofeta** – skunk; **cobaya** – guinea pig; **rata** – rat; **jirafa** – giraffe; **gorila** – gorilla; **pantera** – panther and **cebra** – zebra while a noun like **idiota** defines a masculine or feminine **idiot** depending on whether it is preceded by **el** or **la.** But what must be the most gender-bending word of all is faintly funny, as the diminutive of **father** – daddy is **papá**, as feminine-looking and sounding a word as ever was.

AGREEABLE THINGS

Spanish adjectives are always agreeable because they never contradict the nouns they accompany. When we use nouns, we often throw in extra information: **RED shoe, DRY wine, BAD weather, SPANISH joke.** This extra information is an adjective, which in English is just another unchanging, unchangeable word: **red, dry, bad, Spanish.**

In Spanish, however, an adjective identifies itself with the attendant noun: **zapato rojo** (a singular, masculine noun accompanied by a singular masculine adjective); **vino seco** (a singular, masculine noun followed by another masculine adjective); **tiempo malo** (another singular, masculine adjective) and **chiste español** (yet another singular masculine noun, accompanied by yet another singular masculine adjective).

Silk – seda, **skin** – piel, **luck** – suerte and **onion** – cebolla are all feminine nouns and this femininity dictates the accompanying adjectives: **seda roja; piel seca; mala suerte** and **cebolla española**. Adjectives tend to follow nouns in Spanish as it is generally felt that they lose some of their descriptive clout when preceding them.

English nouns such as the days of the week or the months of the year start with capital letters, together with adjectives that refer to nationality. In Spanish, however, all these lose their initial importance so **French** is written like any other adjective: **francés,** as is **American – americano, Chinese – chino** and all other nationalities.

Obviously, plural nouns need plural adjectives: **zapatos rojos, vinos secos, sedas rojas, pieles secas, chistes españoles** and **cebollas españolas.** As for weather and luck, both can be largely lovely or positively putrid, but they only exist in singular version in both Spanish and English.

Not all nouns end in **-o** or **–a** and it would be unrealistic to expect their agreeable companions to do otherwise, so you are faced with adjectives like **baladí – trifling, fiel – faithful, capaz – capable, hábil – able,** all of which remain the same whether they are wedded to masculine or feminine nouns: **un asunto baladí – a trifling matter, una mujer fiel – a faithful woman, un empleado capaz – a capable employee, una perso- na hábil – an able person.** These plurals are unchanging for both genders: **asuntos baladíes, mujeres fieles, empleados capaces, personas hábiles.**

There are a handful of adjectives which always end in **-a** whether they apply to a masculine or to a feminine noun: **alerta – alert, cotilla – nosey** and/or **gossipy, quejica – whingeing, roña – stingy, hortera – tasteless** and/or **lacking in style, majara – crazy.** Although the last three are slang, it's as well to know them, since these, together with **cotilla** and **quejica,** synthesise qualities that are least-appreciated by the Spanish and consequently are much used in day-to-day insults and snap judgements.

At the same time, and having set out to be agreeable, perhaps it's wiser to turn a blind and tolerant eye to the fact that these characteristics unjustly and permanently appear to be feminine.

THERE YOU ARE

At least four translations exist for **there** but the one in **there is** – translated as **hay** – is short and sweet and problem-free: **hay un gato encima del armario – there is a cat on top of the cupboard**.

Hay remains the same whether singular or plural: **hay dos gatos encima del armario – there are two cats on top of the cupboard**. You aren't restricted to the present tense and can say **there was** and **there were – había** for the recent past and **hubo** for the time the cat hid on top of the cupboard two years ago. There are compound versions, too: **ha habido – there was/there have been, habrá habido – there will have been, había habido – there had been, habría habido – there would have been**.

Inevitably, there are subjunctive versions too: the present tense – **haya** – and the past, which in this case are **hubiese habido/hubiera habido**. They look and sound a little clumsy but still crop up: **si no hubiera habido un gato encima del armario, Elena nunca habría descubierto su regalo de cumpleaños – If there hadn't been a cat on top of the cupboard, Elena would**

If there hadn't been a cat on top of the cupboard.
Elena would never have discovered her birthday present

never have discovered her birthday present.

Apart from **hay,** it is easy to trace the parentage of each version back to the verb **haber.** Tempting as it may seem, take care not to use their plural versions, although these days you hear them in the mouths of those who should know better and read them in the prose of those who should write better.

Having disposed of one **there**, that leaves us with **allí, allá** and **ahí,** three adverbs designed to put something or someone in its place. **Allí** pinpoints a specific **there** so you can point to the top of the cupboard and exclaim **el gato está allí – the cat's there** because you know where it's got to, and are indicating its whereabouts at the same time.

Allá is supposed to indicate a more distant, unspecified **there: por allá debe andar el gato – the cat should be wandering somewhere around there** but you will find that people mostly stick to **allí** if the object under observation is visible, however vaguely. **El gato esta ahí** means **the cat is there** – unlocated but nearer to home than if you'd used **allá**, and the phrase might be accompanied by a wave of the hand in the direction of the highest cupboard.

Allí combines with prepositions to give more detailed information: **allí arriba – up there, allí abajo – down there, allí dentro – in there, allí al lado – beside there**. You find them wedded to **ahí** and less often to **allá** but all accompany **por** to give three versions of a **round there** whose distance from the speaker depends on whether **allí, allá** or **ahí** is used.

Allá followed by **por** appears in constructions like **Elena conoció a Fausto allá por los sesenta – Elena met Fausto back in the Sixties. Por ahí** can be a vague **thereabouts/in the region of: el gato ha estado allí arriba dos horas, o por ahí – the cat has been up there for two hours or so**. A somewhat different state of affairs is **estar por ahí**, which conveys **being out on the town or out on the tiles. Right there is allí mismo: Elena vio al gato allí mismo hace media hora – Elena saw the cat right there half an hour ago.**

The **there it is/there you are** we pronounce on presenting something to someone else is **allí tienes** or **allí tiene** literally **there you have**. The **there you go!** which has overtaken the complacent, accusatory or ratifying **there you are!** is expressed by complacent, accusatory or ratifying Spaniards as **¡ya está!**

as well or the more modern **¡venga!** – literally **come!** A surprised **there!** is very near to a Spanish **¡ahi va!** but **¡anda!** or **¡vaya!** also express the same degree of unexpectedness.

A placating **there, there** is **tranquilo, tranquilo** or the less soothing **tranquilízate/tranquilizaos, tranquilícese/ tranquilícense** which can resemble a brisker **pull yourself/ yourselves together**.

An individual described as being **all there** is **espabilado/a,** literally **wide awake,** and his or her opposite number who is **not all there** would be regarded as **ido/a – gone**. The reflexive **espabilarse** exists as a verb in its own right, meaning **to wake up, look lively, to pull one's socks up** but it is interesting that **ser espabilado** and **estar ido** once again demonstrate what English-speakers see as the consistent inconsistency of **ser** and **estar.**

Allá plus **tú, él, ella, ello** is one way to say **that's your, his, her problem/lookout: si el gato no quiere bajar, allá él - if the cat won't come down, that's his lookout**. The Spanish say **I'm going there – allá voy** when we would say **I'm coming,** while **¡vamos alla!** is **let's get going/let's be off!** Más allá refers to **somewhere further on,** but the addition of the definite object turns **el más allá** into what looks like **the thereafter** but is a less earthbound and far more enigmatic **the hereafter.**

HERE'S LOOKING AT YOU

Here turns few linguistic pirouettes, with translations an undemanding choice between **aquí** and **acá**. It would be convenient and symmetrical if **aquí** and **acá** were to correspond to **allí** and **allá,** but **acá** is something of a poor relation because **aquí** does as well at describing the specific as the unspecified. In fact, you can survive in Spanish without using **acá** at all, with the exception of left-hand-down-a-bit instructions: **mueve esa mesa un poco más hacía acá – move that table a little nearer towards here**.

Aquí can be used whenever you want to say **here: el gato está aquí en el lavadero – the cat is here in the scullery**. Teamed up with **por** it is also suitable if you're not sure whether he's skulking in the scullery or crammed fatly into a drawer: **el gato debe estar por aquí – the cat ought to be around here somewhere.**

Por aquí is useful because it combines vagueness with a sense of direction so someone confronted with a minefield or a muddy street can protest: **no quiero andar por aquí – I don't want to walk through/along here.** Vivo por aquí means **I live round here** while an unadorned **por aquí** is what a waiter murmurs when guiding you towards a table.

Like **allí – there, aquí** is extendable: **aquí dentro – here inside, aquí abajo – down here, aquí arriba – up here, aquí al lado – beside here. Aquí al lado**, incidentally, is a best-loved Spanish phrase and, together with **ahora mismo – here and now**, has no equal for blatant inaccuracy coupled with an inherent reluctance to be tied down to time and distance.

Worthy rivals are **aquí cerca** and **a poca distancia de aquí**. In theory both mean **near here** but they are as fitting for a five-minutes' stroll as a five hours' drive. More frank is **far from here – a mucha distancia de aquí** and **lejos de aquí.** With the addition of exclamation marks, this last doubles for **get out!** although **¡fuera de aquí!** is preferred by husbands who find light-haired cats nestling amongst a drawerful of black socks.

Here and there is a straight translation: **aquí y allá** but there are two versions for **here, there and everywhere: por doquier and por todas partes: cuando tienes gatos, encuentras pelos por todas partes – when you have cats you find hairs everywhere.** In Spanish **that's neither here nor there** loses its links with both **here** and **there** and is translated as **eso no tiene nada que ver.**

Right here is **aquí mismo** and **here I am, here you are** etc. are translated as **aquí estoy, aquí estás** etc. The **here you are** pronounced on **handing something over** is **aquí tienes** but in **a toast – un brindis** the health-conscious Spanish substitute **a tu salud** for our **here's to you.**

De aquí is similar to **thus** or **that's why: a Gilbert se le está mudando el pelo, de aquí el enfado de mi marido – Gilbert's moulting, that's why my husband is cross. De aquí a un tiempo** means **for a while: de aquí a un tiempo, que no vea yo al gato – for a while just don't let me see the cat.**

De aquí en adelante means **from now on: pues de aquí**

en adelante, cierra el armario – well, close the cupboard from now on. And Elena eavesdropping on the cat-and-socks incident later commented: los vecinos han tenido una riña de aquí te espero – the neighbours have had a terrible tiff.

An exasperated Spaniard hits his forehead with the edge of his hand in a gesture resembling a lopsided salute while declaring: estoy hasta aquí – I'm fed up to the back teeth (literally up to here). This exclamation can be enlarged upon by the addition of de plus any noun, pronoun or infinitive: estoy hasta aquí de gatos y calcetines – I'm sick to death of cats and socks. To which a pacific but weary reply might be estoy hasta aquí de discutir – I'm fed up with arguing.

It's not all trouble however, as hasta aquí also occurs in an unexasperated llena mi vaso hasta aquí – fill my glass up to here. The little phrase is the standby of radio announcers too, who like to intone: hasta aquí han escuchado... - (up till now) you have been listening to...

For once it's no big deal if you are an indifferent speller, because an outraged here! can turn into an equally outraged hear! – ¡oiga! if there is no degree of intimacy and ¡oyes! when remonstrating with friends, family and animals... especially animals.

THE GENUINE ARTICLE

The Spanish language, the Spanish assure you, is predictable, reliable and rule-abiding. So you might be disconcerted to read and hear el hacha – axe, el alma – soul, el ancla – anchor, el agua – water, el alba – dawn, el hambre – hunger, el hada – fairy, el ave – bird. These are feminine nouns so you would expect them to be preceded by the feminine article la, but the reason for such waywardness is logical enough. It is as uncomfortable to pronounce la before certain Spanish words as it is to say a before vowels in English. Consequently a Spaniard swaps the feminine article la for the masculine el in el agua while we say an uproar or an earwig.

This only happens with singular, feminine nouns of two or more syllables that begin with a stressed a or ha- and plurals switch back to **las: las hachas, las almas, las anclas, las aguas**, etc.

Differently-stressed feminine nouns starting with **-a** or **ha-** remain obediently tethered to **la: la hamaca** – deckchair, **la hamburguesa** – hamburger, **la agalla** – gill, **la amapola** – poppy, **la alcantarilla** – sewer (drains, not a dressmaker). This also applies in **la albahaca** – basil, **la alcachofa** – artichoke, **la alquería** – farmstead, **la albóndiga** – meatball, **la alpargata** – canvas sandal, **la almohada** – pillow and other words beginning with **al** which are Moorish in origin and generally of a practical, agricultural, homely or edible nature.

You will meet words like **capital, orden, cava corte** and **cura: el capital** is **money** but **la capital** is a **capital city**. **El orden** means **order** of a tidy sort but **la orden** means **order, command** while **la cava** is **the cave** but **el cava** is the **champagne-type Spanish wine** stored in caves until ready to drink. **El corte** is a **cut** but **la Corte** is where aristocrats used to hang out. **El cura** is a **priest** but **la cura** is a **cure in health**. The same thing happens with **modelo: un modelo** corresponds to the **model** that is a representation or prototype but **una modelo** describes a female who models clothes, appears in advertisements or poses for a painter. **Un guía** is **a male guide** but **una guía** is a **handbook, directory** as well as a **female guide,** while **la policía** refers to **the police force** but **un policía** is a **policeman**.

A **lady patriot** is **una patriota** but a **male patriot** is **un patriota** and **un ebanista** is a male **joiner, carpenter** – so a **joiner, carpenter** who happens to be female is referred to as **una ebanista**. A person who looks on the cheerful side of life is **un** or **una optimista,** depending on gender and someone who is inclined to be gloomy will be **un** or **una pesimista**.

This applies to **bromista** – joker, **cuentista** – a tell-tale, **bañista** – swimmer, **carterista** – pickpocket, **caballista** – rider as well as obvious-looking words like **ciclista, futbolista, tenista, dentista** and **oculista**.

Strictly speaking, **azúcar** can be masculine or feminine as the fancy takes you although most people say **el azúcar**. There are no two ways about **la mar** – sea because **el mar** is where we paddle, swim and fish but **la mar** is what people paint or write music, prose and poems about. The latter also provides an enthusiastic superlative: **él es la mar de divertido/crispante**

– he's really funny/annoying.

Old allocations like **pink for a girl and blue for a boy** are outmoded now and even in a sexist language like Spanish you can't always rely on choosing **a** for a girl and **o** for a boy, but you won't go far wrong if you remember that apart from exceptions like **hacha** and **agua** it tends to be **la** for what's feminine and **el** for what's not.

TOIL AND DOUBLE

English is anarchic when forming the plural – look at the way **mouse** becomes **mice** but **house** becomes **houses**. That's why you shouldn't find it odd that Spanish metamorphoses the **-z** in **lápiz** into **-c** when forming the plural **lápices**.

As usual when Spanish takes an anarchic turn, it is for a good reason and on this occasion it is because of the rule that doesn't like a **-z** to be followed by an **-e** (even though the Spanish name for the letter **zed** is **zeta**).

The accent which indicates emphasis on the initial syllable in **lápiz** is retained in the plural, as it is in similarly stressed words like **tree – árbol – árboles** and **chalice – cáliz – cálices**. Some words lose an accent when made plural: **nación, naciones** and **Danish – danés – daneses** but plural adjectives with a stressed first or second syllable hang on to their accent: **fast – rápido – rápidos** and **empty – vacío – vacíos**. Other words succeed in acquiring them: **young man – joven – jóvenes** and **crime – crimen – crímenes**.

The foregoing are subtleties governed by phonetics rather than grammar but the rules for forming plurals are largely trustworthy in Spanish. You can depend on it that a word ending in a vowel only needs the addition of **–s** although those stressful accents make one last guest appearance because a word ending with an emphasised **í** will end in **–es: ruby – rubí – rubíes**. The same rule applies to **-á, -ó** and **-ú** but there are few authentically Spanish words ending in **-á, -ó** or **-ú** and the one you are most likely to meet is **hindú – hindúes**.

A word that ends with a consonant requires **–es** to turn it into a plural and although **y** sounds the same as the vowel **i**, for plural purposes this letter behaves as a consonant: **king – rey – reyes**. And although it might be repetitive, it is not superfluous to mention one again that when a word ends in **-z** this changes to **-c** before adding **–es: blunder – desliz – deslices**.

As in English, some words are plural even when they are singular: **scissors – tijeras, knickers – bragas, underpants – calzoncillos**. All working days end in **–s: lunes, martes, miercoles, jueves, viernes – Monday, Tuesday, Wednesday, Thursday, Friday**, but only the article changes in their plural versions: **los martes, hay mercadillo en Altea – there is market in Altea on Tuesdays**.

Surnames have no plural form, so although you refer to a family named **the Whites**, their Spanish relations are called **los Blanco** while **mothers-in-law** can go plural all round if you say **madres políticas** instead of **suegras**.

Although some English-speakers take the trouble to use Latin plurals for words like **crisis, crises** and **analysis, analyses**, Spanish is conscientiously unpedantic and says **las crisis** and **los análisis** but is undecided about foreign words. Consequently you encounter both **clubs** and **clubes** while the correct plural for **barman** precipitates its own ration of trouble because a Spaniard simply doesn't hear the difference between **barman** and **barmen**.

It would be difficult to replace the use of **club** without radically altering Spain's nightlife and sporting activities. However, there's nothing to prevent your substituting **barman** with **camarero de bar**, not that it's much of an improvement because **bar** is yet another unSpanish word. On the other hand, the plural for **bar** poses no problems and is unanimously agreed to be **bares**, which is appropriate because it's so easy to see double in bars anyway.

TWO THE SAME

Spanish has two words meaning **same: igual** and **mismo** (often extended into **lo mismo**). Sometimes one definition fits a particular bill better than the other, but they are often interchangeable so **me da igual** and **me da lo mismo** are identical in translation: **it's all the same to me**. You can also eliminate **me** to proclaim more anonymous indifference: **da igual, da lo mismo**. There is no obligatory order for the words in these phrases which can be said the other way round if you prefer: **igual me da, lo mismo me da, igual da, lo mismo da**.

Both words appear in different circumstances: **we are the same age** – **tenemos la misma edad** but **somos iguales de edad**. In the first phrase the adjective **misma** applies to the noun **edad** but in the second, **iguales** refers to the **we** implicit in **somos**. If you get bogged down or bored with details of this type of explanation, detour the problem by saying **somos de una edad** – **we are of an age**.

Usually **the same as** is translated as **igual que: tu aljibe es igual que el nuestro** – **your water deposit is the same as ours.** On the occasions when you use **mismo** this tends to be followed by a noun which in turn tends to be followed by **que: es la misma revista que ví ayer** – **it's the same magazine** (that) **I saw yesterday**.

Occasionally it is necessary to stick to **mismo**, as in **next week, come on the same day at the same time** – **la semana que viene, ven el mismo día a la misma hora**. When **at the same time** means **at once**, you continue to use **mismo** and for once **time** is translated as **tiempo: todos hablaron al mismo tiempo** – **everyone spoke at the same time** although it is possible to use another translation for **time** – **vez: todos hablaron a la vez**.

When **at the same time** implies **also**, you can take your pick between **mismo** and **igualmente**. **Al mismo tiempo, quiero dejar bien claro que no estoy de acuerdo** and **igualmente quiero dejar bien claro que no estoy de acuerdo** both imply **at the same time I want to make it quite clear that I'm not in agreement**.

Por igual is another way to convey **equally: respeto a todas las opinions por igual** – **I respect all opinions equally.** **¡Igualmente!** is a courteous response when wished a nice weekend or Happy Christmas, for instance, but a sufficiently insolent tone makes it an insolent **and the same to you! Lo mismo digo** is another phrase that can combine apparent agreement with discourtesy.

Mismamente is less versatile than **igualmente** and nearer to **actually: mismamente, no creo que respetas a todas las**

opinions **por igual** – actually I don't believe you do equally respect all opinions.

Igualdad means **sameness** as well as **equality** in **igualdad de los sexos** – **equality of the sexes** or **igualdad de oportunidades** – **equal opportunities**.

Mismo frequently expresses emphasis, so **yo mismo, tú mismo, ella misma** etc. mean **I myself, you yourself, she herself** etc. so **yo mismo respeto todas las opinions** means **I personally respect all opinions**. On the other hand, if you are asked for help when feeling unhelpful you might snap **¡házlo tú mismo! – do it yourself!**

El mismo día means **the same day** but when **hoy mismo – this very day** is uttered by plumbers it would be more accurately translated as **soon-ish** while **ahora mismísimo** is another wily delaying tactic designed to lull the ingenuous into a false sense of immediacy.

Two the same is **dos iguales** but **the same as usual** becomes **lo de siempre**, a phrase suitable for commenting on continuing rain, drought, cold snap or heat wave as well as requesting your usual drink at your usual bar.

When you grumble about **the same old routine**, call it **la rutina de siempre**. **The same old story** becomes **the same song** in Spanish: **la misma canción de siempre** and despite being set to music, the sinking feeling it creates will definitely be the same. One more **same** that isn't the same is **ditto,** which because Spanish so often likes to be different is translated as **idem.**

FINE HOW-D'YOU-DO

Learning another language often means you have to redesign the way you speak. This is particularly noticeable with the various forms of **do** in statements like **do you have a cat?** and which produce elliptical replies like **I do. You do too, don't you?**

You can ask a Spanish question merely by changing inflection and inserting a verbal question mark: **¿tienes un gato?** or by adding **no: ¿no tienes un gato?** while continuing to sound probing. It's also possible to omit **no** with the lengthier **¿es que tienes un gato?**

As well as eliminating **do** from questions, you will have to wave goodbye to **do you? don't you?** and all the other **dos** and **don'ts** that English adds to statements as well as questions. This doesn't mean that you must throw out the baby with the bathwater and eliminate **to do** because this verb is even more in evidence than it is in English, since **hacer** means both **to make** and **to do.**

But **hacer** can't and won't make an appearance in questions such as **do you like going to tea with Elena? – ¿te gusta merendar con Elena?** Both languages can be insultingly short-winded with a curt **no** if you feel that arsenic with Attila might be preferable to a happy half-hour with **Elena.**

One Spanish answer to **I do** and **I don't,** consists of **yes** or **no,** followed by a repetition of all or part of the question. So if you, together with your pain threshold and your boredom threshold not to mention your tastebuds, are prepared to meet the challenge of **merienda** with Elena, you'd say **sí me gusta – yes, I do** literally **yes, that pleases me** or **no, no me gusta – no, I don't.**

If you want to say **Elena makes dreadful/marvellous cakes, doesn't she?** you'll be able to add any number of appendages to **Elena hace unos pasteles atroces/maravillosos** although they will now be appeals for the listener to agree or disagree with the speaker, rather than confirmations of cake-making ability. **Hace unos pasteles atroces ¿no crees? – she makes dreadful cakes, doesn't she?** (literally **don't you think?**) or **¿hace unos pasteles maravillosos ¿verdad? – she makes marvellous cakes – true?**

I'm going to ask Elena to lunch – voy a invitar Elena a comer will provoke an encouraging **do** or a discouraging **don't** which are still detectable in translation: **yes, do – sí, hazlo** or **no, no lo hagas** although these are slightly more precise as you are now saying **yes, do it** or **no, don't do it.**

In English we use **to do** in the sense of **to get on, to fare** but in Spanish it is necessary to translate this with the verb **ir** and some radical rewording: **how did he do at the interview? – ¿cómo le fue la entrevista?** (literally **how did the interview go for him?**). **Do** in its other sense of **to be acceptable, to be all right** is **estar bien: that will do/that won't do – está bien/no** está bien (that's good/not good).

On the other hand, a Spaniard is also fond of the absolutely-verbally-vital **valer**, whose literal meaning is **to be worth** or **to be equal to,** so he often says **vale** or **no vale**. In non-consensual circumstances my less dogmatic, more long-suffering neighbour Marisa might try to smooth things over with **no nos enfademos – don't let's get cross**. Despite her forbearance, even her patience can become exhausted during neighbourly spats and she is apt to tell both Elena and me **I do wish you would both be quiet! – ¡ojalá os callaseis las dos!**

PUTTING ON AN ACCENT

A Spaniard is as class-conscious as anybody else, although when he opens his mouth you won't always be able to tell which kind of school he went to, how he holds his knife or whether he prefers "pudding" to "sweet".

In Spain, an accent tells you where a person lives or comes from. A marquis who is born, bred and resident in a certain region tends to retain that region's accent, instead of having it ironed out once he stops playing with the housekeeper's children. Tone, volume of voice and choice of words indicate whether a Spaniard is what is described as "educated" regardless of his or her level of education, and they indicate whether he or she is socially acceptable and/or well-off into the bargain.

An accent in Spanish is more a question of the cockeyed little hats that perch over so many words and, unless you intend to write much Spanish, the proper placement of accents may come low on your list of priorities. But it doesn't hurt to know that there are occasions when the addition of an accent gives a word another meaning, beginning with **más** which means **more**.

An accentless **mas** means **although – aunque** and **but – pero** (although don't expect to hear them as often as **aunque** and **pero**): **me gustaría comer más sardinas, mas sospecho que me van a sentar mal – I'd like to eat more sardines although I suspect they aren't going to agree with me. Solo** means **alone** but an accent turns this into **only: le gusta comer solo –**

he likes eating alone but **le gusta comer sólo boquerones** – **he only likes to eat anchovies.**

Porque means **because** but **el porqué** is a noun meaning **the reason why** or **the underlying reason**: **te explicaré el porqué de mi pasión por las sardinas** – **I'll explain the cause of my passion for sardines.**

When devoid of an accent, **por que** is roughly equivalent to **through which, for which** or **because of which,** although these need not be present in an English translation: **el tema por que me interesó** – **the matter I was interested in.** If it is sandwiched between question marks and wears an accent as a topknot, **¿por qué?** means **why?: ¿Por qué te gustan las sardinas? Porque me gusta el pescado** – **Why do you like sardines? Because I like fish**. All of which can be confusing, until you get so used to all versions that you no longer see their similarity, like a woman with quads.

The preposition **de** frequently means **of** and frequently appears where it is not needed in English: **una docena de sardinas** – **a dozen (of) sardines. Dé**, however, is part of the verb **dar** – the third person of the present subjunctive, to be precise – and you use it to say things like **quiero que me dé una docena de sardinas** when you are shopping: **I want him/her/you to give me (serve me with) a dozen sardines.**

Something similar happens with **saber: sé que es fácil** – **I know it's easy** but **se sabe que es fácil** – **it's known to be easy**. In this case **sé** is the first person of the verb **saber**, but in the second phrase **saber** has become reflexive – **saberse** – and **se** is the third person, reflexive pronoun.

There is a long list of apparently identical pronouns and adjectives that undergo a personality change when wearing an accent: **mi/mí; tu/tú** etc. as well as **este** and **éste** –not to mention the subjunctive verb **esté**. Their repercussions on what you say or hear in Spanish are so slight that they can be ignored on a conversational level. Many Spaniards will in any case assure you that accents only ever matter when doing dictation at school. What is more, they continue, they can be omitted entirely when using capital letters, although this sounds suspiciously like the contempt that familiarity breeds. Accents may be something you don't have to worry about too much – but it's still handy for a foreigner to be warned about the upheavals and confusion that could result from not knowing that **te quiero** means **I love you** but **té quiero** means **I want tea.**

ON REFLEXION

There's no escaping the fact that Spanish verbs often do things that ours don't. Reflect upon **a reflexive verb,** which some modern Spanish grammarians now prefer you to call **un verbo pronominal**. They have decided this describes an action that originates with or within the subject of the verb, rather than an action that returns to or reflects upon the subject.

Perhaps reflecting upon a verb, let alone scrutinising its intimate relations with a subject or, worse still, with an object, isn't at the centre of your own private universe. In this case it would be nice to say you can miss out this bit. Unfortunately, you'd better soldier on because when you need to strain greens or intend to do some queue-jumping it's in your best interests to be aware that **colar** means **to strain** but **colarse** means **to enter without permission** or **to push in**.

This isn't because **colar** and **colarse** are unrelated and isn't a case of double definitions, either. It just so happens that marrying the pronoun **se** to an infinitive puts many a verb in an entirely different light.

Thus, **ir** means **to go** but **irse** means **to go away; marchar** means **to walk** as well as **to go** in the sense of **to function** but **marcharse** once again means **to go away. Meter** is the infinitive of **to put** but **meterse** is a not tremendously articulate translation of **to pick on**.

Levantar and **levantarse** illustrate the way verbs change in the presence of a reflexive pronoun. **Levantarse** is the sort of reflexive verb that makes most sense to an English-speaker because **levantar** means **to lift, pick up** while **levantarse** means **to pick oneself up**. Similarly **acostar** means **to put to bed: la madre acostó al bebe – the mother put the baby to bed** but **acostarse** means **to go to bed, to put oneself to bed: yo me acuesto a las once – I go to bed at eleven** and yes, **acostarse** is used as ambiguously in Spanish as in English.

Besar means **to kiss: Nieves besa a su madre – Nieves**

*Nieves and her cousin Esmeralda loathed each other
when they were young*

kisses her mother but **¡que se besen los novios!** is what the guests chanted at her wedding breakfast after she married Blas. They wanted to **see the bride and groom kiss** because **besarse** refers to mutual kissing between couples.

Once you get the hang of reflexive verbs it is easier to understand how **querer** can mean **to want** as well as **to love**. You say **Nieves y Blas quieren encontrar un piso – Nieves and Blas want to find a flat** as well as **Nieves y Blas se quieren – Nieves and Lola love each other**.

It's not all love and kisses, either: **Esperanza aborrece escribir cartas** means **Esperanza loathes writing letters** but **Nieves y su prima Esperanza se aborrecían de pequeñas** means **Nieves and her cousin Esperanza loathed each other when they were little**.

The absence of a reflexive pronoun in **Blas afeita – Blas shaves** might imply he is a barber and shaves the entire male population of his town. In contrast **Blas se afeita** makes it plain that the only person to be shaved by Blas is himself.

This is what **reflexive verbs – verbos pronominales** if you insist – are all about, because a verb with a tell-tale reflexive pronoun reveals who does what to whom, independently of preceding or following waffle. Some verbs such as **jactarse – to brag about, vanagloriarse – to boast about, atreverse – to dare to and dignarse – to deign to** only exist in reflexive form

With infinitives, reflexive pronouns come wagging their tails behind them but once you get round to conjugating, **me, te, se, nos** and **os** all nip round to the front. There they tend to stay until they get bossy and attach themselves to the rear ends of imperatives: **¡levántate – get up! ¡volvéos! – turn round!** and **¡vámonos – let's go!**

English-speakers use the passive all the time to say things like **Esperanza was heard to say it doesn't matter** but Spanish is less fond of it, and often uses a verb's third person, preceded by **se: se le ha oído decir a Esperanza que no importa**.

Nevertheless, what with the continuing spate of Latin American soap operas and the influence of English on transatlantic Spanish, the voice of the passive is heard in our land. Consequently, it is no longer unusual to come across constructions like **la voz de la tórtola fue oída en el campo – the voice of the turtle dove was heard in the countryside.** Luckily most people still stick to **se oía la voz de la tórtola en el campo** and even Nieves's mother, Elena, who is addicted to acquiring soap opera mannerisms remains faithful to **¡esto no se puede aguantar!** or **this can't be borne!** – a lament she mutters twenty times a day and which we all know is only a reflex action.

WELL AND GOOD

When you announce **my cat's had kittens,** your English friends say **good**, a word whose Spanish translation is **bueno**. Then again, your Spanish friends will answer **bien,** which means **well**. In both instances, and whatever the nationality, all can be relied upon to change the subject immediately.

Once the little kitties start to grow and you canvass for happy feline homes, your English friends will ponder your plea and say **well...** while your Spanish friends will also ponder your plea and murmur **bueno...** In both instances they will all turn you down flat.

These reactions have less to do with like or dislike of kittens than a Spaniard's tendency to say **well** where we say **good** and our own tendency to say **well** when he says **good.** It doesn't always happen this way, though, and some of the time you find these words doing what they oughta, like the little white duck sitting in the water.

So **un buen libro** means **a good book** and **un libro bien escrito** is **a well-written book**. When preceding a singular, masculine noun, **bueno** is shortened to **buen** because this is more pleasing to the Spanish ear. When following a noun, **bueno** is unchanged: **un libro bueno,** but a plural is the same whether it comes before or after: **buenos libros** and **libros buenos**.

Some people hold that **buen** and **buena** are more emphatic when preceding a noun while others maintain that they sound better when following but in practice it is a matter of choice whether you place them fore or aft. **Bastante bueno** – literally **good enough** is closer to **quite good** – and this phrase is an example of Spanish understatement because in the right tone of voice it will imply that something is **really very good indeed**.

Sometimes the adjective **bueno** is preceded by **el** and is visible in that recurring street name, **Guzmán el Bueno** – **Guzmán the Good.** If Blas or Nieves promises to take a kitten you will almost certainly refer to them as **el bueno de Blas** or **la buena de Nieves** which, as well as some degree of saintliness, also implies they are okay people: **good old Blas** and **good old Nieves**.

As pronouns, **el bueno/la buena** and **los buenos/las buenas** identify a **good** person or object amongst others that are less so: **de todos estos gatitos espero que me des el bueno – out of all those kittens I hope you give me the good one** or **esta vecina es de las buenas – this neighbour is one of the good ones**.

On the other hand, **lo bueno** is quite colloquial and does not necessarily mean **the good**, but can imply the **best aspect** of something: **lo bueno es que la suegra de Blas tiene alergia a los gatos – the best part/best side of it is that Blas's mother-in-law is allergic to cats**.

The adverb **bien** sometimes corresponds to an English **good/very/fine/** when preceding an adjective: **ese gatito está bien gordito – that's a fine plump kitten**. It can also be similar to **enough: ya está bien de gatitos – that's enough about kittens.**

Bien combines with the verb **venir** to mean something like **to suit** or **to be convenient: me vendría bien si alguien quisiera llevarse un gatito – it would suit me very well if someone were to want to take a kitten**.

As well as being an adverb, **bien** has a shot at being a noun too, so **el bien** means **welfare or good: hacer el bien – to do good. Un hombre de bien** or **una mujer de bien** suggests a **decent, upright sort of person** and **hago esto por tu propio bien** means **I'm doing this for your own good.** The plural **bienes** are **assets** of a financial nature but not the **goods** that are **commodities,** whose translations are **mercancías** or **géneros.**

You can't exclaim an equivalent to **good grief!** or **good gracious!** in Spanish, but **good heavens!** does become a singular **holy heaven! – ¡santo cielo! Good Lord!** is merely **Lord! – ¡Señor!** although this will often be repeated: **¡Señor, Señor!**

Goodness exists as **bondad,** the sort of **goodness** that is **kindness,** not an exclamation: **would you be good enough to hold this kitten for a moment – ¿tendrías la bondad de sujetar este gatito un momento?** Our **goodness!** is similar to **¡caramba! ¡jolín!** or **¡corcho! –** the last two being substitutes for quite strong swear-words which the Spanish use as frequently and insouciantly as an English-speaker's **goodness! For goodness sake!** is closer to **¡for God's sake! – ¡por Dios¡**

and **good!** is **¡qué bien!** despite the use of **well**, although **a goody-goody** is **un beato** or **una beata**.

Good is absent from many phrases: **for good** turns into **para siempre** – **for always** and the resigned **what's the good?** is an equally resigned **¿para qué?** When something is **no good** you say **no está bien** (using **well** once more) or **no sirve** but a **no-good** is **un malhechor** or **un gamberro,** for whom things do necessarily not **turn out well – salir bien.**

The peculiarly English **not to do any good** is the peculiarly Spanish **no hacer nada,** literally **to do nothing: decirme que no te gustan los gatitos no hace nada – telling me you don't like kittens doesn't do any good.**

Spanish **men of goodwill** are still good chaps: **hombres de buena voluntad** but the **good will** with which girls and boys were encouraged to come out and play is **de buena gana.**

You meet **buena** and **buenas** in un-English sayings but international predicaments like **la hemos hecho buena – we've made a mess of it** and **¡la tenemos buena! – now we're in for it! ¡Buenas!** is a lazy, laconic greeting, suitable for any time of the day or night.

Buenas is likewise incorporated into the kind of unlazy, unlaconic leave-taking you get from friends when broaching the subject of love and security for appealing but fast-developing kittens: **¡adiós y muy buenas!**

BAD SHOW

No hay mal que por bien no venga – nothing is so bad that it doesn't bring good is as near as you get in Spanish to **it's an ill wind that blows no good.** In this instance, **mal** is a noun – **badness, evil** – but **mal** can also be an adverb that corresponds to **badly** or **wrong: ¿cómo te fue el examen? – how did the exam go?** If things didn't go too well, the answer would probably be **mal – badly.**

The negative **no estar mal** can indicate **mediocrity** so **no está mal** means **it's not bad** or **it's passable.** However, the same phrase – and especially **no está nada mal** – can also imply an enthusiastic **it's quite good** and **it's really rather good** respectively. **Estar mal** is also the classic Spanish way **to be wrong, not to be in the right** or **to be unacceptable: estas sumas están mal – these sums are wrong.**

Pasarlo mal is **to have a bad time** or **not enjoy oneself. Encontrarse mal** has no connection with not encountering what you seek or being ill-met but means **to feel ill.** Thus, if the prawns you had for dinner turn out to have been suspect, you will probably groan **me encuentro muy mal** as you totter along to the bathroom next morning.

On those occasions when you need to sound insincerely regretful or regretfully insincere, **mal que me pese** does splendidly: **mal que me pese, tengo que decirte que la cena anoche me sentó fatal – much as I hate to, I must tell you that last night's dinner had a ghastly effect on me.**

Mal can be a shortened form of the adjective **malo – bad** that behaves in the same way as its nicer side, **bueno.** You'll meet **mal tiempo – bad weather, un mal asunto – a bad business, mal gusto – bad taste, mal consejo – bad advice.** Once you put the adjective after the verb, it will be necessary to add **-o: tiempo malo, un asunto malo, gusto malo, consejo malo.**

The feminine **mala** cannot be shortened. As a rule, you can put it both before and after a noun but **bad luck** is invariably translated as **mala suerte. Por las malas**, logically enough the opposite of **por las buenas,** means **with a bad grace,** while **"malas"** is called out by children when eliminating someone during a game.

Whether you use **ser** or **estar** inevitably has some bearing on the degree of badness you wish to convey. **Estar mal, malo** or **mala** means **to be unwell** and also **to be off** or **spoilt** (food, drink): **las gambas que compré ayer están malas – the prawns I bought yesterday are off.** Saying **las gambas que compré ayer son malas** suggests that whatever their degree of freshness, they are of poor quality.

As well as **to be wicked, ser malo** can refer to something that is **bad for one: las galletas son malas si quieres adelgazar – biscuits are bad if you want to slim.**

In some verbs, **mal** is incorporated: **maltratar – maltreat; malgastar – to spend unwisely** or **fritter; malvender – to sell unprofitably; maldecir – to curse.** Adjectives and nouns behave similarly: **maloliente – bad smelling; malcontento –**

discontent; **malhumorado** – **bad-tempered**; **un malhechor** – **a wrong-doer. Un malhecho** is **a bad deed** but **mal hecho** describes things or people when they are **badly made**.

Mal educado is the Spanish version of our **rude, bad mannered** and also serves as a noun: **un mal educado** or **una mal educada** – and yes, **mal** is now an adverb qualifying an adjective and can be situated before the feminine **educada**. **Mal educado** does not automatically involve having been **badly taught**, which is translated as **mal enseñado. Mal pensado** describes a person who **thinks the worst** in an uncharitable but not a fatalistic sense.

El mal exists as a noun and, as you'd imagine, means **evil** or **badness**, two nasty concepts that can also be translated as **maldad,** and which it is to be hoped has nothing to do with **el mal de ojo** – **the evil eye. Un malo** is **a villain** and **una mala** is no better than she should be, either. You'll come across **lo malo** which means something approximate to **the worrying, annoying** or **worst thing: lo malo es que no puedo pensar en un ejemplo** – **the annoying thing is that I can't think of an example.**

Last of all, instead of **thank goodness** or **that's good,** a Spaniard tends to say **menos mal** – **less bad**, a phrase that says much about Spanish propensity to hope for the best while expecting the worst.

MUCH OF A MUCHNESS

The comfortingly recognisable **mucho** proves to be less than accommodating to English-speakers because it will not always correspond to **much**. So although **with much respect** is **con mucho respeto**, you will find that **much respected** is an unobliging **muy respetado**.

Mucho is an adjective when accompanying a noun like **respeto** and retains the meaning of an English **much: le trataron con mucho respeto**. But when **much** precedes yet another adjective as it did with **much respected** it promptly becomes an adverb to be translated as **muy** – **very**.

This is a two-way process because **BEING very hungry,**

sleepy, afraid in English involves adjectives but in Spanish you will find yourself complaining about **HAVING** much **hunger, sleepiness, fear**. These are nouns and therefore preceded by **mucho: mucha hambre, mucho sueño, mucho miedo**. As with all Spanish adjectives, **mucho** must agree in number and gender with its lawful wedded noun. Occasionally it acquires a translation specific to the word it keeps company with: **mucho tiempo – a long time; mucho mar – rough sea, mucha mujer – quite a woman**.

Adverbs are easier because they are unchangeable and unchanging. As a rule, they are found in the company of verbs and **mucho** will be translated as **very, very much, a lot: cocinar mucho – to cook frequently** or **me parece que discutimos mucho – it seems to me that we argue a lot**.

Spanish can be more effusive than English, but the smoothest way to translate **Do you like my new shoes? Yes, very much** omits **very**: **¿Te gustan mis zapatos nuevos? Sí, mucho**. For a palpably enthusiastic **very much**, use the superlative **muchísimo** instead. Something similar happens with **I miss you very much – te echo mucho de menos** and **I miss you very, very much – te echo muchísimo de menos**. When wanting to say **I miss you SO much** you need a quite different word, **tanto: te echo tanto de menos**. Should you decide you're not so lonely after all, say **no te echo tanto de menos como antes – I don't miss you so much as before**.

Having warned you to look out for **mucho** as an adjective and a noun, it's only fair to tell you that it is also a pronoun corresponding to **many**. It will almost always be plural and take the gender of the noun it replaces: **no tires las revistas porque hay muchas que no he leído – don't throw the magazines away because there are many I haven't read**. Or **muchos creen que ciertas revistas son mezquinas – many think that some magazines are silly**.

Mucho has no part in **too much – demasiado** or **de más: me dio demasiado cambio – he gave me too much change** or **le diste diez euros de más – you have given him ten euros too much**.

Much is a non-starter in **how much,** which in all its guises is translated as **cuánto: ¿cuánto valen los zapatos? – how much are the shoes?** or **se le había olvidado cuanto le gustaban los**

garbanzos – he had forgotten how much he liked chickpeas.

Much more is a predictable **mucho más: hay mucho más trabajo de lo que me imaginaba** – there's much more work than I imagined. It's time to nag about **mucho** in the phrase **mucho más** taking the number and gender of a noun it precedes: **hay muchas más revistas de las que me imaginaba** – there are many magazines than I imagined. On the other hand, when **más** precedes an adjective, **mucho** is unchanged: **es mucho más guapa que su hermana** – she's much prettier than her sister.

Mucho menos is **much less, far less** and the basis of a favourite pleasantry – **ni mucho menos** – which is a very civil way of saying **not at all**. It is also a favourite put-down that remains civil but conveys a differently flavoured **not at all: ¿Me echas de menos? Ni mucho menos** – Do you miss me? Not in the least.

Como mucho is not unlike **at the outside** but should not be taken seriously when used in connection with time, since **como mucho, tardaré veinte minutes** invariably precedes an hour's wait: **I'll be twenty minutes at the outside**. A confident phrase like this needs only slight modification to put things in the right perspective, though: **por mucho que insistas que no tardarás, no te creo** – **however much you insist you won't be long, I don't believe you**. Note, too, the presence of the subjunctive – always a sure sign of disbelief or an iffy situation.

YOU'D BETTER!

Better improves itself into a Spanish **mejor** and, just as **better** in English is usually followed by **than, mejor** will have **que** in tow: **Nieves es mejor cocinera que Esperanza** – **Nieves is a better cook than Esperanza**.

When comparing unnamed things or people, **mejor que** will be followed by any of the pronouns: **ella es mejor cocinera que tú** – she is a better cook than you; **estos libros son mejores que aquellos** – these books are better than those; **él dice que esa corbata es mejor que la suya** – he says that tie is better than his.

If what you compare is plural, remember to make **mejor** plural, too: **las lentajas son mejores que las judías** – **lentils are better than beans**.

Sometimes **que** is omitted and comparison made while only implying what has been put in the balance: **hoy hace mejor tiempo** – **the weather is better today; es mejor andar** – **it's better to walk** or **es mejor pasar hambre** – **it's better to go hungry**. Adding **que** suggests something obliquely opposite: **es mejor que andar** – **it's better than walking and es mejor que pasar hambre** – **it's better than going hungry**.

The noun **una mejora** describes **an improvement** in looks, temper, circumstances or weather but the nearest Spanish gets to the outdated collective noun, **betters**, is **superiores** and refers only to someone with superior authority – not more money or social position.

Better can be an adverb in Spanish and English: **házlo mejor** – **do it better; ella cocina mejor que tú** – **she cooks better than you; se come mejor en el campo** – **one eats better in the country**.

The plural should be pondered because, as an adverb, **mejor** does not undergo changes in gender or number: **ellas guisan mejor las lentejas** – **they cook lentils better**. If you get it wrong you will continue to make sense, however: **ellas guisan lentejas mejores** – **they cook better lentils** and the difference is so subtle as to be barely visible.

The verb **mejorar** means **to better, to improve: puedo mejorar su oferta** – **I can better his offer; el nivel de vida en España ha mejorado significamente** – **the standard of living in Spain has improved significantly; ese peinado te mejora** – **that hairstyle makes you (look) better. To get the better of** is **aventajar, llevar ventaja** and, if you really succeed in coming out on top, **vencer**.

The reflexive **mejorarse** means **to get better: espero que te mejores de la indigestión** – **I hope your indigestion gets better**. On the other hand, **to get better in health** is translated as **curar: Esperanza cree que el nuevo médico le curará a su padre** – **Esperanza believes the new doctor will cure her father**. The past participle, **mejorado**, is an adjective meaning **better, improved** and **estás muy mejorada** (heard after a holiday or Botox injections, perhaps) is understood to mean **you're looking very much better**.

Both **mejor aún** and **mejor todavía** mean **better still**, while **tanto mejor** is **so much the better.** Any of these provides a suitable reaction to a statement like **he decidido planchar tus camisas en vez de leer el periódico – I've decided to iron your shirts instead of reading the newspaper**.

Mejor para tí is harder to translate than it looks. Its literal meaning is **better for you** but it can imply resigned acceptance of unwelcome news: **no puedo planchar tus camisas porque salgo a comer – I can't iron your shirts because I'm going out to lunch**. A magnanimous, shirtless response to this would be **mejor para tí – well bully for you**.

A lo mejor goes off at a tangent by meaning **perhaps: ¿a lo mejor no tienes hambre? – perhaps you're not hungry? Así mejor** and **mejor así** are the same as **that's better, it's better that way,** so **he decidido hacer caldo en vez de paella – I've decided to make consommé instead of paella** might be greeted by indigestion sufferers with **mejor así** while a dedicated dieter might exclaim **¡mucho mejor! – much better!**

It's better to is translated as **es mejor** or **más vale: es mejor hacer regimen** and **más vale hacer regimen** both mean **it's better to diet**.

Occasionally **mejor** is preceded by a possessive adjective or one of the definite articles, an addition which turns it into a superlative: **esta es mi mejor receta – this is my best recipe; sacaron los mejores vinos – they brought out the best wines**.

Lo mejor is the **best part, the best thing: lo mejor de la paella es el arroz – the best thing about paella is the rice. Lo mejorcito** isn't quite slang and despite the diminutive suffix implies **the very best, really the best: lo mejorcito de una paella es lo rascado – the very best part of a paella is the crust at the bottom**. As any serious paella expert will tell you, **no hay nada mejor – there's nothing better**.

FROM BAD TO WORSE

What's best about **worse** is the way it behaves like **better: Esperanza es peor cocinera que Nieves – Esperanza is a worse cook than Nieves; su estofado es indiscutiblemente peor** que el mío – her stew is indisputably worse than mine.

When making comparisons in the plural, it's necessary to use the plural form of **peor: las lentejas que hace Esperanza son peores que sus judías – Esperanza's lentils are worse than her beans**.

As with **mejor**, it is not always necessary to drag another party into the conversation: **hoy hace peor tiempo – the weather is worse today; es peor andar – it's worse to walk; es peor pasar hambre – it's worse to go hungry.** Again, popping in **que** makes a difference: **es peor que andar – it's worse than walking; es peor que pasar hambre – it's worse than going hungry.**

Peor does its obligatory stint as an adverb: **Esperanza y su prima Nieves guisan peor las lentejas que Elena – Esperanza and her cousin Nieves cook lentils worse than Elena**. As before, you still won't sound incoherent if you addle an adverb and turn it into an adjective: **guisan peores lentejas – they cook worse lentils.**

Hacer peor translates **to make worse: esa medicina ha hecho peor mi indigestión – that medicine has made my indigestion worse.** You get across the same idea with **poner peor: creo que esa medicina me pone peor – I believe that medicine makes me worse.**

Empeorarse and **empeorar** mean **to be worse, to worsen, to make worse: se empeorará el tiempo – the weather will get worse** or you might say to a bad-tempered individual: **no empeores las cosas – don't make things worse.**

Empeorar isn't the most apt verb to use when a person **is** or **looks worse** and even a hypercritical person like Esperanza would have the good grace to say **te veo peor –** literally **I see you worse** when what she really means is **you look worse.** For this reason, **hacer peor** is often preferred to **empeorar: ese peinado te hace peor – that hairstyle makes you (look) worse.**

Un empeoramiento is a noun that means **a worsening: noto un empeoramiento en el tiempo – I detect a worsening of the weather**. The past participle **empeorado** can be used as an adjective but you'll hear **desmejorado** just as often, especially when describing someone whose aspect is **worse: Esperanza dice que ve muy desmejorada a Nieves – Esperanza says that Nieves looks worse to her.**

Ir de mal en peor means **to go from bad to worse. Peor aún, peor todavía** and **tanto peor** all mean **worse still.** Like **mejor para ti**, you will find **peor para tí** hard to translate but easy to use. It is superficially commiserating but double-edged, so when I inform my husband **salgo a comer con Esperanza – I'm going out to lunch with Esperanza** he is likely to respond **¡pues peor para tí! – tough for you!**

With the addition of the definite article or a possessive adjective **peor** descends deeper into the depths and turns into **worst: son las peores lentejas que ha hecho nunca – they're the worst lentils she's ever made** or **ni las ofrecería a mi peor enemigo – I wouldn't offer them to my worst enemy.**

On its own, **lo peor** means **the worst, the worst thing: lo peor de las lentejas de Esperanza es que siempre se pegan – the worst thing about Esperanza's lentils is that they always stick (to the saucepan)** and note that Spanish is more economical with words in this situation. **Llevar lo peor** means **to get the worst of a situation,** something I am resigned to when Esperanza invites me to lunch, and although a philosopher might say **podría ser peor – it could be worse,** not being of a philosophical turn of mind, I can't help sighing **¡peor imposible!**

MORE THAN YOU KNOW

Más que ayer, menos que mañana is what those in love like to hear. It means **more than yesterday, less than tomorrow** and is a standard declaration of long-term devotion.

Más means **more: ¿quieres más café – do you want more coffee?** Or **voy a hacer café – ¿quieres más? – I'm going to make coffee – do you want some more?**

To say **more than,** add **que: el café-café me gusta más que el instantáneo – I like real coffee more than instant** (**café-café** may not figure in your dictionary, but exists in the personal vocabulary of every coffee-drinking Spaniard). However, when **más** is followed by a number, **que** is substituted by **de: he tomado más de cinco tazas de café – I've had more than five cups of coffee.**

You nearly always need **más** to make comparisons. There are exceptions such as **grande – mayor, bueno – mejor** and **malo – peor** which mean **big – bigger, good – better** and **bad – worse** respectively. However, the usual procedure is to put **más** in front of the adjective, noun or adverb, followed by **que** if needed: **este café es más caro – this coffee is dearer; bebo más café que té – I drink more coffee than tea** or **bebo más rápidamente que tú – I drink more quickly than you.**

You form the superlative by putting a definite article – **el, la, los** or **las** – in front of **más: es la más cara de todas las marcas – it's the most expensive of all the brands**. If, as the Spanish often do, you put the noun before the adjective, the article goes before the noun: **es el café más horrible que he bebido nunca – it's the most horrible coffee I've ever drunk.**

Some Spanish phrases incorporating **more** correspond to a few we use in English: **más o menos – more or less; no more – no más; nevermore – nunca más** and **ni más ni menos – no more and no less.**

On the other hand, some phrases – **más bien,** for instance – are completely foreign to English: **este café es más bien soso – this coffee is rather insipid**. **Más** will sometimes translate **so** in an exclamation: **¡es más rico el café! – coffee is so good!** or **¡estaba más cargado! – it was so strong!**

Su más y su menos is another uniquely Spanish phrase: **el café tiene su más y su menos – coffee has its good and its bad points.** **A lo más** is one way to say **at most**, while **cuando más** is another. **De más** means **too many, extra** and is the same as **de trop** in French (and English, come to that). As well as meaning **to be in the way, to be the odd one out, to be superfluous**, the verb **estar de más** sounds pretty martyred in an observation like **no estaría de más fregar las tazas sucias – it wouldn't hurt to wash up the dirty cups.**

Venir a más implies **to come up in the world, rise above one's station: una que ha venido a más ya no querrá fregar las tazas sucias – someone who's bettered herself won't want to wash dirty cups now.**

That's **more** more or less sorted and you'll be able to dispose of **less** in more or less the same fashion. **Bebemos menos té – we drink less tea; te pondré menos té – I'll pour you less tea; este té es menos caro – this tea is less expensive; he tomado** menos de cinco tazas – I've had less than five cups.

Comparatives and superlatives behave predictably: **bebo menos té que café – I drink less tea than coffee; bebo menos rápidamente que tú – I drink less quickly than you; es la menos cara de todas las marcas – it's the least expensive of all the brands; es el té menos horrible que he bebido nunca – it's the least horrible tea I've ever drunk.**

Venir a menos means **to come down in the world** and **cuando menos** means **at the outside, at least. Ser de menos** undergoes the kind of change you'd expect when switching from **estar** to **ser**, so that **es de menos que no hayas fregado las tazas** implies **the fact that you haven't washed up the cups is the least of it.**

A menos means **unless: me voy, a menos que hagas más té – I'm off, unless you make more tea. Menos mal,** literally **less bad** is similar to **thank goodness: menos mal que hayas comprado otra marca – thank goodness you've bought another brand. Echar de menos** means **to miss: no echo de menos el clima inglés – I don't miss the English climate.**

And to conclude, another stock declaration of undying Spanish love: **hoy y siempre – today and always.** So what has that got to do with **more and less?** Nothing really –but it's more or less what those in love like to hear.

IN DEPTH

An English **in** will often be a Spanish **en,** so **in all,** for instance, tots up to **en total.** If you're **in danger** you'll be **en peligro** and with characteristic Spanish pessimism, **in trouble** plunges into plurality and worries itself into **en dificultades. In transit** transfers itself into **en tránsito, in motion** moves over to **en movimiento** while **in vain** becomes **en vano** or **en balde. En vilo** isn't the slightest bit vile and means **up in the air** (ideas or plans, not aeroplanes).

Sometimes matters are predictable, so **en mi vida** means **in all my life: en mi vida he visto un gato más guapo que Gilbert – in all my life I've never seen a more handsome cat than Gilbert.** You find **en** where you do not in English, and a fitting answer to a question like ¿es Gilbert un gato activo? – is Gilbert an active cat? would be en absoluto – absolutely not. En resumen means to sum up or briefly but the tempting en breve is closer to shortly, soon. En curso corresponds to current: el año en curso – the current year. En directo is a live performance, en forma is on form and en este momento means at the moment while a notice saying "en obras" advises "men at work" or "under repair."

En replaces how in that frequent, solicitous question ¿en qué le puedo ayudar? – how can I help you? (literally in what can I help you?). Occasionally you translate en as on: ¿por qué está el periódico en el suelo? – why is the newspaper on the floor? Or, lo dejé en la mesa – I left it on the table.

There are times when in appears in English but not Spanish: in fact turns into de hecho and in the end into al final. Occasionally an English in changes to a built-in en: in love – enamorado; to fall in love – enamorarse but it's not all blue skies and starry eyes as there is also endeudarse – to get into debt and encarcelar – to jail, to put in prison.

With reference to time, in often becomes dentro de: dentro de diez minutos, hago café implies in ten minutes' time I'll make coffee. When you use en – hago café en diez minutos - you could also be explaining I make coffee in ten minutes because that's how long the process takes. Another in that goes out is the one in café instantáneo es la peor cosa del mundo – instant coffee is the worst thing in the world.

En definitivo is closer to definitively than definitely but when you wish to sound affirmative and particularly when your attention wanders you'll sound impressively Spanish if you throw in the odd en efecto which is the nearest there is to definitely. An English-Spanish dictionary might maintain otherwise, but en efecto is not really the same as an English in effect although if this is one of your habitual phrases, you can produce a similar effect with en realidad and de hecho, even though both mean in fact.

En principio looks straightforward but doesn't mean on principle, so if someone says en principio no tomo café instantáneo he or she is telling you for one thing I don't drink instant coffee or principally I don't drink instant coffee. Alternatively, a person with strong prejudices might

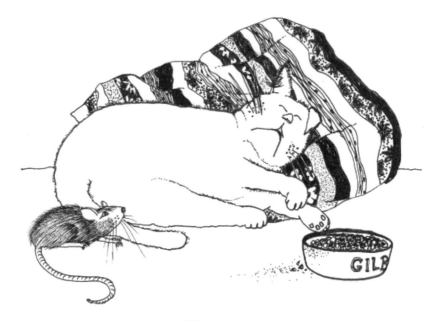

Is Gilbert an active cat?

declare **por principio no bebo café instantáneo** – I don't drink instant coffee on principle.

In time can be translated three different ways: **al compás** – in time to music; **con el tiempo** – in time or eventually and **a tiempo** – in time when this implies **on time: espero que llegue a tiempo el café** – I hope the coffee arrives in time.

En fin means **finally** but often signifies **after all** or **well, then**. This is another exceedingly Spanish expression and is useful for winding up overlong conversations, in which case an inconclusive **en fin...** is generally preceded by a smile and sometimes followed by a rather insincere sigh.

WHAT'S WHAT

Spanish-speakers learning English claim that **que** produces translation headaches, even though it's a mousy, nondescript little word. Like so many of the mousy, nondescript little things that litter our lives, it is deceptively complicated in

80

both languages and can bewilder English-speakers learning Spanish, too.

Que means **that, which, what, who, than, for** and **because** but despite this abundance of meanings it is occasionally hitched to a preceding preposition or article: **fue nuestro conejo** *el que* **comió las plantas de Fausto** – **it was our rabbit** *that* **ate Fausto's plants. La manera** *en que* **mordisqueó alrededor de los pinchos del cactus era** *lo que* **más le irritó** – **the way in** *which* **he nibbled round the cactus spines was** *what* **annoyed him most** (and there you get two for the price of one).

The troubled episode with Fausto and the rabbit continues to illustrate the versatility of **que** in Spanish: **Fausto,** *que* **dice que le gustan los animals, quiere matar a nuestro conejo** – **Fausto,** *who* **says he likes animals, wants to kill our rabbit. Fausto dice que un conejo no es tan importante que su huertecita** – **Fausto says that a rabbit isn't as important as his vegetable patch**.

¡Dáte prisa, que viene Fausto! means **hurry up because/ for Fausto's coming!** a warning that nearly came too late for our rabbit. **Que** is frequently used to give more weight to phrases like **¡que te des prisa!** which is translated as **hurry up!** but is actually a subjunctive-heavy **that you should hurry!** This could be expanded to **¡que te des prisa, que viene Fausto!** **Que** also appears in **¡que aproveche!** which is what one Spaniard says to another Spaniard who is tucking into a meal that he himself is not eating.

Que turns up before **sí** and **no** in **¡que si!** and **¡que no!** which are emphatic ways of saying **yes** and **no**. **Qué** wearing an accent turns into an exclamation beginning with **how** or **what: ¡qué glotón es ese conejo!** – **how greedy that rabbit is!** or **¡qué hombre más antipático** – **what an unpleasant man!**

In English we can omit **which** and **that: the rabbit we own** or **the problems we've had** but you can't get away with this in Spanish. Instead it is vital to have your **que** prominently in view: **el conejo que tenemos** and **los problemas que tuvimos.**

With so many options for mousy, nondescript **que** it is easy to see why translating it into English should also be the cause of so many Spanish headaches. That's why Fausto's immortal rendition in English of **the plants what he devoured** for **las plantas que devoró** was some compensation for the rabbit incident. Even so, and being the way he is, any comment on his grammatical error would have been countered with a belligerent **¿y qué? – so what?**

EVERY WHICHWAY

Having promised you that **who, which, whom, that, what** etc. can all be translated by the same word **que**, now's the moment to stir things up by mentioning that **which** can also be translated as **cuál**.

Cuál is used when you are faced with a choice: **¿cuál de los vinos quiere? – which of the wines does he want?** Or **¿cuál día quieres que venga? – what day do you want me to come?**

When you are shopping or suffering agonies of indecision regarding pears or pumpkins the assistant might (if he or she were in a not particularly good mood) demand **¿cuál?** in the same irritable way an exasperated shop assistant would demand **which?** in English. And if you can't tell the turnips from the tomatoes, you'd grumble **no distingo cuál es cuál – I can't tell which is which.**

Cuál applies to masculine and feminine words alike: **¿cuál mesa? – which table? ¿cuál mes – which month?** The plural for both genders is **cuáles: ¿cuáles mesas?** and **¿cuáles meses?**

There are Spaniards who want to invent their own feminine version and at some time or other you are going to hear **¿cuála?** Answer out of politeness but turn a deaf ear to this hybrid and to its entirely illogical, completely uncalled-for brother version **¿cuálo?** and the totally superfluous **¿cuálos?** because they are as unnecessary as they are incorrect.

Cuál also occurs in phrases like **cada cuál** where it is the equivalent to **each** and **everyone: cada cuál tiene sus propias ideas – everyone has his** (or **her**) **own ideas.**

Expect to encounter **lo cuál**. It still means **which** but joins two separate but connected phrases in the same sentence: **llegó tarde, lo cuál nos irritó – he arrived late, which was annoying** (literally **the which irritated us**).

Por lo cuál means **for which** and is one of the not-so-

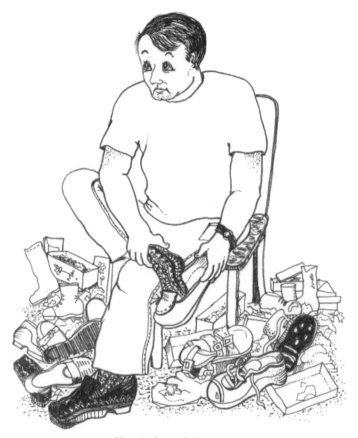

He tried on all the shoes

frequent occasions when you can actually translate **por** as **for**, even though it could be substituted by **so: ya no llueve, por lo cuál debéis estar contentos – it's not raining now, for which you should be glad**.

Con lo cuál means **with which** when this implies **at which, upon which: empezó a llover, con lo cuál se levantó y se fue a casa – it started rain, upon which he got up and went home.** When translating **of which,** you usually encounter a plural: **había zapatos de todos los colores, de los cuáles eligió los rojos – there were shoes of every colour, of which he chose the red.**

You don't need to be a translating whiz to realise that **después de lo cuál** means **after which: probó todos los zapatos, después de lo cuál decidió que no le gustaba ninguno – he tried on all the shoes, after which he decided he didn't like any of them.**

Con lo cuál, después de lo cuál and **por lo cuál** may strike you as being too much like hard work, but they can be banished as readily as they have been conjured up. A lot of people settle for different constructions involving **que** but **that's a matter of taste,** of course: **allá cada cuál...**

WHILE WE'RE ABOUT IT

The **while** that is a **period of time** can be translated as **tiempo** or **rato** but as well as conveying its own measure of heartache and heartbreak, translating **it's a while since I saw him** (or **her**) requires minor surgery. It needs the verb **hacer,** which means **to make** or **to do** and always crops up in time or weather conditions, plus the insertion of a negative to arrive at **hace tiempo que no le veo.**

Verb-spotters will appreciate the substitution of the present for the past tense, a common occurrence when **hacer** is followed by a noun connected with **time** and which in turn is followed by **que.** If you feel less tense when leaving tenses alone, put it another, still negative way: **no le he visto en tiempo,** literally **I haven't seen him in time**.

Your second choice, **un rato,** sounds more immediate and although **no le he visto en un rato** still means **I haven't seen him for a while,** it's clear he was around until a short time ago. You are as likely to hear **hace un rato que no le veo** as **le ví hace un rato** and in both cases it is again understood that the elusive non-appearer was in evidence shortly before.

You'll have to make use of different adjectives when translating **a long while** and **a short while** because length is eliminated and you settle for quantity instead: **hace mucho tiempo que no le veo – it's a long while since I saw him** as well as **hace mucho rato que estoy esperando – I've been waiting for a long while. Short** becomes **little: hace poco rato que**

estoy esperando: I've been waiting a short/little while. Rather or **quite** turn into **bastante – enough, sufficient: hace bastante tiempo que no nos vemos – it's quite a while since we've seen each other.**

Accustomed as we are to Spanish prolixity, it's unexpected when an English word can be eliminated, as happens in **hace mucho que estoy aqui – I've been here a long while; hace poco que estoy esperando – I've been waiting a short while** or **hace bastante que no le veo – it's quite a while since I've seen him**. In fact, there is no need for either **tiempo** or **rato**, so whether or not you get round to translating **while** often depends on whether or not you feel like it.

While isn't only a noun and sometimes it enters your orbit as an adjective, a conjunction or an adverb. If you don't consider nouns, adjectives, conjunctions or adverbs to be fit topics for conversation, keep calm and merely remember that when **a while** implies a **period of time** you say **un tiempo** or **un rato** and when it doesn't, you can often use **mientras: escuchaba a Bach mientras le esperaba – she listened to Bach while she was waiting for him.**

Mientras que is also suitable in a sentence like **while she likes Bach, he likes Berg – mientras que a ella le gusta Bach, a él le gusta Berg** (which might explain why he always keeps her waiting or doesn't turn up at all). The most suitable translations for **while** when this means **although** are **aunque** or **bien que** and both require the subjunctive mood for the following verb: **aunque parezcan incompatibles tienen mucho en común / bien que parezcan incompatibles tienen mucho en común – while they appear to be incompatible, they have a lot in common.**

The adverb **meanwhile** as in **meanwhile back at the ranch** is **mientras tanto** or **entretanto: mientras tanto/entretanto, ella intenta escuchar a Berg – meanwhile she tries to listen to Berg.** The adjective **worthwhile** requires some reshuffling and the predictable introduction of **valer** which in these circumstances actually means **to be worth** for once: **ella dice que no vale la pena escuchar a Berg – she says it's not worthwhile listening to Berg**, while the Bach-hater has been heard to mutter **no me interesa seguir viéndole – it's not worth my while to go on seeing her.**

There's a verb, too, so it's still easy to **while away** your time, although translations might make you ponder Spanish attitudes towards time, its use and abuse, because you can say **pasar el rato** as well as **perder el tiempo.** Significantly, they imply the same thing although one means to **pass** time, while the other means to **lose** it.

MINEFIELDS

People tend to be attached to their belongings, so it is essential to know the words that indicate who has what. They are **mi, tú, su, nuestro, vuestro** and again **su** but since possessions are not necessarily singular you will also encounter **mis, tus, sus, nuestros, vuestros** and **sus.** Accordingly a bird fancier says **mi periquito** unless he has an aviary full of budgerigars in which case he would say **mis periquitos.**

These words spend their lives as pronouns or adjectives but if a statement of this kind leaves you in the dark there is no need to be anxious because when the moment comes to use them, all you need to remember is that the all-purpose **mi, tú, su** have no feminine versions and just have to be made plural when accompanying a plural noun or replacing one. However, **nuestro** and **vuestro** do have feminine versions: **nuestras** and **vuestras.**

Amongst other things **a budgerigar** is a noun, so in keeping with the demands of Spanish grammar it will live in eternal agreement with neighbouring adjectives and pronouns. Thus proud owners of more than one budgerigar refer to **mis peri-quitos, tus periquitos, sus periquitos, nuestros periquitos** and so on down the long, cheeping list.

Birdless owners of other objects refer to **nuestro plumero – our feather duster** but **vuestras hormigoneras – your cement mixers** and **vuestras aspiradoras – your vacuum cleaners.**

Having learnt to establish ownership of budgerigars by saying **mis periquitos** you might like to say **that budgerigar is mine, yours, his** etc. For this you need **mío, tuyo, suyo, nuestro, vuestro, suyo: este periquito es mío, tuyo** and so on and so on.

All these words end in **-o** in masculine form, and once again they should agree with the word they accompany or replace. When someone points to a phalanx of cement mixers and asks **¿de quién son aquellas hormigoneras: whose are those cement mixers?** - keep your head, tell the truth, don't muddle your numbers and genders and admit **son mías – they're mine**.

Mío, tuyo etc. are used in the same way as **mine, yours** etc. but you sometimes find **mío** or **mía** following a noun as in **¡madre mía! – mother mine!** an exclamation you hear a hundred times a day encompassing anything from **good gracious!** to **curses!**

Muy señor mío and **muy señores míos** correspond to Dear Sir and Dear Sirs, while **muy señor nuestro** and **muy señores nuestros** are an entrepreneurial **we**. **El Padre Nuestro** is what the Spanish call the **Our Father** or **Lord's Prayer**.

Mi hijo, mi hija mean **my son, my daugher** but the more emphatic **hijo mío, hija mía** as well as an unaccompanied **¡hijo!** or **¡hija!** are employed as conversational signposts or punctuation. **Hijo mío** and **hija mía** are used paternally, condescendingly or affectionately by parents, priests or older people but young people use them amongst themselves somewhat sarcastically and tongue-in-cheek.

Whether or not possession still constitutes nine-tenths of the law it is helpful to know how and when to use **mi, mío** etc. when laying claim to cement mixers, feather-dusters, budgerigars or vacuum cleaners. And when the waiter in your local bar has a drink on his tray and looks round to see where it belongs, just pipe up, **¡es el mío – that's mine!** and it will find its way safely to your table. Occasionally, though, you'll hear **¡mis, mis, mis!** and might wonder what possession is being referred to. In fact, it will be a cat, because **¡mis, mis, mis!** is the Spanish equivalent of **puss, puss, puss!** (and responded to in the same primadonna manner of cats the world over).

THIS, THAT AND THE OTHER

When the Spanish complain about the mysterious rules of English pronunciation and the quaint way we formulate our questions, you realise it's an advantage to have learnt English at your mother's knee and not in the classroom.

Occasionally, however, English is blissfully straightforward – especially when it comes to an undemanding, unchanging little word like **this,** for instance. In Spanish, sex will always come into the proceedings somewhere, which is why **this** must be translated as **este** or **esta,** depending on the gender of what follows. **This steak** becomes **este filete** and **this chop** turns into **esta chuleta.** When you are ravenous and one steak isn't enough, you say **estos filetes – these steaks,** likewise **these chops – estas chuletas.**

Once you get the hang of **this,** you might as well keep things symmetrical and get the hang of **that**, which is translated as **ese** or **esa** when singular: **ese filete y esa chuleta – that steak and that chop.** Their plural versions are **esos** and **esas: esos filetes y esas chuletas – those steaks and those chops.**

Spanish has a further way to say **that** and **those: aquel/aquella** and **aquellos/aquellas.** They are used when you wish to differentiate between **that here** and **that over there: aquel filete – that steak over there** or **aquellas chuletas – those chops there.** In other words, the ones you see on someone else's plate that always look more appetising than your own.

You will also find **aquel** in phrases like **en aquel entonces – at that time, then: en aquel entonces la carne era barata – at that time meat was cheap. That time** is also translated as **aquella vez** when the time referred to is **over and done with** and past: **¿te acuerdas de aquella vez cuando comímos esos solomillos tan ricos? – Do you remember that time when we ate those delicious fillet steaks?** This doesn't mean you can't use **esa,** however: **no queríamos chuletas esa vez – we didn't want chops that time**.

Aquellas tiempos means **in those times, in those days: en aquellos tiempos, comíamos más carne – in those days we ate more meat**.

As in English, you can expect to encounter **este, ese, aquel** etc. as substitutes for a person, object or animal: **quiero una chuleta como aquella, no ésta – I want a chop like that one, not this one. Un filete como aquel es lo que quiero – what I want is a steak like that**. When used as a pronoun in this way, it is a matter of choice whether **este, ese** and **aquel** etc. wear an accent which is only obligatory where there might otherwise be confusion: **comieron esos filetes tiernos** translates as **they ate those tender steaks.** In contrast, an accented **comieron ésos filetes tiernos** tells you that **those** (implying those people) **ate tender steaks.**

The Spanish language doesn't believe in equality of the sexes, so when the plural **these** or **those** have masculine and feminine components, for example – **filetes** and **chuletas** - the resulting **these** or **those** will always be translated as a masculine **estos**, even though there might have been six hundred feminine chops and only one masculine steak.

You'll also make the acquaintance of **esto, eso** and **aquello** which are used, as they are in English, to refer to something that is understood but unspecified: **no sabía eso – I didn't know that, ¡esto es inaguantable! – this is intolerable!** and **no creo que aquello tiene gracia – I don't think that's funny.**

You may find you resent the necessity of handling countless Spanish mutations of words that are comfortably immutable in English. On the other hand, remember that ours is an acquisitive, material society and you stand a better chance of getting what you want once you know how to point and say **I'd like this, I need that** or **I want that over there…**

EITHER WAY

Together with twenty other little girls, I used to be rather wary of a formidable nun whose name was Sister Imelda. Nevertheless, she ironed out many potential problems for us, including how to marry **either** and **neither** to **or** and **nor**, a dilemma whose hash she settled with the nice mnemonic **either or, neither nor.**

If you had no Sister Imelda to solve this one for you, it won't matter in Spanish since **either** compresses itself into the perfectly circular **o** and **neither** is shortened to **ni. Either you do as I say or I'll be angry** becomes **O haces lo que te digo o me enfado** and **neither Cato nor Pushy wants sardines** is **ni Cato ni Pushy quiere sardinas. Neither one nor the**

other is a handily literal translation: **ni uno ni otro quiere jamón – neither one nor the other wants ham.**

Nothing in this world is all black or all white and not all **eithers** and **neithers** will be **o** or **ni**, so **Pearl doesn't want sardines, either** is translated as **Pearl tampoco quiere sardinas. Tampoco** is just as happy before a verb as after although you'll need to add **no: Pearl no quiere sardinas tampoco**.

Words like **either** and **neither** occur as adverbs, conjunctions, pronouns and adjectives but what most people want to know is how to translate a word without stopping to analyse its grammatical function. We've already crossed two off our list with the conjunctions **o, ni** and the adverb **tampoco,** which considerately provides the translation for **neither: tampoco le gusta a Cato la leche – neither does Cato like milk.** Should you want to say **neither do I** this is an uncomplicated **ni yo tampoco** or the terse **ni yo**. By now you will probably have twigged that from a Spanish point of view our translations of **either** and **neither** are merely unnecessary complications.

For the adjective **either,** the Spanish use **cualquiera** which immediately before both a masculine and feminine noun is allowed to drop its –a: **lleva cuálquier gata de las dos – take either of the two (female) cats** or **puedes leer cuálquier libro de estos dos – you can read either of these two books.** In a sentence containing a negative, **either** is **ninguno: he didn't take either cat – no llevó ninguna gata** although this amounts to saying **he didn't take any cat.**

When **either** is a pronoun you need **cualquiera** again: **me gustaría llevar cualquiera de los dos – I'd like to take either of the two.** Or you might say **send it to either of us – mándalo a cualquiera de nosotros.** What won't be mentioned is a specific noun and yet again, **cualquiera** looks – but isn't – an exclusively feminine pronoun and substitutes masculine nouns, too.

Either of us turns into **ninguno de nosotros** if there is a negative in the vicinity, and takes the gender of what is usurped: **no habló a ninguna de las dos – he didn't speak to either of the two (women).** Obviously, the accommodating **ninguno/ninguna** also translates **neither of the two, neither of us** etc.

There are people who never take no for an answer and say things like **either way, I think you ought to read that book**, where **either** needs to be translated from an entirely different angle: **de todas maneras, creo que debes leer ese libro.**

Sometimes **either** signifies **each** so **there are trees on either side of the street is hay árboles en cada lado de la calle.** It might look as though **cada** isn't fulfilling its adjectival duty of agreeing with **lado**, but this is because it is an easygoing word that remains the same whatever the gender of the noun.

Many of us communicate via exclamations and you'll find **ni** helpful when translating **not on your life!** which can be expressed as **¡ni hablar!** even though **hablar** means **to speak. ¡Ni pensarlo!** is pretty much the same as **I wouldn't even consider it!** while **¡ni en sueños!** corresponds to **I wouldn't dream of it!**

Not an exclamation but a verdict is the slangy, disillusioned **ni chicha ni limoná**, a distortion of **ni salchicha ni limonada – neither sausage nor lemonade**, the prosaic, food-orientated lament of a Sancho Panza rather than a Don Quijote – corresponding to an ambiguous **neither one thing nor the other...**

ALL CHANGE

All is an all-enveloping **todo.** As an adjective it frequently lends itself to straight translation but, naturally, acquires the number and gender of the noun it accompanies: **Elena dice que todos los hombres son difíciles de entender – Elena says all men are hard to understand** and **¿por qué has comido todas las galletas? – why have you eaten all the biscuits?** The distraught disclaimer **I've never done anything like that in all my life** dispenses with **all** and is no longer negative: **en mi vida he hecho una cosa así.** However, **all** reappears in **with all haste** and **in all haste,** both of which become **con toda prisa.**

Occasionally, **todo** corresponds to **proper** or **real: era todo un drama – it was a proper drama.** In Spain **es toda una mujercita** has always evoked the kind of little girl who bustles her uncomplicated way towards womanhood and housewifery: **she's every inch the little woman.** At the same time, omission of the article **una** indicates a female who got there long before: **es toda mujer – she's all woman.**

The plural **todos** can convey **every: todos los martes voy al mercado – every Tuesday I go to the market.** It can be similar to **any: I shan't go in any case – de todas maneras, no iré,** although **all** is retained if this is translated as **all the same, I shan't go.** Another version of **todo** is **very: el tren iba a toda velocidad – the train was going very fast.** More idiomatic and colourful would be **el tren iba a todo meter** or **el tren iba a toda pastilla**, both of them similar to **the train was going like the clappers.**

Foreign-sounding to an English-speaker is **con todo, me sigue gustando – in spite of it all, I still like him/her/it.** The similarly magnanimous **a pesar de todos sus defectos es buena persona** means **despite all his faults, he's a good sort,** while **después de todo** boils down to **still and all** as well as the obvious **after all: después de todo, me gusta – still and all, I like him/her/it.**

All is forgotten in **no es para tanto – it's not as bad as all that** while the subjunctive **que yo sepa, no va** is **for all I know, he's not going.** The **not at all** which the polite lob back at you on being thanked for something turns into **de nada** or **no hay de que.** The **not at all** that implies disagreement, once again loses **all: no le gusta el cava en absoluto – he doesn't like cava at all.**

For an obliging **by all means,** a Spaniard obliges with **por supuesto** together with the somewhat effusive, somewhat insincere **no faltaba más** although this phrase can transmit exasperation, too. **De todas maneras** looks as if it could also be useful in translating **by all means** but is nearer to **in any case/anyway: de todas maneras, preferiría vino tinto – he'd rather have red wine, anyway.**

A todo esto is a tremendously Spanish little phrase that means **by the way/incidentally/meanwhile: a todo esto, ¿te has acordado del cava? – by the way, did you remember the cava? A todo esto, tengo sed – in the meantime, I'm thirsty.**

Sometimes it is English that dispenses with **all** as happens with **del todo: no me convence del todo este cava – I'm not entirely impressed by this cava** or **no es del todo horrible – it's not completely horrible.**

The prerogative of the organised, **to be on top of it all** is **estar en todo** – literally **to be in/on it all**. Meanwhile, the conversationally disorganised are not denied the handiness of tailing off sentences with the inelegant **and all** or the more acceptable **everything – habrá canapés y todo – there will be canapés and everything...**

Above all is **sobretodo: sobretodo, tengo que decir que me habría gustado verle – above all, I must say I would have liked to have seen him. Un sobretodo** exists as **a dustcoat** or **overcoat** but the **overall** that means **all in all** is **en conjunto** or **en resumen**. A workman's **overalls** are **un mono** when incorporating **trousers** but the **overalls** worn by a cleaner, shop assistant or doctor are **una bata**.

Todo can become a pronoun, or to put it another way, it saves your having to repeat a noun in sentences like **¿Has comido las galletas? Si, todas – Have you eaten the biscuits? Yes, all (of the biscuits).** As a pronoun **todo** is easy to deal with and you only need to remember to make it take the number and gender of the substituted, unspoken noun.

There will be canapes and everything

93

A phrase like **all three of us like cava** can lose **three: a todos nos gusta el cava** or it can lose **all: el cava nos gusta a los tres** – but however you juggle it, you won't fit **all** and **three** in the same sentence. As well as meaning **all,** the pronouns **todos** and **todas** will translate **everybody, everyone: ¡todos a cantar!** – sing, everybody!

Hay de todo is a dual-purpose phrase with a literal meaning of **there are all sorts of things** and the question **¿aquí se vende cava?** – **is cava sold here?** might prompt a response of **hay de todo** – **there are all (kinds of things)**. This is sometimes the reply of someone who prefers not to go into boring details but you can also expect to meet the resigned **hay de todo…** a resigned fragment resembling **it takes all kinds…**

Todo sometimes slopes off to become a conjunction, although to non-grammarians this amounts to name-dropping. More important are the occasions when **todo** is an adverb. Many people believe that they can manage perfectly well without adverbs. If your linguistic horizons are modest, you can avoid close analysis of the roles carried out by the words you translate. Still, you'll be doing yourself out of the subtle pleasure of appreciating the difference between **todas las medias están rotas** – **all the stockings are torn** and **están todo rotas las medias** – **the stockings are all torn.**

Since you should be getting accustomed to Spanish use of repetition by now, you won't be amazed to learn that an affirmative answer to a question like **is that all?** – **¿es todo?** is rarely a monosyllabic **sí** and what you will hear most is **es todo,** or an expansive **todo, todo.**

SUMWHAT

In the past, adults who read or wrote with difficulty would have less trouble when counting. Is it really easier to agree that two plus two makes four than to accept that the letters C-A-T conjure up something furry, four-legged and feline? Possibly it had a lot to do with knowing that understanding money requires arithmetic so people were aware that learning to count was literally worth their while.

Counting is one of the first things that is taught in another language, particularly in Spain where cheques require both the amount and date to be written in words as well as figures.

You will already have made friends with the indefinite articles **un, uno, una** which as well as **a** and **an** can also mean **one: un año – one year; una quincena – a fortnight**. You use **uno** mainly when counting: **uno, dos, tres** etc. It also occurs when you are asked **¿cuántos terrones? – how many lumps?** and you answer **uno, por favor – one, please** if you're not particularly sweet-toothed.

Nearly all numbers are adjectives, but apart from **uno** and numbers ending in **–uno** they won't do anything in the way of agreeing in number or gender below two hundred: **diez vacas – ten cows; treinta días – thirty days; tres deseos – three wishes**.

Once you reach a hundred it starts to get more fiddly and you say **noventa y nueve; cien, ciento uno; ciento dos – ninety-nine; a hundred; a hundred and one; a hundred and two** and so on until you run out of breath or things to count.

One is one and all alone but when it's accompanied a Spanish **one** loses its tail which is why **one hundred and one days** is **ciento un días**. This happens only when what you are counting is masculine in gender, as feminine nouns are consistent: **ciento una libras – a hundred and one pounds**. The same thing applies to numbers under and over a hundred: **cincuenta y un cocodrilos – fifty-one crocodiles** but **cuarenta y una hienas – forty-one hyenas** or **ciento sesenta y una horquillas – one hundred and sixty-one hairpins**.

Unlike English you don't refer to nouns like **one hundred** or **a hundred** but to **cien** without a handle of any kind: **cien euros – a hundred euros; cien años – one hundred years; esos guantes cuestan cien euros – those gloves cost a hundred euros**.

Because they are adjectives, plural **hundreds** end in **–os** or **–as** as the case may be: **doscientas mujeres – two hundred women; trescientos hombres – three hundred men; cuatrocientas palomas – four hundred doves; quinientas buitres – five hundred vultures; seiscientas hormigoneras – six hundred cement mixers; setecientos periquitos – seven hundred budgerigars; ochocientas ardillas – eight hundred squirrels; novecientos elefantes – nine hundred elephants**.

The vague **hundreds** is a masculine noun and needs to be followed by **de: cientos de periódicos – hundreds of newspapers** and **cientos de personas – hundreds of people**.

Everyone knows that **mil** is **a thousand**. English-speakers in Spain were very attached to this word before the advent of the euro and used it when speaking English although most pronounced it as **mill,** so something costing **siete mil pesetas** would be described as **seven mill** instead of **siete mil**. Once again you don't refer to **one thousand** or **a thousand**, merely **mil** which does not undergo changes of number of gender: **mil libros – a thousand books** and **dos mil libras – two thousand pounds**. When used vaguely it is a masculine, plural noun **hay miles de libros en la biblioteca – there are thousands of books in the library**.

We all know the rich are different so it's not surprising that **a million** should be different too by being a noun, so you can say **a million or one million** because in both cases it will be **un millón**. As a noun, instead of agreeing it is agreed with and exists as a plural when there is more than one million to take into account: **veinte millones – twenty million**. Since it is different, **un millón** also needs to be followed by the preposition **de** even when being particular: **tres millones de buitres – three million vultures**.

You might find your adjectives and nouns are out of kilter to start with, but that won't stop you cashing a cheque – and the bothersome letter **O** that appears and disappears in your twenty-ones and your one-hundred-and-ones won't matter when checking lottery coupons. Nonetheless it probably won't take you long to get them under control, because people go to more bother with numbers than verbs: it's money that makes the world go around and keeping count of it is possibly the most absorbing business of all.

SOME INFORMATION

Once you start to understand a foreign language, you stop noticing the things that initially struck you as eccentric. Take the indefinite article, **un.** It doesn't take long for an English-speaker to accept this as the Spanish way of saying **a** or, in the case of words beginning with a vowel, **an.** Once he or she has swallowed the idea of gender, this same English-speaker happily refers to a man friend as **un amigo** and a woman friend as **una amiga**. They'll find transvestite words like **un mapa** or **una mano** both interesting and amusing.

As in English, a plurality of friends in Spanish can be an article-less **amigos/amigas – friends** or **unos amigos/unas amigas – some friends**, although this sociable circumstance can also be translated as **algunos amigos**. Nevertheless, that's not much help when assessing the various implications of **necesito zapatos, necesito unos zapatos** and **necesito algunos zapatos.**

Necesito zapatos – I need shoes sounds as though you're in need of a pair of shoes, any shoes at all so long as they come into the footwear category. **Necesito unos zapatos** provides much the same information but, having bunged in that article, it will be understood that you'd appreciate some new footwear but are neither barefoot nor down-at-heel.

Necesito algunos zapatos still means **I need some shoes** but a listener gets the message that you're not short of shoes but could do with, or would like, another pair – with higher heels perhaps, or squarer toes.

English-speakers can be wrong-footed by the similar meanings but different inferences of **unos** and **algunos** although it will assist in making up your mind if you take your cue from the singular **uno** and **algún**. **Un día tendré esmeraldas – one day I'll have emeralds** sounds more confident and definite than **algún día tendré esmeraldas – some day I'll have emeralds**. **Alguno** continues to demonstrate its indefinition with **a algunos gatos no les gustan las sardinas – some cats don't like sardines**. **A unos gatos no les gustan las sardinas** is another dish of fish because the speaker is almost certainly acquainted with certain cats that turn up their whiskers at sardines.

Algún, alguno and **alguna,** together with their plural versions **algunos** and **algunas** are either adjectives or they are pronouns which precede and substitute nouns and always take the same number and gender as these nouns. Both as an adjective and a pronoun **algún** behaves in the same way as **mal/malo** and **buen/bueno**, which is why the singular, masculine adjective **alguno** drops its **–o** before the singular, masculine no **un día** in **algún día tendré esmeraldas.**

As pronouns, **un, uno** etc. and **algún, alguno** etc. cause no more hassle than they do as adjectives: **¿Ves aquellas esmeraldas? Pues quiero unas – You see those emeralds? Well I want some.** Or in a bar: **¿Tiene usted sardinas? ¿Me puede poner algunas por favor? – Do you have sardines? Could you serve me some, please?**

Algún combines with **que** for a careless **some or other:** **algún que otro día tendré que colocar los armarios – some day or other I'll have to tidy the cupboards.**

Although Spanish pays unashamed homage to the double negative, it is possible to avoid betraying your grammatical heritage by using **alguno** and at the same time you will be rewarded with the unlooked-for bonus of an implicit **at all:** **colocar los armarios no me supone dificultad alguna – tidying cupboards holds no difficulty for me at all**, not that this construction is favoured by plain-talking Spaniards, who remain faithful to their beloved double negatives and prefer the sound of **no me supone dificultad ningúna colocar los armarios.**

In English **some** can occasionally imply awed approval but the Spanish version of **that's some emerald you've got there** is **vaya esmeralda que tienes allí.** Using the subjunctive of the verb **ir** to convey admiration may appear weird, but makes fewer demands on the imagination than the alternative, **menuda esmeralda que tienes allí,** since **menuda** is an adjective usually understood to mean **small.** All of which can only be due to the fact that **Spanish is quite some language – el español es todo un idioma...**

YES BUT...

But is usually translated as **pero**, and if you want to say **I love you darling but...** you say **te quiero, cariño, pero...** before dropping the little bombshell this statement often precedes. There are times when it is necessary to use **sino,** however, so when wishing to murmur, **not only are you rich but handsome too**, murmur **no solo eres rico, sino guapo también.**

Sussing **sino** consists of using it to say **but also, as well** or **instead**. It is equally efficient at rejecting anything from shoes to sugar: **no sólo son caros los zapatos, sino feos también – not only are they expensive, but the shoes are ugly as well.** Or **no quiero azúcar blanco sino moreno – I don't want white sugar but brown instead.**

Not all phrases containing **no** require **sino** but all phrases with **sino** must have a **no** in them somewhere. **No quiere hígado pero lo tendrá que comer** means **he doesn't want liver but he'll have to eat it** while **no quiere hígado sino mollejas** means **he doesn't want liver but sweetbreads**.

Pero is always followed by some kind of clause containing a verb: **hacía buen día, pero ahora llueve – it was a nice day but now it's raining or pensaba que era rico pero no tiene dinero – I thought he was rich but he doesn't have any money.**

Sino can be followed by a noun, pronoun, adjective, adverb or verb: **no es lluvia sino nieve – it's not rain but snow; no me gustan estos zapatos, sino aquellos – I don't like these shoes, but those over there; no creo que eres rico, sino interesante – I don't think you're rich, but interesting; no lo hace mal, sino bien – he doesn't do it badly, but well.**

When the infinitive of a verb follows **sino** the construction is simple: **no quiere andar, sino correr – he doesn't want to walk but run.** Simplicity is absent when things get more personal: **que la causa del accidente sea un error humano no minimiza sino que acrecienta responsibilidades – that the accident should be a human error does not minimise, but increases, responsibilities.** It's the kind of mouthful you don't encounter when popping out for bread or the paper, but useful because it shows what you can expect of **sino.**

Sino has further but less-used translations of **only, except** or **save** (exception not rescue). When writing, try not to confuse **sino** with **si no** as many Spanish people do. If it is split into two separate words, **si no** severs its ties with **but** and means **if not** or **otherwise: si no acabas todo el higado, no tendrás un helado – if you don't finish all the liver, you won't have an ice cream.**

Finally there is another type of **sino**, a noun that means **destiny** and which makes only rare appearances in most everyday vocabularies. Returning to **pero,** you can still remonstrate with **but me no buts** in Spanish, although now you will say **no hay pero que valga.**

THE BE-ALL AND END-ALL

When **be** is part of an imperative or command, don't anticipate a clash with **ser** and **estar**, because this time they won't cause much trouble.

For instance, I know that the moment I go out, Gilbert will sharpen his claws on the corner of the sofa. Despite this, and displaying a touching amount of trust and self-deception I habitually tell him: **sé bueno – be good,** as I close the door.

When you say **be good** or use the imperative form of **to be** you tell someone how to behave while appealing to what you hope is one of their nicer characteristics: **be patient, punctual, nice, polite, brave, sincere, gentle, affectionate, sensible, reasonable, agreeable, obedient, generous**.

Since it would be edifying to regard these qualities as inherent, you use **ser** to translate **to be**, although considering them immutable is as ingenuous as my telling Gilbert to be good. Nonetheless, **be** followed by an adjective will nearly always be translated by **ser: sé paciente, sé puntual, sé simpático, sé valiente, sé suave, sé cariñoso, sé sensato, sé razonable, sé agradable, sé obediente, sé generoso.**

If you are being polite as well as bossy, use **usted: sea paciente, sea puntual, sea simpático, sea valiente, sea suave, sea cariñoso, sea sensato, sea razonable, sea agradable, sea obediente, sea generoso.** For large-scale, plural bossiness use **seamos – let's be: seamos pacientes, seamos puntuales** etc. Naturally all these adjectives can be preceded by the familiar second person plural imperative, **sed** (which in other circumstances means **thirst**), as well as the polite form **sean**.

Since **estar** is used when referring to position or one-off, impermanent situations, it won't figure in appeals to anyone's better nature or inner reserves. Consequently you'll use **estar** far less when telling people to be this, that or the other. If you do, it will nearly always be wedded to a reflexive pronoun, so when Gilbert weaves and purrs and rubs his cheek against my ankle, even though I am grateful for his attentions I know what's on his mind. **Estáte quieto – be still**, I tell him as he ambushes me on the way to the fridge. Unlike **ser, estar** can also be followed by an adverb as well as an adjective: **estáos   allí** – the plural version of **be there**.

When you've worked out that you should choose **estar,** you still find that the **be** which is present in English can be eliminated and you can dispense with **estar, too: callad – be quite; dáte prisa – be quick** (literally **give yourself haste**); **tengamos cuidado – let's be careful; prepárense – be prepared; diga la verdad – be truthful** (literally **tell the truth**); **calláos – be silent**.

Half the commands and demands you give and receive will probably be negative so you need to know how to prohibit and dissuade, too. This is done with the present subjunctive of the appropriate verb: **no seas impaciente – don't be impatient; no llegues temprano – don't arrive early**. Reflexive pronouns should be incorporated and, what's more, in negative imperatives they precede the verb: **no te calles – don't keep quiet or no te des prisa – don't hurry**.

Having established that **be** followed by an adjective is generally translated by **ser**, it's only fair but not very reassuring to point out that **be happy – sé feliz** or **sé content** can also be translated as **éstate feliz** and **éstate contento** depending on the circumstances and the quality of the happiness.

It's tempting to regard this inconsistency as Spanish ambivalence concerning happiness and sadness but, whatever the reasons, as soon as you tangle with **ser** and **estar** be prepared to philosophise, analyse and agonise at least once in the course of the encounter. So here it is – your token ration of philosophy, analysis and agony, because **don't be sad** has its positive side as it is always translated as **no estés triste**.

IS IT OR ISN'T IT?

Graciosilla la gatita, ¿verdad? – sweet little cat, isn't she? said an acquaintance the other day about my cat, Pushy. She is little, she has a few chic grey and ginger patches on her very white coat and she is very clever but not particularly sweet. To tell the truth she is the most disruptive cat I have ever owned. Not wishing to hurt the compliment-payer's feelings I smiled faintly and murmured **¿a que sí?** while manoeuvring Pushy out of range before she could sail into his lap and anchor herself claws-first.

Verdad, verdad que sí and **a que sí** are the ways you continue in Spanish to state or ask **isn't he, isn't she,** and **isn't it.** In each instance you seek confirmation from your interlocutor without mentioning gender although in the first two, **verdad** is an appeal to **truth.**

Tiene hambre tu gata, ¿a que sí? and **tiene hambre tu gata, ¿verdad que sí?** or **tiene hambre tu gata, ¿verdad?** are all asking **your cat's hungry, isn't she?** In each case, I could agree with **pues sí** or dissent with **pues no.** If I had been asked **tiene hambre tu gata, ¿verdad?** then I might choose ¿a que si? as confirmation.

¿A que no? and **¿verdad que no?** appear in negative observations: **no es muy obediente esta gata, ¿verdad que no?** **– this cat's not very obedient, is she?** Only the hardest-hearted, most disloyal cat-owner would answer **pues no** or ¿a que no? **– she's not, is she?** and some would protest **¡sí que lo es!**

A que sí or **a que no** at the beginning of the sentence also do the job of **isn't he, isn't she** and **isn't it.** It is possible to eliminate the **yes** from ¿a que sí? but not the **no** from ¿a que no? so you say **¿a que la gata está debajo del sofá? – the cat's under the sofa, isn't she?** but **¿a que no la estás buscando con mucho interés? - you're not looking very hard, are you?**

Although one is negative and the other affirmative **¿es así?** and **¿no es así?** – which mean **is it so?** and **isn't it so?** – are virtually identical. They allow you to say **tienes miedo a mi gata ¿es así?** and **tienes miedo a mi gata ¿no es así?** Spanish constructions mean that **being afraid** turns into **having fear** and there is the same subtle difference between these two sentences as there is in **you're afraid of my cat, are you? and you're afraid of my cat, aren't you?** And anyone with his or her wits about them would reply **sí que lo tengo** where Pushy is concerned.

In the conditional tense **¿a que sí?** remains unchanged:

The cat's under the sofa isn't she?

quejarías si Pushy te arañara ¿a que sí? – you would complain if Pushy were to scratch you, wouldn't you? To this perceptive statement there comes a predictable answer: **sí que lo haría** – yes, I would (do).

It's all right if I stroke Pushy, isn't is? is translated as **está bien si acaricio a Pushy ¿verdad?** but anyone who knows her, knows also that there is only one rational answer to this. Strangely enough, while Spanish subjects you to the subjunctive morning, noon and night an English-speaker who is largely unaware of its existence now uses it unhesitatingly where a Spaniard doesn't: **yo que tú, no lo haría** – I wouldn't if I were you...

VERILY, VERILY, VERILY

You can translate **very** as **muy,** but the same effect can be obtained with **-ísimo,** a suffix added to adjectives and adverbs: **mi tarea es difícil/mi tarea es dificilísima** – my task is very

difficult. Or **la mujer de mi vecino ríe muy poco/la mujer de mi vecina ríe poquísimo** – My neighbour's wife laughs very little.

Addition of **-ísimo** makes it necessary to modify any word ending in a vowel, but **poco** not only divests itself of **o,** but its **c** turns into **qu,** a deviation that obviates creating the non-existent and meaningless **pocísimo.**

Words ending in **l** and **r** give the least bother: **regular – regularísimo; frágil – fragilísimo.** On the other hand, those ending in **n** give more trouble than the rest put together: **young – joven/jovencísimo; greedy – glotón/glotoncísimo.** Once again, this occurs for the sound of it, the **c** being slipped in to make the entire word slide more easily off the Spanish tongue.

However, the majority of Spanish adjectives end in a vowel and have their tails docked before acquiring **-ísimo: beautiful – guapo/guapísimo; sad – triste/tristísimo; soft – blando/-blandísimo; much – mucho/muchísimo.**

Adverbs behave identically so you go through the same routine with words like **soon - pronto/prontísimo; much – mucho/muchísimo** (and you're not seeing double because, as it does in English, **mucho** leads the double life of an adverb and an adjective); **far – lejos/lejísimo** although in this case the final **s** does a disappearing act together with the **o.**

Many Spaniards are so attached to **-ísimo** they manage to wedge it into the kind of adverb that ends in **mente: generously – generosamente/generosísimamente; quickly – rápidamente/rapidísimamente.** In these cases **-ísimo** is added according to the rules before changing its final **o** to an **a,** also according to the rules that must be observed when forming an adverb ending in **–mente.** A word with an accent somewhere about its person loses this when coupled to the accented **-ísimo,** which is why **frágil** becomes **fragilísimo** and **rápidamente** becomes **rapidísimamente.** These words needed accents in the first place because of the rules governing the way syllables are emphasised in Spanish; however, the addition of **-ísimo** means stress now falls on the accented **í** in **-ísimo** instead, overriding the original emphasis.

An English-speaker invariably regards **-ísimo** as **very,** but grammatically it denotes the superlative **most,** so strictly speaking **fragilísimo** means **most fragile** and **guapísimo** is **most handsome**. You also come across irregular superlatives, as you do in English: **óptimo – best; pésimo – worst; ínfimo – lowest;** nevertheless **buenísimo** is equally acceptable for **best,** as is **malísimo – worst** and **bajísimo – lowest**.

Only one noun – **general** – has habitually been transformed into a superlative: **generalísimo,** which is the reason why many streets were named **Calle** or **Avenida del Generalísimo** in honour of Francisco Franco who during his lifetime was, amongst other things, the country's **highest-ranking general**.

There are people who will and people who won't add onion to Spanish omelette. Likewise, there are people who are more devoted to **-ísimo** than others. Some employ the **–ísimo** formula only in enthusiastic circumstances, so they refer to a man or woman as **guapísimo/guapísima**, to wine as **buenísimo** and to a book as **interesantísimo,** reserving **muy** for what inspires less enthusiasm.

Since there are quite as many gloomy Spaniards as jolly Spaniards, the former might reserve **-ísimo** for the things they like least: **feísimo – most ugly** or **aburridísimo – very boring**, saving up **muy** for what gives them a buzz. Either way, and regardless of whether something or someone meets with favour or disapproval, Spanish emphasis on emphasis means you can expect to hear **-ísimo** and **muy** very, very, very often.

GEDDIT?

The best way to translate the sort of phrase we were advised to avoid as children:, **have you got my book? – ¿tienes mi libro?** usually involves **tener** and, as you can see, Spanish is more elegant than English because you now say: **do you have my book?**

A vital **got to** also relies on **tener: I've got to be at the airport by eleven – tengo que estar en el aeropuerto a las once.** There is another version using **haber** but it is less current in conversation although it frequently appears in print: **hemos de hacerlo cuanto antes – we've got to do it as soon as possible.**

Most of us use **get, got** and **getting** incessantly: **get back!**

he got the bus in the evening; get out of those wet clothes; let's get out of going to the theatre tomorrow; she got off the train; I just want to get away from everything; that woman will get to be a nuisance; it's getting late; your cat gets in the way; get down from that tree; his daughter got the first prize; he didn't want to get into trouble; I can't get into this book; the food got cold; get happy; I told him to get on with what he was doing; I don't get it; could you get Blas for me? and so on and so on into what looks like infinity.

The preceding little gems of everyday English turn into corresponding little gems of everyday Spanish. The best of the bunch is **¡atrás!** for **get back!** because it is short and logical (it means **back!**) but the lack of a Spanish **get** means that the others require an English alternative before translating.

Get can mean **catch, take** so **he got the bus in the evening** can be translated by **coger** and **tomar: cogió el autobús por la tarde** and **tomó el autobús por la tarde**. **To get out of** is another way of saying **remove,** so **get out of those wet clothes** could be translated with **quitarse: quítate esa ropa mojada** but **let's get out of going to the theatre tomorrow** uses **evitar – to avoid: evitemos ir mañana al teatro.**

To get off/alight is **bajar/apearse: bajó del tren/se apeó del tren – she got off the train,** while **to get away from** is nearer to **leave – irse** or **escaparse,** which is less dramatic in Spanish than it sounds. Thus **I just want to get away** is **simplemente quiero irme** if you're not keen on returning but **simplemente quiero escaparme** if you've a jaunt in mind.

That verbal jack-of-all-verbal-trades **poner** is useful when **get** implies **to become: that woman will get to be a nuisance – esa mujer se pondrá pesada.** To translate **it's getting late,** use **hacer** plus the reflexive **estarse: se está haciendo tarde.**

To get in the way is **estorbar** so **your cat gets in the way** is **tu gato estorba** and if the cat is like Gilbert and he's in a garden like Fausto's, you'll hear: **bájate de ese árbol – get down from that tree.**

When **to get** signifies **to receive,** although you can use the logical **recibir,** a more roundabout **to give** is also used and **his daughter got first prize** becomes **they gave his daughter first prize: a su hija le dieron el primer premio.**

Meterse is often adequate for **to get into: he didn't want**

to get into trouble – no quería meterse en un lío. This verb is also used for an unusually straight translation for a colloquialism: I can't get into this book – no me puedo meter en este libro. However, the food got cold is translated as la comida se enfrió but you return to poner for get happy – ponte contento. You need the subjunctive for I told him to get on with what he was doing and this time you use to go ahead: le dije que siguiera con lo que hacía. When I told him to get on with it is a touch rude and dismissive, you'd perhaps address the object of your scorn directly and say ¡allá tú!

The bemused complaint I don't get it is understandably translated by comprender and entender: no comprendo or no entiendo. Alternatively you can use caer, literally to fall: no caigo. To get in the sense of get hold of someone is llamar (to call): me podrías llamar a Blas – could you get Blas for me? as well as localizar: ¿me podrías localizar a Blas?

Finding translations for get is liable to get you down – agobiarte but it may console you to learn that the Spanish find it hard to get to grips with – resolver translations entailing get, got and getting. And if you were to explain that they are also a headache to translate into Spanish you would receive an old-fashioned look and a sceptical ¡ande! ¡ande! – get away with you...

ACCENTUATE THE NEGATIVE

When a fractious, feverish child croaks don't want nuffin' to eat, loving mothers murmur ANYTHING to eat even as they reach for the thermometer, since minor illness and double negatives are common during childhood. However, although measles is an internationally unpopular ailment, you may be surprised to learn that double negatives are so popular in Spanish that you can double them up to your heart's content.

Nothing is nada in Spanish and to translate I don't want anything, you must grit your grammatical teeth and say no quiero nada, literally I don't want nothing. If you simply can't be happy pronouncing a double negative, it's possible to avoid one by saying **nada quiero,** not that you'll be applauded for doing so. Nonetheless, it is worth noting that when a word like **nada, nadie (no-one), ninguno (none), nunca (never)** precedes the verb, **no** is eliminated: **absolutamente nadie quiere comer nada** – **absolutely nobody wants to eat anything.** Although you're saying **anything** in English, you are saying **nothing** in Spanish and there you are – stuck with a double negative again.

Spanish is the proud possessor of triple negatives, too, so if that **no** steals a march on the verb you'll find yourself saying **no quiere comer nadie absolutamente nada.** There are rules concerning negatives, so in any permutation of negating words only one should be placed before the verb. Thus **nobody ever tells me anything** must become **nadie me dice nunca nada** or **nunca me dice nadie nada**, although this is a rule that not all Spaniards take seriously themselves.

Algo, which means **something** as well as **anything,** is used affirmatively in phrases like **quiero algo** – **I want something; dale algo** – **give him** or **give her something.** You rarely find **algo** in a negative sentence like **don't give him anything,** which has to become **don't give him nothing: no le des nada.** You find **algo** in company of **no** in **eso es algo que no me agrada** – **that's something I don't like**, but sentences like these are other kettles of grammatical fish.

When **at all** appears in negative circumstances, it can be translated as **nada,** so someone who is hard to please might snarl **no me gusta nada lo que has hecho** – **I don't like what you've done at all.** This could produce a pathetic response like **¿de verdad que no te gusta nada?** – **you really don't like it at all?,** to which an overcritical reply might be **nada de nada,** a super-emphatic **not at all.** And it won't matter how many toes are trodden just so long as those negatives are duly doubled.

Again, you won't find **algún/alguno/alguna** – **some, any** in a negative sentence like **don't give him any books** and they are replaced by their opposite numbers **ningún/-ninguno/ninguna: no le des ningún libro** (and note the English plural but Spanish singular). However, it is as correct to say **¿no tienes ningún libro interesante?** – **don't you have any interesting book(s)?** as **¿tienes algunos libros interesantes?** – **have you any interesting books?** Ask this begging question of a non-lender and he or she is sure to answer, **lo siento, pero no tengo ninguno – I'm sorry but I (don't) have none.**

To start with, you will almost certainly find that double negatives stick in your throat. Nonetheless, all that's required is the presence of mind not to choke on them – and the ability to shed your inhibitions and say **no** and **no** again.

HOW ABOUT IT?

Como is an unexceptional Spanish word that can be defined by a standing army of unexceptional English words: **as, like, such as, since, because, unless, how** and **why**. **Como** is both an adverb and a conjunction but you can forget I mentioned this because adverbs and conjunctions do not vary – unlike people, the weather or the price of cat food.

In phrases like **mis gatos son tan listos como tus perros, como** means as: **my cats are as smart as your dogs.** This could be reworded as **mis gatos son como tus perros de listos**, a very Spanish, most unEnglish, construction which still means **my cats are as smart as your dogs.**

People who rabbit on tediously about their cats frequently make unverifiable claims about them: **es como si fueran personas – it's as though they were people,** yet another word-for-word translation which uses an obvious subjunctive in English as well as Spanish.

People who rabbit on super-tediously about their cats are capable of making further totally inaccurate and patently partisan assertions about them: **como estos, hay pocos – there aren't many like these** although what you are actually saying is **like these, there are few.**

Sometimes **como** is nearer to the phrase **something like** when preceded by **algo: Gilbert tenía algo como seis semanas cuando lo encontramos – Gilbert was something like six weeks old when we found him.** Preceded by **así, como** signifies **that's how, that's why: así como ya tenemos cuatro gatos – that's how we now have four cats.**

Equally often, though, **así como** means **as well as, and also:**

le gustaban los gatos, así como los pingüinos y las ardillas – he liked cats and also penguins and squirrels. You can similarly refer to animales tales como los pingüinos y las ardillas – animals such as penguins and squirrels but remember to make the adjective tal agree with the noun animales.

Occasionally como corresponds to because, since: como tenemos poco tiempo, no hablaremos de gatos – since we've little time, we shan't talk about cats. A promise like this tends to be met with gale-force sighs of relief, prompting a cat-owner to confide: no me explico como no quieran escuchar – I don't understand how they can't want to listen. Even easier to fathom are the sentiments of dog-lovers who snarl between gritted teeth como no te calles, voy a hacer algo desagradable a tus dichosos gatos – unless you shut up, I'm going to do something unpleasant to your wretched cats.

Since there have been previous examples of como followed by the subjunctive, you might as well be subjected to another: como sigas así, Gilbert te morderá – if you go on like that, Gilbert will bite you. This unpleasant prophesy provides a good opportunity to point out that when como can be translated as unless, if, as if or as though and is followed by a verb, you can rely on said verb being in the subjunctive.

Much of the time, the interrogative ¿cómo? corresponds to how? as in ¿cómo te encuentras? – how do you feel? ¿cómo estas? - how are you? or ¿cómo quito los gatos del sofá? – how do I get the cats off the sofa? There are times when ¿cómo? is translated as what? as in ¿cómo dices que se llaman tus gatos? – what did you say your cats were called?

Then there are constructions like ¿a cómo es el bacalao? – how much is the cod? or ¿cómo es de caro? – how dear is it? There are plural versions of these phrases: ¿a cómo son las pescadillas? – what are the whiting like for price? and ¿cómo son de caras – how dear are they? You will also run into como with other adjectives such as ancho – wide; alto – high; profundo – deep and anything referring to price or dimensions: ¿cómo es de profundo – how deep is it?

¿Cómo? is excluded from some questions: how much – ¿cuánto? as well as how about it? – ¿que te parece? or how long? – ¿cuánto tiempo? Neither will you detect it in all exclamations: how funny! – ¡qué divertido! how hot! – ¡qué calor! **how good!** – **¡qué bien** or **¡qué bueno!** and even **how nice your cats are!** — **¡qué simpáticos son tus gatos!** When you do find **como** in an exclamation it is always immediately followed by a verb: **¡cómo nos reímos! – how we laughed!** or **¡cómo estaba de furioso! – how cross he was!**

A Spanish person begs your pardon if he treads on your toe but when he doesn't catch what you have just mumbled, he tends to look perplexed and asks **¿cómo?** – an interjection that on its own is a favourite one-word reaction to surprise, outrage, confusion or incredulity.

Como quieras and **como usted quiera** is an easy-going way to be compliant and helpful. It means whatever you want, whatever you wish, although delivery can be modified to make this off-hand or even rude. Another amenable-sounding phrase is **¿cómo no?** literally **how not?** Once again, delivery is all since this is a phrase that lets you be accommodating, resigned, blasé or cynical too. Once **que** is popped into the middle of **cómo no** you arrive at **¿cómo que no?** This is as indignant and tetchy a question as you'll find: **¿cómo que no quieres sentarte en el sofá con los gatos? –how can you not want to sit on the sofa with the cats?** which is an enquiry prompted not only by indignation and tetchiness, but querulous incomprehension, too.

COMATOSE

A Spanish **full stop - punto final** does not mention full, nor does it stop. **Final** is self-explanatory while translations for **punto** start with **stitch, point, fleck, speckle, pip,** progressing to the **spot** and **dot** that are closer to what we're looking for. In English we often use **full stop** to sound emphatic and so do the Spanish, although they omit **final: I said I wasn't going, full stop – dije que no iba, y punto.** You also meet **punto** in the Spanish version for **start a new paragraph,** the rather terse **punto y aparte.**

Grammar is grammar wherever you are and whatever language you speak and subjects, objects, verbs and other parts of speech carry out similar roles in all European languages.

The Old Woman said come back soon

On the other hand, **punctuation – puntuación** is allowed to be **an entirely different matter – harina de otro costal.**

The arbitrary and random commas in private letters, business letters, magazines and newspapers – but not books – often look as though they have been scattered at the discretion of the writer. A flip through my daughter's primary school Spanish Language textbook (she is now an adult and it was printed nearly thirty years ago) reveals that commas should correspond pretty well to those learnt or forgotten by English-speakers. Nevertheless, it was startling to read that "...a comma can replace a copulative co-ordinate" but closer investigation rules out erotic togetherness, and a copulative co-ordinate is an untitillating **y – and.** Evidently this may be replaced with a comma, as in English: **el gato era gordo y peludo – the cat was fat and long-haired** or **el gato era gordo, peludo – the cat was fat, long-haired.**

Colons and **semi-colons** behave in much the same way as ours, although their habitual Spanish names sound rudimentary compared with ours: **colon – dos puntos** and **semi-colon – punto y coma.** This may be due to the fact that a Spanish **colon** is usually part of the large intestine rather than a sentence.

A colon is used after the salutation in a letter, instead of our comma: **Estimada Elena: hace tanto tiempo que no te escribo – Dear Elena, It's so long since I've written to you.** Business letters usually start **Muy señor mío/Muy señores nuestros – Dear Sir/Dear Sirs** as well as the no-nonsense **Señores:**

Colons appear before quoting what is spoken or written, although inverted commas may be omitted: **La vieja dijo: vuelve pronto – The old woman said, "Come back soon."** Written dialogue used to be indicated by a colon, followed by a rather longer dash: **Fuensanta miró a César: ¿Qué piensas hacer?** and eliminated our own laborious opening and closing of quotation marks: **Fuensanta looked at César: "What are you going to do?"** This formula is still observed in books, but newspapers and magazines tend more and more to use inverted commas. These are also used for quotations, nicknames, for emphasis and to indicate foreign words.

A question or exclamation in Spanish is preceded as well as followed by a **question mark – punto de interrogación** or **exclamation mark – punto de admiración** as the case may be. The use of **interrogación** cannot be accidental in a country where neighbourly interrogation is part and parcel of daily intercourse but the unexpected substitution of **exclamation** with **admiración** by the hypercritical Spanish is less easy to assimilate. When writing, the opening question mark or exclamation mark only precedes the question or the exclamation itself: **sé que tiene razón pero ¿cómo se lo voy** a decir? – I know he's right, but how can I tell him? or **sé que tiene razón pero ¡no se lo voy a decir!** – I know he's right, but I'm not going to tell him!

Anyone who is only minimally observant, and receives both business and personal correspondence or reads the local or national Spanish press, will be protesting by now that most of these rules are broken daily. That's more or less where we came in, because not only is it virtually arbitrary, but Spanish punctuation is obviously more random than Spanish punctuality which is now virtually on a par with everyone else's.

PART TWO
WATCH YOUR STEP

Having been warned to take care where you put your feet, don't feel you must approach this section on tiptoe. Its aim is to help you avoid the pitfalls, potholes and hurdles that can turn learning Spanish into a bumpy slog instead of a smooth journey. Acquiring another language involves more than substituting one word for another and too often the right word isn't the one you think it's going to be. On some occasions Spanish is comfortingly similar to English, on others it can seem so alien that a little guidance doesn't come amiss. But on second thoughts, don't be too cautious because if you put your foot in it you'll still learn – the hard way.

OBVIOUS LINKS

It's fun to glimpse obvious links between Spanish and English in words like **proeza – prowess** or **destreza – dexterity**. It's equally amusing to tally the adjective **dependent on** with the adjective **dependiente** but it's irritating not to be able to match the noun **un dependiente** to a **dependant**. This is because the Spanish version is **a shop assistant** whereas the English **dependant** translates as **un familiar**. Similarly, **una asistenta** is **a charlady, cleaning woman** but **an assistant** is **un ayudante**.

There is an explanation for this apparent waywardness, because **asistir** means **to serve, wait on, attend** – all redolent of charladies – while **ayudar** means **to aid, help, assist** – all expected of an assistant (and a charlady if you're lucky).

Easy-to-spot words in both languages frequently decline to correspond, so **dilapidar** means **to squander, waste** and although **to waste** *is* one of the definitions of **to dilapidate**, this is more often associated in English with allowing a building to go to wrack and ruin. Consequently, the adjective

Blonda... a mantilla... the veil that is worn with a tall comb

dilapidated is translated as **desmoronado, desvencijado, ruinoso**. And although **a ruin** *is* **una ruina** don't be misled by the adjective/noun **ruín**, which means **despicable, mean, low, heartless, callous**. You also encounter **ruin** in what amounts to our **talk of the devil** in **hablando del ruín de Roma, por la puerta se asoma**.

Different shades of meaning acquired by what should be recognisable words probably have much to do with national temperaments. The super-impatient Spanish have a short, sharp verb like **urgir – to be urgent, to be pressing: me urge encontrar un ayudante cuanto antes – I must find an assistant urgently**. What we describe as **an urge** has a variety of non-**urgir** translations, depending on context: **impulso, deseo, ansia, ambición, antojo,** this last also being the word for the **craving** of a pregnant woman.

"Urgencias" is the sign you see outside a hospital's **Emergency Department** although latterly most other **emergencies** do you a favour by being **emergencias**. Nonetheless, hair-splitters will remind you that strictly speaking (although few speak strictly anymore, whether in English or Spanish) **an emergency exit** should not be called **una salida de emergencia** unless it leads from a basement and allows you to **emerge** from the bowels of the earth. Otherwise it is the more legitimate **salida de urgencia**.

Then there are the words that aren't what you think they're going to be, so **la competencia** turns out to be **competition, a rival** and not **competence,** while **blonda** is the type of **lace** that makes up a **mantilla** – the veil that is worn with a tall comb.

Our adjective **parochial** is synonymous with narrow-mindedness, but its Spanish version, **parroquial** means what it says and appears only in a **church** or **parish** context. A Spanish **discusión** is an English **argument** but a Spanish **argumento** is an English **plot** (storyline, not a piece of land) and the familiar-looking **escuálido** means **emaciated** or **weak**, with **squalid** translated as **vil, miserable**. The former is still unappetising but now means **villainous, foul, rotten** and although its translations include **vile**, the Spanish do not use it as frequently or in the same context as English-speakers. As for our dejected **miserable,** choose from **triste,**

abatido, desdichado and desgraciado.

You can often find yourself being tripped up by the presence or absence of one measly letter in what should be identical twins. **Fragrance** loses an **-r** to become **fragancia,** along with **appropriate – apropiado** and **orchestra – orquesta**. Occasionally an **-r** isn't lost but put in a different place, as in **crocodile – cocodrilo**. You'll have fun and games with **-n** as well, since many English-speakers are seemingly unaware that **Vincent** loses an **-n** in **Vicente** but gains one in **cemetery – cementerio**.

Now and again you slip up with pairs of words which look or sound like each other, but have unsimilar meanings. It is pretty hard for the ear to differentiate between **la cera – wax** and **la acera – pavement,** as the **–a** in the latter is often swallowed which means you hear **la cera** for both. There are lots more of these little darlings: **jabón** and **jamón** which mean **ham** and **soap** respectively and could easily make a hash of your **tapas** order as well as **lechuga** and **lechuza – lettuce** and **owl. Una orca** is a **killer whale** and the indistinguishable-sounding **una horca** is just as dangerous, because it is **a gibbet.**

Other tripwires are **polilla** and **palillo – moth** and **toothpick, stick; abeja** and **oveja – bee** and **sheep; obispo** and **avispa – bishop** and **wasp; carbón** and **cartón – coal** and **carton, cardboard**. While we're about it, don't let's forget **consumir – to consume** and **consumar – to complete, consummate**.

It helps to know that opening a tap marked **"C"** produces a gush of water that is **caliente – hot** and not **cold – frío** which emerges from the one marked **"F"**. And it won't do any harm to keep an eye – and an ear – open for **el tilde** (the ~ sign that resides over an **-ñ**) because it can turn **ano – anus** into **año – year** and **cono – cone** into a blush-making word to say the least. And be careful with **-e** and **-i** when they are joined together. Although they can still sound like a solitary **–e** to a non-Spaniard, their incorrect pronunciation in **peine – comb** might get you more than you bargained for in your friendly neighbourhood **perfumería**.

FEELING YOUR WAY

If he treads on your toe, a Spaniard says **lo siento, perdóname** or **perdóneme** depending on his mood and speech patterns. It's easy enough to work out that these are ways to **beg pardon**, although **lo siento** actually means **I feel it**.

The verb **sentir** means **to feel, sense, perceive, regret, be sorry** and tardy answers to letters invariably begin with **siento no haberte escrito antes – I'm sorry not to have written to you before.** The kind of **sorrow, regret** that is detectable in a threat is similarly translated by **sentir: si no haces lo que yo te digo, lo vas a sentir – if you don't do as I say, you're going to be sorry. Sentir** can also translate **to feel, note, perceive, sense etc.,** although **notar** does equally well: **sintieron/notaron cierta frialdad en su contestación – they felt a certain coldness in his answer.**

Occasionally you encounter **sentir** with the unexpected implications of **to hear, to smell: creí sentir una llamada a la puerta – I thought I heard (felt) a knock at the door; después del incendio sentía aún un leve olor a quemado – after the fire he still noticed (felt) a slight smell of burning.**

The reflexive **sentirse** also conveys abstract feelings and sensations. **Me siento incómoda – I feel uncomfortable** might be prompted by an uneasy conscience or a sentimental lump in one's throat rather than a lump in the sofa which is expressed as **estar incómodo. Sentirse** does you some favours by providing easy, straightforward translations: **se sentía ridículo llevando sombrero – he felt ridiculous wearing a hat** or **¿te sientes nerviosa cuando estás sola en casa? – do you feel nervous when you're alone at home?**

Sentir is not the right choice for translating the **feel** that in English precedes **thirsty, hungry, full, happy** and other states of mind or body. For these it necessary to use **tener: I feel thirsty – tengo sed** although, as always, there can be exceptions, as in **se sentía cansado – he felt tired.** In contrast, a Spaniard would be equally inclined to complain **tengo sueño – I feel sleepy, estoy cansado** or **me encuentro cansado.** If he is driven to admitting **I don't feel too good** – inevitable in a country where men are encouraged to be rampant hypochondriacs –

119

there are many ways to say so, starting with **encontrar: no me encuentro bien, me encuentro mal.** There is also a childish **estar/encontrarse pachucho** which is nevertheless often groaned by many an adult, as well as the moody, martyred **tener malestar,** this last word incorporating the magnificent opposite of **well-being: ill- being.**

The **feel** that has no connection with emotion, sentiments, health or state of mind but gauges the bathwater or the quality of the material, is **tocar – touch: toqué el sombrero para ver si estaba mojado – I felt/touched the hat to see if it was wet.** You can also use **palpar: palpó el paquete, intentando adivinar que había dentro – he felt the parcel, trying to guess what was inside.** With regard to feelings, **resentir** need not necessarily indicate sulky resentment: **mañana te resentirás del atracón de esta noche – tomorrow you're going to feel the effects of over-eating tonight.**

Plural **feelings** are **sentimientos** while a singular **feeling, sensation** is the similarly labour-saving **sensación: me da la sensación de que hago el ridículo llevando este sombrero – I get the feeling I look ridiculous wearing this hat.** The **feel** of something is **el tacto: me gusta el tacto del terciopelo – I like the feel of velvet.** The **feel** that implies **knack** would be translated as **tranquillo: todavía necesitas coger el tranquillo del nuevo ordenador – you still need to get the feel of the new computer.**

On the occasions when your conscience pricks and you **feel guilty,** use **saber,** one of whose literal translations is **to taste: me sabe mal decírtelo, pero ese sombrero te sienta como un tiro – I feel badly about saying this, but that hat makes you look awful.** Having said this, you might also have the good grace to add a lame **lo siento...** while risking that petulant stock reply, **más lo siento yo...**

A LOT TO TELL YOU

Despite its not overwhelmingly articulate image, most of us are unable to avoid using **lot** an... umm... awful lot. **Lot** has a Spanish lookalike – **lote** – but there all resemblance ends.

Starting at the fount of sometimes misleading wisdom, your dictionary will probably tell you that **un lote** is **a portion** or **share**. Strictly speaking it is, but you more often meet it as a special offer consisting of more than one item, while in a saleroom it continues to be the **lot** that you associate with **an auction – una subasta.**

If yours is a long-winded yet modern dictionary, it might be indelicate enough to divulge the further information that **darse el lote** means **to have it off.** Personally, I would say that in the everyday language and usage of Spanish over-forties, proceedings are not generally expected to reach this stage: almost, but not quite. Nevertheless, nothing dates as rapidly as slang and if you were to ask a teenager's opinion he or she would look blank while trying not to snigger with pitying embarrassment.

The **lot** that might be substituted by luck is also regarded as **luck – suerte** by the Spanish, so **to cast lots** (which is much the same as trying your luck) is **echar suertes.** To **throw in one's lot with someone** is **unirse a la suerte de alguien** and the policeman´s **lot** that Gilbert and Sullivan proclaimed not to be a happy one would be **la suerte de un policía.** You'd need to go a long way to hear an English-speaker lament **would that my lot were otherwise** but gloomy Spaniards can be heard to lament **ojalá mi suerte fuera otra** in connection with lack of enthusiasm for whatever they are having to tolerate at any particular moment.

It falls to my lot is the kind of thing we expect only to hear in a speech: **me incumbe informarle que no nos vamos a rendir – it falls to my lot to tell you that we shall not give in**. Still, **incumbir** is a popular choice in Spanish when used negatively and **no me incumbe hacer eso,** which could be held to mean **I'm not really obliged to do that,** is the favourite refrain of an Iberian jobsworth.

The other kind of **lot**, a trans-Atlantic **parking lot** turns into the unSpanish but unavoidable **parking** or the more acceptable **aparcamiento.** A **vacant lot,** (waste land not a load of morons) is **un solar.**

The **lot** you are probably most interested in is the **lot** we use all the time: **he loved her a lot** or **a lot of people do that, don't they?** If you want your Spanish to sound reasonably acceptable it will be necessary to separate an adverb from an adjective because there's no escaping the fact that the **lot** which pops up in **a lot of people do that, don't they?** is an adjective but an adverb in **he liked her a lot.**

It makes little difference in English and you might feel it should make little difference in Spanish since both are translated as **mucho.** Unfortunately you must have twigged by now that a Spanish adjective needs to agree in both number and gender with the noun it describes, while an adverb does not. Therefore **he loved her a lot** becomes **la quería mucho** but **a lot of people do that, don't they?** is **mucha gente hace eso, ¿verdad?**

It isn't a matter of life and death, of course, and those who can't or don't want to separate adjectives and adverbs need not suffer unduly because they will still be understood. Most Spaniards would possibly be too courteous to comment on an error, anyway. Besides, many themselves aren't aware of the existence of adverbs and adjectives, but get them right because they learnt at their mothers' knees instead of the hard way.

Lastly, two more words containing a totally unrelated **lot: el loto** of the lotus-eater and meditators and **la Loto** of would-be lotus-eaters, **the lottery** we all want to win, because it pays out **a lot of money – muchísimo dinero.**

TO HAVE AND TO HOLD

When you want to say **have** in the sense of **holding, owning** or **possessing** the word to choose is **tener: tengo cuatro gatos – I have four cats; tendremos vacaciones – we shall have a holiday** or **tiene un recado para tí – he has a message for you. Tener** is also used for illness: **mi prima tiene sarampión – my cousin has measles.**

Tener followed by **que** is exactly the same as **have to** or **must: tienes que leer este libro – you must read this book** or **me tengo que ir – I have to go.** If you have a weakness for sonorous little phrases, **tener** provides a nice one: **Es buen libro? Ni que decir tiene – Is it a good book? It goes without saying.**

Tener occurs in situations without an English parallel. For instance, a Spaniard *has* **cold: tiene frío** although as far as an English-speaker is concerned this means **he is cold**. Neither will he **be hungry, thirsty, sleepy or afraid and** instead he will take discomfort to heart and say **tengo hambre, tengo sed, tengo sueño and tengo miedo**. Where an English-speaker says **I feel sick** he'll **have sickness: tengo náuseas** – and in the plural for good measure.

You aren't **lucky** in Spanish but **have luck: Pushy tiene la suerte de tener unos dueños muy consentidos** – **Pushy is lucky to have very indulgent owners**. You'll have a monopoly on righteousness, too: **tengo razón** – **I am right** but you'll rarely hear **no tengo razón** for **I'm wrong**. Instead, a Spaniard says **estoy equivocado** – **I'm mistaken**. He could be less hesitant about informing someone else **no tienes razón** although he might be magnanimous enough to announce **estás equivocado**.

Tener entendido is an elaborate way of saying **to understand: tengo entendido que es muy buen libro** – **I'm given to understand that it's a very good book**. **Tener en cuenta** is similar to **bear in mind: tenga usted en cuenta que es un escritor muy bueno** – **bear in mind that he's a very good writer**.

When you **have a fancy for** something, add **ganas** to **tener: tengo ganas de leer ese libro** – **I've a fancy to read that book**. **Gana** means **appetite, wish** or **desire** but when combined with **tener** it is always used in the plural, in keeping with Spanish reluctance to do things by halves.

Haber appears as an auxiliary verb in the compound, double-barrelled kind: **he hablado** – **I have spoken, you have answered** – **has contestado, habrá comido** – **he will have eaten, habíamos esperado** – **we had expected**.

Haber plus **de** also means **to have to, must or ought: he de ser seria** – **I ought to be serious** but it sounds faintly old-fashioned and occurs more often in print than chat.

An important by-blow of **haber** is **hay** which means **there is** or **there are: hay cuatro gatos en la terraza** – **there are four cats on the terrace. Hay** is an irregular component of **haber** but has past and future versions which are strictly conformist: **ha habido** – **there has been/there have been, había** – **there had been** and **hubo** – **there was/there were**. With these there is a temptation to use their quite illegitimate plural versions – a temptation not always resisted by the less literate.

Hay que means **should** and conveys the need or obligation to do something but the exclamation ¡hay que ver! corresponds to something like **would you believe it!**. Because Spanish is unenthusiastic about the passive voice, **hay que**, as well as its future and past versions, is often used to avoid it: **habrá que decirle – he will have to be told**.

Sometimes the infinitive **haber** appears alone and, yet again, implies **should, ought, have to** as well as a regretful **if only!** as in ¡no habérmelo dicho! – **if only you hadn't told me!** This is spoken more often than written and usually in the second person **tú** or the polite **usted,** although you sometimes meet it in the third person: **no haberlo hecho ella – she ought not to have done it**.

Tener and **haber** are pretty straightforward and demand only a fraction of the attention demanded by those other quick-change artists, **ser/estar** and **por/para**. Besides, in an unfair and anxious world of have-nots, it makes a welcome change to come across two such unabashed **haves**.

CON GAME

Con exists in both Spanish and English but many of our varieties are slang and consequently appear in rather different circumstances. In Spanish, **con** is a well-bred, well-spoken, unslangy preposition usually corresponding to **with**. Putting a preposition in its place can be tricky in Spanish and often obliges you to use constructions or do some thinking that English doesn't require, so we might as well commence with **conmigo – with me** and **contigo** (the intimate, second-person equivalent of **with thee**) – **with you.**

These words present such a perfect picture of grammatical togetherness that they have become pronouns. They are less formidable than you'd imagine and aren't affected by gender: **ven conmigo al cine – come to the cinema with me** or **mañana cenaré contigo – I'll have dinner with you tomorrow**. This applies only to the first and second person because **with you** (polite), **with him, with her, with us, with you** (plural), **with you** (polite) and **with** them become **con usted, con él, con ella, con nosotros, con vosotros, con ustedes, con ellos/ con ellas** respectively.

This doesn't mean you won't come across the third person **consigo** although it will be in different circumstances, implying **with himself/herself: César está irritado consigo mismo** – **César is angry with himself.** Or you might hear **Fuensanta llevó un maletín consigo** – **Fuensanta took a briefcase with her. Consigo** would not be appropriate if the two were to meet up for dinner: **César invitó a Fuensanta a cenar con él** – **César invited Fuensanta to dine with him.**

A Spanish **con** is sometimes needed where it is often absent in English: **café con leche** – **white coffee** (although hair-splitters will point to **coffee with milk); un filete con patatas** – **steak and chips.** More and more European English-speakers favour the rather transatlantic **talk with/speak with** and neither do the Spanish look askance at **quiero hablar contigo** – **I want to talk with/to you** particularly with regard to meandering, idle chat. On the other hand, the quite different **quiero hablarte** also means **I want to talk to you** but indicates that you have something specific in mind.

All these fine shades of meaning cut both ways so a Spaniard who speaks presentable English can still get his or her prepositions puckered up, too. That is why you are liable to hear **are you cross at me?** or **are you angry at me?** even though he or she would use **con** – **with** in Spanish.

In English **con** is slang for **a convict** – **un preso/recluso/presidiario.** To **con** is **engañar, estafar, timar,** while the **con** performed on the unwary is **un engaño, una estafa** or **un timo.** Another supremely scornful word for a **con-man** is **un engañabobos,** a word that is also suitable for the **con** or **scam** itself.

To **con** is also an antiquated way to **study** or **revise** but the far older but closely-connected **ken** is mainly confined to Scotland, although its definition of **to know** is closely related to its Spanish cousin, **conocer.** Of course, another translation for **to know** is **saber,** a verb covering the other kind of **knowing, knowledge** or **cleverness** that should help prevent the sagacious from falling victim to a **con-game** – **un chanchullo.**

A MATTER OF TASTE

Sabe bien means **he, she, it knows well** as well as **he, she, it tastes good** although you'll probably refer more often to **it** than **he** or **she** when describing your flavour of the week.

Saber is a verb that means both **to know** and **to taste** but the tasting performed by a wine or tea taster – **un catador** – is translated as **catar or probar**. **Taste** does not only involve **taste buds – pápilas gustativas** but also reflects preferences and both are translated as **gusto**. So you could say **esta remolacha tiene un gusto raro – this beetroot has a strange taste** and on seeing my neighbour's new sofa I might comment: **Nieves tiene muy buen gusto – Nieves has very good taste**. At the same time not everyone agrees and Esperanza has been heard to say **Nieves tiene mal gusto**. When she really wants to get her knife into Nieves, Esperanza bungs in an article and a superlative for good measure: **Nieves tiene un gusto malísimo – Nieves has the worst taste**.

In English, **food tastes of...** but in Spanish it swaps prepositions and **food tastes to...** so **la comida sabe a...** If the beetroot is truly appalling, you splutter **esta remolacha sabe a rayos,** which is a tricky little phrase to paraphrase, since the literal meaning of **rayos** is **lightning.**

Saber mal is one way to express discomfort, not because your shoes pinch but because your conscience pricks: **me sabe mal no comer la remolacha que me dio Esperanza – I feel guilty about not eating the beetroot Esperanza gave me**.

It doesn't require much imagination to identify **saborear** as **to savour** while the adjective **sabroso** means **tasty** but does not necessarily correspond to an English **savoury**. **Sabroso** also occurs in the sense of **juicy** when connected to an interesting piece of gossip or scandal.

When translating **in good taste** or **in bad taste**, Spanish again chooses a different preposition – **de: es de mal gusto no agradecer un regalo, aunque sea una remolacha – it's in bad taste not be grateful for a present, even though it's a beetroot.** To which it would be tempting to reply: **sin embargo, es de gusto dudoso regalar una remolacha – nevertheless, it's in dubious taste to give a beetroot.**

However, since this is a hypothetical conversation with Esperanza and since she is averse to ceding the last word, at this point she would no doubt smile and inform you **allá cada cuál con su gusto – it's all a matter of taste.**

ENOUGH SAID...

In Spain it's forgivable to **lose one's temper – enfadarse** but it's not easy to win potentially angry arguments. Why? Because if things get sticky and your opponent feels you're getting the better of the encounter, he or she is apt to pronounce an authoritative **¡basta!** which truncates further verbal warfare.

¡Basta! means **enough!** and is often sufficient to nip squabbling in the bud. You don't only hear it in the course of disagreements, as mothers snap **¡basta!** to grizzling children and cat owners also yell **¡basta!** at over-enthusiastic claw-sharpeners.

Basta is the third person singular of the present tense of the verb **bastar – to be enough, to be sufficient, to suffice.** It's appropriate in situations like those where you dump a plain omelette and a bowl of soup on the table while asking a leading question like **con eso basta ¿verdad? – that's enough, isn't it?** Depending on mood and circumstances, this can be met with a cowed **sí, sí** or a stony **basta con decirte que odio tanto la sopa como la tortilla francesa: suffice it to say that I loathe both soup and plain omelettes.** (And the attentive will detect from the foregoing that where we often use the plural in generalised references like **omelettes,** Spanish sticks to the singular).

An unquarrelsome but slightly urgent **that's enough** when a glass is topped up or a plate sufficiently heaped with food is likely to be **¡ya!** or a tranquilly-pronounced **basta** or **es bastante.**

Having identified **bastar – an** undemanding verb, as it is nearly always limited to the third person singular – it is easy to pinpoint the origins of **bastante.** As well as **enough, bastante** can be translated as **rather** and **fairly: ¿tienes bastante con una tortilla francesa y sopa? – is a plain omelette and soup**

enough for you? In some households this might be met with a pained **esa es una pregunta bastante tonta – that's a rather silly question.**

At the risk of making your eyes cross with boredom and provoking jaw-cracking yawns, don't forget that **bastante** is an adjective when signifying **enough** or **sufficient: preparas bastantes comidas – you make enough meals, you make a lot of meals.** When it means **rather, somewhat etc.** it is an adverb – not because it provides more information about a verb, but because it tells you more about an adjective: **preparas comidas bastante sosas – you make rather insipid meals.** This turns it into an adverb and adverbs are nicer than you might suspect because there is no need to make them agree with adjectives and/or nouns.

As well as the little-used first person singular of the present tense of **bastar, basto** is an adjective meaning **coarse** and is as appropriate for describing texture as a person's manner or appearance. Plural **bastos** correspond to the **clubs** you see on Spanish playing cards and which bear an striking resemblance to the **clubs** brandished by cavemen in cartoons.

The English **to baste, tack** (sewing, not sailing) has no connection with **bastar** and is translated as **hilvanar**. For the **basting** required of a leg of lamb, the dictionary suggests a hard-to-swallow **pringar.** A more modern translation for **pringar** is **to splash, spatter** with the sort of dirt that sticks after mud-slinging and these days **un pringado** is likely to be a politician or businessman with a blotted copybook and a huge bank balance.

Returning to the Sunday joint, the way to **baste** in Spain is **mojar la carne con su jugo** but you won't have to sever all food connections with **pringar** as it also means **to dip bread** into sauce, gravy or egg-yolks. In Spain this isn't a shameful or solitary vice but a pleasure that may be indulged in when eating out in all but august, un-**basto** establishments. Less tolerantly regarded in public is **rebañar,** which is closer to **mopping up the very last remains** of sauce or whatever is left on your plate. **Pringar** and **rebañar** are important parts of the Spanish way of eating that allows you to **dunk – mojar** biscuits and cake in tea, coffee or drinking chocolate, too. Naturally, this self-indulgence is abhorrent to those on diets or with exquisite manners, all of whom dismiss such permissiveness with an appalled **¡basta ya! – enough of that!**

AT LENGTH

Long is locatable in some Spanish words and occasionally bears some resemblance to an English **long: longaniza – a long**(ish) **sausage; longevo – long-lived; longitud – longitude.** But by and large an English **long** becomes a Spanish **largo** and has few connections with **large: un discurso largo – a long speech; una novela larga – a long novel.**

A lo largo del día could be translated as **all day long** but is subtly closer to **throughout the day. Crecen amapolas a lo largo de la carreteras** allows **long** to raise its head once more and describes one of the joys of Spain in the spring: **poppies grow along the side of the roads.**

The **long** that lacks measurement is translated as **mientras** and is often entangled with the subjunctive mood: **I don't care what flowers you give me, so long as they're not carnations – no me importa que flores me des, mientras no sean claveles**.

It's doubtful that it will ever figure prominently in your compendium of vital-to-know information, but **la puesta de largo** is an unproletarian and virtually extinct **coming-out dance,** the occasion when a Spanish girl **puts on a long frock for the first time** and is presented in society. **Esto viene de largo** has no relation with dress or trouser lengths, however, and means **this goes back some time. Un café largo** is a **big, black coffee** and not the usual tiny thimbleful although you will find that **una comida larga** doesn't necessarily promise mountains of food but will be **a long meal.**

Larguirucho used to be a not particularly admiring adjective to describe someone **long and lanky** but, curiously, it is less heard now that young Spanish people are strikingly tall when compared with their grandparents and even parents.

In other circumstances **long** will be translated by **mucho,** especially with reference to time: **you've taken a long time**

Poppies grow along the road

to mend that – **has tardado mucho en arreglar eso. A long time ago** needs the addition of the verb **hacer: hace much tiempo. A long way away** becomes a brief **lejos – far** or **a mucha distancia** but when you want to know if Madrid, for instance, is **a long way** off, you would ask **¿está lejos Madrid?** – literally **is Madrid far away?** When you're nearly there you'd make use of the unexpected **faltar – to lack: falta poco para llegar a Madrid – it's not long until we reach Madrid** although you're really saying **it lacks little to arrive at Madrid.**

As well as **largo** there are alternative words with a built-in, unspoken **long** so **long hair** can be **pelo largo** but also **melena,** which is a specific noun for a **head of long hair. Melenas** is a nickname for anyone with unusually or inappropriately **long hair** while **melenudo** is the adjective **long-haired** and can sound a touch critical when used by a short-haired gentleman to describe a long-haired youth. **Melenudo** also corresponds to the English **long-haired** applied to people or activities considered intellectually demanding.

The way **to long** or **yearn** is **anhelar** and although the verb **alargar** sounds like **to enlarge** it means **to lengthen**. **Largar** is another matter and variously means **to pay** or **give out** (a cable or rope, not money), **unfurl, let fly** (an insult, not a kite). It also implies to talk too much or too long: **César nos largo un rollo que duró una hora** – César gave us a spiel that lasted an hour. In reflexive form, **largarse** suggests **to leave abruptly** so that **bueno, me largo** means **well, I'm off,** to which a fitting reply would be **hasta luego** – **so long.**

TIME & TIME AGAIN

We all know that time is relative – kind of you, Albert – but the Spanish already knew that anyway, because five minutes here can correspond to seven and a half elsewhere. The Spanish are not nearly as unpunctual as they were, but their perception of the passing of time is still not in line with the trans-Pyrenean model.

This could be influenced by the fact that the Spanish use three words to translate **time: tiempo, vez** and **hora. Tiempo** also means **weather**, of course, but if you say **¿llevas mucho tiempo esperando?** you are asking **have you been waiting a long time?** And a peevish **no tengo tiempo para entretenerme** means **I haven't got a lot of time to waste**.

When you want to know if it's ten to nine or twenty past three, you use the word for **hour,** as you would in France: **¿qué hora es?** – **what's the time? Hora** is necessary in constructions such as **it's still not time to go to bed** – **todavía no es hora de acostarse,** or **about time too!** – **¡ya era hora!** as well as the wordier **¡ya va siendo hora!**

Vez translates **time** in phrases like **this time** – **esta vez** and **that time**, which is as likely to be **aquella vez** as **esa vez.** **Sometimes** has three versions: **a veces, algunas veces** and **de vez en cuando.** The singular **sometime** is singular in Spanish too: **alguna vez iré a ver a Nieves** – **I shall go and see Nieves**

sometime. From time to time can be translated once more as **de vez en cuando** or the less-frequent but closer translation of **de vez en vez**.

Once and for all is as final in Spanish as it is in English but they manage to drag time into it too: **una vez para siempre,** literally **one time forever**. You have a choice with **at the same time** or **both at once**, either of which can be variously translated as **a la vez, a la misma vez** or **al mismo tiempo: veré a Nieves y Esperanza a la vez – I shall see Nieves and Esperanza at the same time.**

When **at the same time** implies **all the same** you can only use **al mismo tiempo: at the same time I suppose I'd better go and see Fuensanta too – al mismo tiempo, supongo que debo ir a ver a Fuensanta también.**

Once a week is **una vez a la semana, twice a day** is **dos veces al día** and **three times a year** becomes **tres veces al año**. Instead of the **once upon a time** that all the best stories begin with, the Spanish say **érase una vez...** or **there was a time...**

Spanish attitudes towards punctuality have improved considerably and Mass, bullfights and football matches are no longer the principal functions that start at the announced time. Even so, attitudes towards time are still sufficiently unrealistic for the Spanish not to recognise the incongruity of a phrase like **ahora después**, literally **now afterwards** a contradiction that in practice means **at some unspecified time in the near, or possibly distant, future but in any case not right now**.

Right now, incidentally, is frequently translated as **ahora mismo**, a stock phrase that promises speedy attention to any problem, request or proposal without actually saying when.

To take a long time is usually translated as **tardar** but it also means **to be late**, which might lead you to suppose that **apresurarse – to hurry** could double up as **to be early**. Instead, this is translated as **llegar temprano** or **llegar pronto**.

Pronto means **early, speedy, prompt** or **ready** but it is also a noun meaning **a sudden impulse** or **a fit of anger**. So the next time you are subjected to unpunctuality, remember this will almost certainly be due to a Spaniard's belief that it is better to travel hopefully and get there late than to arrive early and bad-tempered.

ABOUT TURN

Translations for **to turn** are **girar, hacer girar, dar vueltas** or **volver** and it is personal preference which decides whether you say **Fausto giró la manivela, Fausto hizo girar la manivela** or **Fausto dio vueltas a la manivela** for **Fausto turned the handle.**

The noun **vuelta** is the past participle of **volver** but this verb doesn't do a particularly good job of turning handles and implies **to turn back, turn round, return.** Even so, **to turn back the clock** is **retrasar el reloj** while **Fausto dio una vuelta** is standard Spanish for an old-fashioned **Fausto took a turn**

All these verbs have reflexive versions so **turn round!** is **¡hazte girar! ¡dáte la vuelta!** or **¡vuélvete!** although **¡gírate!** is less common.

Doblar means **to double over, bend** but can imply **to turn: Elena dobló la esquina** – **Elena turned the corner.** The reprehensible reader's **dog-eared book** is **un libro con las esquinas dobladas** but to **turn the pages of a book** is **pasar la página.**

To turn something into something else requires **transformar, convertir: una bruja sabe convertir un príncipe en una rana** – **a witch knows how to turn a prince into a frog.** Both verbs can be reflexive: **los renacuajos se transforman en ranas** – **tadpoles turn** (themselves) **into frogs. Volverse feo/ponerse feo** or **hacerse feo** mean **to turn** or **become nasty, ugly;** you also use these when something or someone **turns a different colour: se puso pálido cuando me vio** – **he turned pale when he saw me.**

Volverse en contra is **to turn against** but **to turn to** (in the direction of) is **volver hacía: el príncipe volvió hacía la bruja** – **the prince turned towards the witch. To turn to** drink, religion or another person is **recurrir: no recurras a César si necesitas dinero** – **don't turn to César if you need money.** But if you do and your appeal is fruitless, you're liable to whimper **no sé a qué atenerme** – **I don't know which way to turn.**

To turn aside is **desviar, apartar** or, when you're the one who's avoiding and evading, the reflexive **desviarse, apartarse.** If **to turn out** means **to evict,** the Spanish use the merciless **desahuciar,** also used for conveying terminal illness: **le han**

133

desahuciado los médicos – the doctors have given up all hope for him. Should **to turn out** be synonymous with **to happen**, choose between **resultar** or **suceder**: resulta que César y Blas ya no se hablan – it turns out that César and Blas don't talk to each other now.

To turn up is **llegar** or **aparecer**: apareció Elena con un nuevo peinado – Elena turned up with a new hairdo. However, there are other ways **to turn up** and queasy distaste is translated by **repugnar, repeler**. They also translate a **turn-off: a Nieves le repugnan los hombres demasiado musculosos – muscle-bound men turn Nieves off** (just as well, bearing in mind Blas's physique) but **to turn off** an electrical or mechanical appliance is **desenchufar, apagar**.

To turn on is **enchufar, encender** but in its modern acceptance it would be **entusiasmar** or the colloquial **chiflar, pirar**. If the turning-on is sensual or sexual, use **excitar** and **encender** or the reflexive **excitarse** and **encenderse**; there is also super-colloquial, not-in-front-of-the children **poner cachondo** and **ponerse cachondo**.

Turnar and **hacer por turnos** both mean **to do something in turn/by turn but tornar** and **tornear** mean **to return, restore** and **to turn on a lathe** respectively. You await your turn – **esperar el turno** when shopping or playing a game but **un turno** is also **a work shift** and **a dining room sitting. A turn** at a show or circus is **un número** and **a bad turn** is **una mala jugada** although, depending on the context, an adjective-less **jugada** could still be a disservice, while **a good turn** is **un favor. A trouser turn-up** is **la vuelta del pantalón, a turncoat** is **un chaquetero** and **a turnstile** is **un torniquete,** which is also a medical **tourniquet**. An edible turnover is **una empanadilla,** a business turnover is **la facturación** and **a turnip is un nabo**. (Turnip? Turnip? What's a turnip doing here?).

MAKE-DO

Hacer is as likely to mean **to do** as **to make,** so a Spanish-speaker sees no difference between **¿qué estás haciendo? – what are you doing? and estamos haciendo mucho ruido – we are making a lot of noise**.

That is why a Spanish painter with not-tremendously-good English might translate **en este momento estoy haciendo acuarelas** as **at present I am making watercolours** instead of what we regard as the more logical **at present I am doing watercolours.** .

Generally you can depend on translating **to make** as **hacer: vender sus acuarelas le hace feliz al pintor** – selling his watercolours makes the painter happy; **ella está haciendo paella** – she is making paella and **¿vale la pena hacer el esfuerzo?** – is it worth making the effort?

Hacer is used when **to make** entails **obligation: ¡no me hagas esperar!** – don't make me wait! You also use **hacer** for **make** in the sense of **to add up to: siete y nueve hacen dieciseis** – seven and nine make sixteen.

To make known has the predictable translation of **hacer saber** and **to make room** is **hacer sitio. To make up** or **to make one's peace with somebody** turns plural: **hacer las paces** but **to put on make-up** severs links with **hacer** and is **maquillarse** instead. Neither does **to make fun of** always require **hacer** because as well as **hacer burla** this can be expressed as the reflexive verbs **burlarse** and **mofarse**.

The Spanish do not regard themselves as racist and in the past had no qualms about saying **hacer el indio**, literally **to make like an Indian**, for **to play the fool** although most would think twice before using it now.

Hacer also does a full-time job of translating **to do: haz lo que él te diga** – do what he tells you; **tengo demasiado que hacer** – I have too much to do. There are always more specific verbs for **to do** so as well as **en este momento estoy haciendo acuarelas,** there is no reason why a painter should not say **estoy pintando acuarelas – I am painting watercolours**. He'd be on the pompous side if he used **ejecutar, realizar** or **efectuar** but these are all synonymous for **doing** a watercolour or even the washing-up.

No doubt by now you will have got the message that anything connected with the climate, meteorology or temperature is expressed with the verb **hacer** although Spanish-speakers are not forthcoming as to whether they regard this as **doing** or **making**. The phrase **hace tiempo**, however, refers to **time** rather than **weather: hace tiempo, el** pollo costaba caro – in the past, chicken was expensive.

Hacer can be used when being more precise about time: **hace tres días regresé de Madrid – three days ago I came back from Madrid**. It can be used in the past tense: **hacía tres meses que no le habíamos visto – it was three months since we had seen him** as well as the future: **mañana hará tres años que no le vemos – tomorrow it will be three years since we've seen him** (but literally **that we don't see him**).

The reflexive **hacerse** means **to become**: **te estás haciendo un poco arisco – you're becoming a little surly.** You will also encounter **hacerse con** with the meaning of **to get hold of**: **Blas se hizo con una foto de Nieves – Blas got hold of a photo of Nieves. Hacer como si**, followed by the subjunctive would be translated as **to act as though, to behave as though** or **to pretend: aunque sea arisco, yo hago como si no lo fuera – even though he's surly, I behave as though he weren't.**

Hacer mal efecto is the way to say that something **looks bad: Nieves cree que hace mal efecto comer chuletas con los dedos – Nieves believes it looks bad to eat chops with the fingers. Hacer falta** is **to be wanting** in the sense of **to lack**, a construction little used by your average English-speaker but much-favoured by Spanish-speakers: **hacen falta cubiertos – cutlery is required.**

Hacer daño means **to harm** but **hacer tiras** means **to make strips out of something** and **hacer pedazos** is **to smash to smithereens, to shatter.** However, **hacer polvo – to reduce to powder** is an inarticulate way to announce the state of **being shattered: limpiar los cristales les hace polvo a algunas amas de casa – cleaning windows makes some housewives really tired** and at the end of a weary working day, it is customary to exclaim or hear **¡estoy hecho polvo! – I'm exhausted!**

Hacer is discarded when translating **to do with,** whose Spanish version is **tener que ver: cocinar no tiene nada que ver con comer – cooking has nothing to do with eating.** When **to do** implies **to be sufficient, to be enough,** this can be translated by **valer con, bastar con: ¿vale con un poco de paella? – will a little paella do?** or **no basta con paella, quiero cocido también – paella isn't enough, I want cocido, too.**

To which an appropriate answer would be the awesomely

colloquial **pues que le vamos a hacer...** a verbal shrug of the shoulders and a philosophically resigned comment implying **oh well, what the hell...**

BELIEVE IT OR NOT

Look up **creer** in a Spanish dictionary and the first definition you see is **to think** and not the expected **to believe.** The Spanish regard these two activities as interchangeable for reasons involving more than semantics but instead of wondering **why** and getting bogged down in philosophy and mired in metaphysics, it's easier to have a look at **how**.

No soul searching and analysis are necessary for this as the interchangeability of **creer** and **pensar** boils down to sticking to **creer** when **think** can be substituted by **believe.** **Thinking** *about* is always translated as **pensar: ¿en qué estás pensando? – what are you thinking about?** In the absence of **about,** you can still use **pensar** although **¿piensas ir mañana?** is as close to **do you intend to go tomorrow** as **do you think you'll go tomorrow?** Again, you use **creer** when belief enters the picture: **¿crees que podrás ir mañana? – do you think** (believe) **you'll be able to go tomorrow?**

Sometimes both **pensar** and **creer** get across the idea of **to feel: no pienso/no creo que es buena idea beber tanto cava** are adequate translations for **I don't think (feel) it's a good idea to drink so much cava.** An improbably, admirably austere reply along the lines of **I think you're right** sounds more conciliatory with **creer** however: **creo que tienes razón.** In phrases like **I think you're right,** English can omit **that,** but omission isn't optional in Spanish and **que** is always present.

A briefer way to express agreement – **creo que sí: I think so** – still requires **que**, together with **creo que no – I don't think so. Ya lo creo** is close to a super-affirmative **I'll say** or **you bet.** In fact the often untranslatable **ya** – principal definitions are **already, now** – is a typical way of saying **yes.**

You can use either **creer** or **pensar** for opinion-seeking **¿tú qué crees?** or **¿tú qué piensas? – what do you think?** Make **creer** reflexive, however and belief doesn't come into it because you're speaking a brusquer language. **¿Qué te crees?**

137

is an impatient reaction to ingenuousness or lack of guile while **¿tú que te has creído?** insinuates **who on earth do you think you are?** as well **as what the hell are you thinking of? No me lo creo** is spoken refusal to **believe** what doesn't warrant belief: **I can't believe it. Creerse** is also a most un-English way to **believe in oneself to the point of conceit;** consequently the past participle **creído** is also an adjective synonymous with **conceited.**

As often as not, **creer** is a straightforward **to believe: Elena dice que no cree ni una palabra de lo que dice Esperanza – Elena says she doesn't believe a word of what Esperanza says or de pequeña Nieves creía en las hadas – when she was little Nieves believed in fairies.**

Creer translates **to believe** in the religious sense. A Spaniard understands **un creyente** as **someone who believes in God** but despite Spain's modern status as an officially non-confessional state, **un creyente** is generally understood to refer to **a Catholic. A belief** is **una creencia** but you often find this referred to as **una opinión,** two abstractions not necessarily identical in an un-dogmatic English-speaker's book.

Words like **credibilidad, crédulo** and **creíble** are easily traced to **creer** and correspond to their English cousins **credibility, credulous** and **credible,** together with **incredibilidad, incrédulo, increíble.** Those with scant faith in their finances find it hard to credit a verb like **creer** with a noun like **crédito,** which in Spanish implies **a bank credit** and crops up in **tarjeta de crédito – credit card.**

You encounter **crédito** in constructions such as **no pude dar crédito a lo que oía – I couldn't believe** (literally **I couldn't give credit to) what I heard.** Apart from this, Spanish disbelief does not need to be expressed with **creer** and can range from a flat **no puede ser – it can't be** to an outraged, querulous **¿sea posible? – can it be possible?** Equally indignant is **¿hábrase visto?,** which means **have you ever seen anything like it?,** and must be one occasion when **seeing** certainly doesn't imply **believing.**

WISHING WELL

There's no Starlight, Starbright wish in Spain, nor are you allowed a wish on finding two almonds in the same shell or eating the first strawberry of the season. Even **a wishbone** loses its magic once it becomes **un espoleto**.

You can put this down to the non-existence of a nice, comfy verb like **wish**. The nearest to it is **desear – to desire**, and very nice, too, but somehow it does put things on a different footing.

Desear is used to **wish** someone **a happy birthday** or **saint's day**, especially in writing: **te deseo muchas felicidades – I wish you much happiness**, although a Spanish person is likely to limit spoken **best wishes** to **felicidades**.

As you'd imagine, **deseo** is also the **wish** that is synonymous with **aim** or **good intentions: mi único deseo es hacerte feliz regalándote estos pendientes de esmeraldas – my sole wish is to make you happy by giving you these emerald earrings**. It is easy to connect **mejores deseos** to **best wishes: te regalo estas galletas de chocolate con mis mejores deseos – I'm giving you these chocolate biscuits with my best wishes**.

Matters get more complex with the introduction of **querer,** which means **to love** and **to want** but often fulfils the same role as an English **wish**. If you're given to snapping **I wish you wouldn't do that!** you'll be able to translate exasperation with **¡ojalá no hicieses eso!,** which amounts to **I wish to goodness you wouldn't do that! ¡Ojalá!** is a remnant of Spain's Moorish past and means **would that Allah!** It is used hopefully or wistfully, as in **quizás nos tocará La Primitiva – perhaps we'll win the Lottery,** and to this the usual answer is **¡ojalá!**

The subjunctive crops up all the time when it comes to wishing. English-speakers have a bee in their bonnets about the subjunctive and bringing it out is something of a drag at first. You'll survive, though, if you remember that **querer** followed by a noun is always in the indicative mood: **quiero esmeraldas, no galletas de chocolate – I want emeralds, not chocolate biscuits**.

If you **wish** and it's not a dead cert you're going to get what you're after and **querer** is followed by **que** plus yet another verb, the subjunctive is called for in both (and not the present tense, either): **quisiera que me dieras esmeraldas – I'd wish you to/I'd like you to give me emeralds.** When **I wish** is really a peremptory **I want**, use the indicative but follow it with the present tense of the subjunctive: **quiero que me des esmeraldas.**

Gustar provides a roundabout, very Spanish way of translating **wish** even though its literal meaning is **to please**. When using **gustar** followed by a noun, you are again spared the subjunctive but **gustar** plus **que** plus another verb will need the conditional for **gustar** and the subjunctive for whatever follows. **Me gustaría que me dieras galletas de chocolate** means **I'd like it if you were to give me chocolate biscuits** but will usually be understood as a wish or a hint and not an outright request for something. Any verb following ¡ojalá! always toes the same subjunctive line: **¡ojalá me diera esmeraldas! – if only he would give me emeralds!**

On the few occasions when a Spaniard feels entitled to **make a wish – formular un deseo** he closes his eyes and says **pido,** followed by the object of his desire. While they might sometimes be considered interchangeable, **to wish for** and **to request (pedir)** do not necessarily amount to the same thing, and as any level-headed non-Spaniard can see, this is just another combination of Mediterranean confidence tempered by Latin wishful thinking.

KNOW-HOW

A synonym for **saber** is **conocer** – but one of the synonyms for **conocer** is **saber**, which is the sort of information that gets you not very far at rather high speed. The verb **saber** generally conveys **knowledge** or **knowledge of facts** while **conocer** suggests **knowledge of** or **acquaintance with people or places**. This means you would say **Nieves sabe inglés pero no conoce Inglaterra – Nieves knows English but doesn't know England.** Or you could mutter **¿Conoces al padre de Nieves? Pues seguramente sabrás que no le gustan los gatos – You know Nieves' father? Well you're sure to know he doesn't like cats.**

If something is **bien sabido** it will be a **well-known fact** but **bien conocido** describes **a well-known person: es bien sabido que a mi bien conocido vecino, Fausto, no le gustan los gatos** – it's well known that my well-known neighbour, Fausto, doesn't like cats.

Conocimiento involves **consciousness** in a purely physical sense, and **perder el conocimiento** means **to lose consciousness.** Perhaps this cerebral connection is why **knowledge** or **anything you have been taught or have learnt,** however unspecialised, is closer to **conocer** than **saber** and plural for good measure: **los conocimientos. Fausto está orgulloso de sus conocimientos de agricultura** means **Fausto is proud of his agricultural knowledge** although there is little left to show for it since our rabbit ate all the plants in

It's well known that... my neighbour Fautus doesn't like cats

la huertecita – **vegetable patch** at the bottom of his garden.

Un reconocimiento is a medical **check-up** or **examination** but as well as **to examine medically**, the verb **reconocer** also implies **to admit, to recognise: reconozco que disfruto discutiendo con Fausto – I admit that I enjoy arguing with Fausto**.

Where we use the French word, **connoisseur**, Spanish prefers a logical **conocedor: Fausto, el padre de Nieves, es buen conocedor de vinos – Fausto, Nieves' father, is a wine connoisseur** (which he should be, considering the vast amount he gets through).

Sabiduría means **wisdom** and **un sabio** is **a sage**. Used as an adjective, **sabio** means **wise, knowing** but **sabihondo** implies **someone who is not as clever as he makes out** and also describes **a too-knowing, not always pleasant child**, someone similar to Perfecto, Nieves' little brother. Not long ago he persuaded his cronies to raid Fausto's melon patch but left them in the lurch when his father made an unscheduled appearance. **¿Y yo qué sabía?** he later protested when accused of treachery: **How was I to know?**

To do something purposely or **to know what you're doing** is **hacer a sabiendas** and as Perfecto's betrayed friends told him: **lo hiciste a sabiendas de que no dormía la siesta – you knew full well that he wasn't having a siesta**.

Un sabelotodo is **a knowall**, which inevitably conjures up Fausto. There are days when it seems I can't avoid him – and there goes the doorbell and Pushy is jet-propelling herself under the sofa. **Ya lo sabía yo: aquí está Fausto otra vez – I just knew it: Fausto's here again.**

FREE SPEECH

It's easy to recognise **libertad** as **liberty, freedom** but an old warning about not confusing **libertad** with **libertinaje – licentiousness, profligacy** reveals earlier Spanish doubts regarding the former's advisability. Liberty need not involve high or low moral tones, however, so **libertad** appears in less contentious situations such as **he tomado la libertad de darle** tu dirección – I've taken the liberty of giving him your address or la pélicula toma libertades con el libro original – the film takes liberties with the original book.

Libertar and the noun libertad appear in situations where English uses to liberate and liberty respectively, although you will hear and use the noun more often than the verb. Poner en libertad means to set free and another option – ser puesto en libertad – is an infrequent example of the Spanish passive voice. To *be* free is ser libre, but to be free after a spell of captivity is estar en libertad, demonstrating that liberty of this kind is strictly physical, possibly recent and not necessarily permanent. The still more transient estar en libertad condicional is to be on bail, parole or probation, depending on the legal circumstances.

We use free where the Spanish might not, so I'm not free to tell you his phone number is translated as no estoy autorizado darte su número de teléfono, no me es permitido darte su número de teléfono or the bald no puedo darte su número de teléfono.

Liberar also means to free, exempt from or release while the past participle liberado – not the more obvious libertado – corresponds to a feminist liberated. Liberar is also responsible for liberal, an adjective whose use in other times and other regimes was not necessarily a compliment. The almost identical librar yet again means to free/set free and suggests rescue or delivery from: Fuensanta librará a César de su promesa – Fuensanta will release César from his promise. It is also favoured by the articulate and/or financially-orientated in constructions such as to issue a cheque – librar un talón as well as the articulate and/or military: librar una batalla – to fight a battle.

¡Líbrame Dios! is God deliver me! but the relieved and reflexive ¡de lo que te has librado! implies what a narrow escape you've had!, while the similarly reflexive librarse por los pelos signifies to escape by a hair's breadth. Less trouble and more relaxing, librar can also mean to have time off: César libra los martes – César has Tuesdays off; alternatively you can say César tiene el día libre los martes.

Ir por libre means to work or do something on one's own account but can evoke a whiff of waywardness: Fuensanta

siempre va por libre – **Fuensanta always does her own thing.**
Al aire libre is the Spanish version of **open air** but **entrada libre** means **free entry,** a term also translatable as **entrada gratis** or **entrada gratuíta.** As with the English adjective **gratuitous, gratuito** also signifies **unnecessary** but **gratis** only ever means **free of charge.**

Tax-free is **libre de impuestos, exento de impuestos** or **sin impuestos.** You find this last formula in phrases like **sugar-free** – **sin azúcar; fat-free** – **sin grasa;** as well as **trouble-free** – **sin problema,** a phrase now understood by the Spanish to convey **no sweat** when communicating with **extranjeros** – **foreigners.**

Libremente and **liberalmente** are more or less inter-changeable for **freely** but it is sometimes possible to detect different shades of meaning, since **dar libremente** implies **to give of one's own free will** while **dar liberalmente** gets across the idea of **giving liberally.**

Even though **ser libre** means **to be free,** it also suggests **to be generous** or even **extravagant.** Thus **César es muy libre con su dinero** is similar to the half-empty or half-full glass and, depending on one's inherent generosity or parsimony, can be translated as **César is very free with his money** or **César wastes his money.**

DONE AND DUSTED

Like people, some words look alike, sound alike, yet have nothing in common and although there are not many of these in Spanish, one or two could trip you up. **Hecho,** for instance, looks very much like **echo** and sounds identical. **Un hecho** is a noun that means **deed** or **fact** and is derived from the past participle of the verb **hacer** – **to do** or **to make. Has hecho bien** is what they tell you when **you've done the right thing** but **has hecho mal** is what you'll hear when **you've done it all wrong** and **hemos hecho una buena labor** means **we've done a good job.** Owing to the duality of **hacer, ¿qué has hecho?** not only means **what have you done?** but also **what have you made?** although commonsense and knowledge of what you have been up to should indicate which you are being asked.

As well as existing in tandem with the auxiliary verb **haber,** **hecho** crops up in **¡bien hecho!** which means **well done!** But **muy hecho** is the way to ask for your steak if you like it **well-done,** while **poco hecho** should ensure that it's brought to you **rare.**

Hecho appears again in **hecho a mano – hand made** and someone crass enough to tell you **estás hecho un asco** should be crossed off your list of favourite people because this means **you look awful.**

Estar hecho una furia is the Spanish way to be **tremendously angry: Elena está hecha una furia porque Fausto no le compra un lavavajillas – Elena is absolutely furious because Fausto won't buy her a dish-washer.**

The exclamation **¡hecho!** corresponds to **done!** meaning **that's a deal!** or **agreed! Dicho y hecho** is the Spanish version of **no sooner said than done** and **hecho y derecho,** literally **done and right,** is frequently pronounced by people who are outright, forthright and downright: **necesitamos ciudadanos hechos y derechos – we need fine, upstanding citizens.**

De hecho is the same as **in fact** or **as a matter of fact,** so **de hecho, yo tampoco tengo un lavavajillas** is the way to say **as it happens, I don't have a dish-washer, either.**

And what about **echo?** For a start, it's not an **echo,** which loses a letter to become **un eco.** The only time you ought to meet **echo** is as the first person singular of the present tense of **echar: echo la pelota – I throw the ball; te echo de menos – I miss you** and **¿echo las cartas? – shall I deal the cards?** Since the **h** is not pronounced in Spanish, many people confuse **hecho** with **echo** when writing. You may be heartened to learn that deciding when there should and when there should not be an **h** in a word is usually easier for a foreigner to sort out than a Spaniard, who is often inclined to shrug and admit **estoy hecho un lío – I'm confused.**

PLAYING THE GAME

The Spanish are famously dignified but sometimes turn uncharacteristically **skittish** or **playful**, in which case they are described by the adjectives **juguetón** and **juguetona** as the case may be. This carefree word is also appropriate to kittens and other fluffy nuisances and can easily be traced back to the verb **jugar – to play**. It can be relied upon to appear in the same situations and circumstances as its English counterpart: **to play on the beach – jugar en la playa; to play at cards – jugar a las cartas; to play football – jugar al fútbol**.

The aspect of **playing** that involves a tuba or bassoon is translated from a totally different angle by the verb **tocar – to touch: I learnt to play the piano when I was small – aprendí a tocar el piano de pequeña**.

It would be naïve to expect life to be all plain sailing and straight translations, so an English **game** turns into a Spanish **juego** but this is also the first person of the present tense of **jugar**. There is added confusion because the Spanish don't distinguish between playing and the game they play, and succeed in killing two words with one stone while they're about it. On the other hand, the **play** they go to see at a theatre is **una obra de teatro** or **una representación teatral**.

Una jugada sounds fun but usually turns up as **a shot** or **a stroke: Ferrero ganó el juego con una jugada preciosa – Ferrero worn the game with a lovely shot**. This word is less sporting when it means **to play a dirty** (rarely amusing) **trick upon** or **to do a bad turn to**. This will be enlarged upon as **una mala jugada** although adding **mala** isn't essential for conveying nastiness and can be substituted with the mini-adjective, **menuda – small: menuda jugada que me has hecho – that's quite a bad turn you've done me**. Some prefer **jugarreta** if they want the small-sounding suffix to remove part of the sting of **jugada**.

Fair play reverts to **juego limpio**, literally **clean play**, with **foul play** a corresponding **juego sucio. Estar en juego** means **to be in play** in a sporting sense, but **mi reputación está en juego** is a risky **my reputation is at stake**.

In tricky circumstances you often feel the need to

proclaim **this is no game** and in Spanish you proclaim **esto no es ningún juego**. At this stage you tend to use **jugar** to trot out panicky clichés like **él está jugando el todo por el todo** – he's **playing for high stakes** and the reflexive **me juego el pellejo** – **I'm risking my skin**. Still reflexive, **te la estás jugando** is a frequent admonition approximate to **you're going too far** in situations that are neither sporting nor playful.

These phrases are redolent of gambling but although **jugar** still conveys **gaming**, someone actually **laying out money on a bet** might prefer the specific **apostar**. However, **estoy apostando muy fuerte** can still be interpreted in cliché mode: **I'm playing for very high stakes**.

To be game is **estar dispuesto** but **to be on the game** has little direct connection with sport or gambling as far as the lady who earns her living this way is concerned and which she would describe as **hacer la calle**, literally **to do the street**. The **game** that appears on the dinner table is known as **caza** while the **big game** that is slaughtered in the name of fun and enjoyment is **caza mayor**.

The **juego** that crops up as **un juego de café** is a **a set of coffee pot and cups** – but don't get too many ideas about **un juego de cama**. As well as being what it sounds like, this also reaches shops and department stores as an unexciting, singularly unerotic **set of sheets**.

TRY IT

Intento looks and sounds like **intent** but the two rarely, barely coincide and, although they do belong to the same family, their relationship isn't noticeably intimate. To convey the **intent** implied by **absorbed, intense, attentive,** you can use the handy **absorto/a, intenso/a, atento/a**. The noun **intento** is invariably translated as **an attempt, a try: logré hacerlo al tercer intento: I managed to do it on the third attempt**.

The English **intent** coupled with **to loiter** is translated as such: **merodear con intenciones criminales** but because a Spanish person tends to equate **intent/intention** with **consummation**, he might prefer **ends: merodear con fines**

criminales – loitering with criminal ends. When he is less certain of motive or outcome, he chooses **propósito: ¿qué será su propósito? – what's his intention/what's he playing at?** The tentative-sounding **tentativa** sometimes, but not always, suggests a **failed attempt: el mes pasado hubo una tentativa de paz – there was an attempt at making peace last month**. Sometimes you encounter **pretender** which in Spanish has less to do with pretence than **endeavouring** or **trying**, albeit with an ulterior motive: **¿qué es lo que pretende? – what's he after?**

The verb **intentar** means **to try, attempt, endeavour**, particularly when sweat, strain and struggle are involved: **no puedo abrir esta botella de cava, inténtalo tú – I can't open this bottle of cava, you try**. Another option is **procurar** although this is closer to **endeavour** or **seek: procuré encontrar la mejor marca – I tried to find the best brand**.

Intentar is often substituted by **tratar** and the preposition **de: estaba tratando de abrir el cava – he was trying to open the cava**. This is one of many translations which at one time would have been considered not-quite-spot-on – for example **retirado** instead of **jubilado** for **retired**. The practice is comparatively recent and can be blamed on trans-atlantic Spanish, plus the need to dub films, soap operas and television series with words that look as though they could be issuing from the actors' mouths.

Tratar usually means **to treat, handle** objects and / or people: **le están tratando con antibióticos – they're treating him with antibiotics; esos vasos son muy caros, asi que trátalos con cuidado – those glasses are very expensive, so handle them with care.** As usual, prepositions modify meanings, so **tratar** followed by **en** means **to deal in, trade: trataba en cerdos antes de abrir el restaurante – he used to deal in pigs before opening the restaurant.**

With the addition of **de**, the reflexive **tratarse** is approximate to **concern/involve: sólo se trata de abrir el cava, nada más – it's just a question of opening the cava, nothing more**.

This verb also applies to **dealing with a subject: ese libro trata de cerdos – this book is about pigs.** Still hitched up to **de, tratarse de tú, tratarse de usted** mean **to use the familiar second person/polite third person when talking to someone.**

Tratar con is another way of saying **to deal or trade with a person** rather than to **deal or trade in a commodity**: no le gustaba tratar con una mujer – he didn't like dealing with a woman.

To try in the legal sense is **procesar** while **to try/cause to suffer/afflict** is an easy **hacer sufrir/afligir**. When **to try** means **to test/taste/sample,** use **probar: ¿habeis probado esta marca de cava? – have you tried this brand of cava?** In reflexive form, it also translates **to try on: me voy a probar esos zapatos – I'm going to try those shoes on**. The Spanish are as likely **to try it on over someone else** as we are but there's no specific expression for this, apart from an admonitory **no me vengas con esas,** which is virtually the same as **don't come it.**

SINGLE-MINDED

When the noun **single-mindedness** and the adjective **single-minded** are equated with obstinacy they can be described inelegantly but serviceably as **cabezonería** and **cabezón** respectively. **Cabezón** exists as an adjective as well as a noun meaning anatomically **big-headed,** so **tu tío es un cabezón** can mean **your uncle is an obstinate, single minded person** as well as **your uncle has a large head**. Having a **big head** in Spanish is not synonymous with being **conceited** as it is in English, and this failing is expressed as **presumido, creído.**

The single-minded are not always dismissed as **obstinate** but can be portrayed in both English and Spanish as the more flattering **resolute, determined, decided – resuelto, determinado, decidido**. Spanish goes one better, though, by linking **empecinado** to the memory of the legendarily stubborn Juan Martín Diaz *"El Empecinado"* who, during the Napoleonic occupation of Spain, led a guerrilla unit. Having got a taste for persistent resistance he was reluctant to call it a day when Napoleon did, and continued in arms after the overthrow of the French. He was finally captured and executed in 1828.

When **single** attaches itself to other English words it can be translated by **mono** or **uni: single seater – monoplaza; single cell – unicelular**. This isn't hard and fast, though, so **single-**

handed is **sin ayuda** (literally **without help**) as well as **solo** accompanied by **yo, tú, él** etc. as the case may be: **he regado el jardín yo solo – I've watered the garden single-handed**.

A **single-masted boat** is **un barco de palo único** and **single-figure interest rates are tipos de interés de una sola cifra**. On the other hand, a **single-sex school** avoids uniqueness with **una escuela feminina** or **una escuela masculine** because **una escuela de un solo sexo** sounds androgynous rather than segregated.

Sólo sometimes appears wearing an accent and this is to differentiate the adjective **solo – single, sole** from the adverb **sólo – only and solely,** which is an abbreviation of **solamente**. To put it another way, a man tends to proclaim **he colocado la casa yo solo – I've tidied up single-handed** or **all on my own** while his partner might sigh **he colocado la casa yo sola**. But regardless of gender a man, woman or child would say **sólo he colocado la casa – I've only tidied up**.

There's less uncertainty with the adjective **único** and the adverb **únicamente** whose suffix **–mente** proclaims it as an adverb, anyway.

Solo is appropriate for exasperated comments: **¡ni un solo día sin fregar platos! – not a single day without washing up!** although when **solo** is missing from **¡ni un día sin fregar platos!** the same message still gets across. Both **solo** and **único** are suitable for enumerating, so **había una sola cama en toda la casa** and **había una única cama en toda la casa** mean **there was only one bed in the whole house**.

A **single, unmarried man** is **un soltero** and a **single woman** (do we still dare call her a spinster?) is **una soltera**. Unfairly but unsurprisingly, an enlarging suffix always turned **solterona** into an **old maid** but **un solterón** was merely a confirmed bachelor. Both words are falling into disuse now that marriage is no longer the goal of every young Spanish woman or the nemesis of every young Spanish man.

A **single ticket** is **un billete sencillo – a simple ticket** or **un billete de ida – an outward bound ticket**. You might come across **un billete simple** but although you come upon **simple** with the meaning of **ordinary** be prepared to meet it as **slightly backward**.

Tennis **singles** are **individuales** and a **single bed** is **una**

Not a single day without washing up

cama individual although older people still refer to **un camero,** which is bigger than a single bed but smaller than a double bed. **A double bed** is **una cama de matrimonio** and its translation of **marriage bed** illustrates who could and couldn't share a double bed until not so long ago.

The verb **to single out** has no Spanish equivalent but is near to **elegir – to choose** or the less-used **entresacar – to pick out.** A grammatical **singular** is the same in English and Spanish and in both languages retains the additional definition of **strange, peculiar** but **singladura** is the **distance travelled by a boat or ship in one day.** If you have lived here long enough you might remember **un single,** pronounced **un sin-guel** and which was, of course, **a single record.** For once the built-in obsolescence of hybrid Spanish defeated its own purpose

151

and however attentively you listen you will not hear the word, and however diligently you search for a single, the only place you might find one is at a car-boot sale.

ODDLY ENOUGH

How odd is odd? This is what you need to decide before translating **odd** because a Spaniard associates the **odd** that does not **match** with lack **of similarity** or **difference**. This is particularly noticeable as regards socks or shoes. More than one semi-martyred Spanish husband has been heard to exclaim: **no puedo salir a la calle con estos calcetines porque cada uno es diferente – I can't go out in these socks because each is different.** What they mean but aren't exactly saying is **these socks are odd.**

An English **odd sock** or **odd shoe** lacks an exact Spanish translation and becomes **different from, not equal** to or **not the same as** its partner. There is an apparently handy word – **impar** – which sounds as though it should fit the bill, especially when a Spanish-English dictionary confirms that **odd** is **impar.** Once in a while, particularly when you are in hair-splitting mode over how best to translate and if your Spanish is up to it, it's not a bad idea to consult a Spanish, not a Spanish-English dictionary. In the case of **impar,** for instance, you will learn that it means **without equal,** which brings us back to those wretched socks again as **impar** clearly isn't the best way to describe an **odd** sock. Pity about that.

In contrast, **impar** is just the job for **odd numbers,** which are **números impares. Even numbers** are **números pares** because, as with the socks, you can make **a pair – par** out of them. The **pairs** in question generally refer to a **pair** of **things,** not **people** whose different kind of togetherness is normally translated with **una pareja.**

A synonym for **impar** is **non,** not that you'll often meet it, except in the game **pares y nones – odds and evens.** It also appears in **quedar de non,** and this time you can use **odd,** because it means **to be the odd one out/the one without a partner/to be** *de trop.* **Estar de más** is another way of putting this unwanted state of affairs although it does not necessarily entail being unwelcome or having to play gooseberry, as it also illustrates what is **odd** because it is **a left over.** That treasure trove of shoe-fanatics, the coveted **odd pairs,** which nevertheless match and can be bought for knock-down prices at **mercadillos – open-air markets** are **pares sueltos.** Pre-euro, this would have gone for around **a thousand-and-odd pesetas – mil-y-pico pesetas,** with **pico** doing the work of **odd.** These days, prices have risen and the currency has changed, so they will probably cost you **twenty-odd euros – veintitantos euros.**

Odd job introduces the **chapuza,** a mainstay of the Spanish, and sometimes submerged, economy. Describing an **odd-job man** as **un chapucero** is not likely to meet with his approval as the shift from noun to adjective heralds a shift in competence, so **chapucero** means **crude, shoddy. Chapuzas** can occasionally disintegrate, collapse or explode but although they frequently defy description, they should not be uniformly described as crude or shoddy.

The **odd** that is **peculiar, strange** is invariably translated as **raro** or **curioso.** That is why **un libro raro** is rarely **a rare book** and more likely to be **an odd book.** When translating **odd,** as well as **raro** you will encounter the adjective **extraño,** not too hard to recognise as **strange.** It also doubles as a noun meaning **stranger** and is closely related to the noun **extranjero – foreigner.** This says a little – possibly a lot? – about former viewpoints concerning strangeness and foreignness and which in the non-Spanish prompts a reflective **qué curioso – how odd...**

BORDERLINE CASE

Whatever type of **border** you have in English, it is always a bit edgy and the same situation applies in Spanish, so there is a nice selection to scratch your head over. In English, **border** does triple duty as a noun, verb or adjective and the corresponding Spanish nouns are **borde** (edge); **frontera** (frontier); **margen** (margin); **cenefa** (a decorative, sewn edging) and **orla** (again, a sewn edging) and **orilla.** It's not too taxing to spot the family connection between the last two, but although **orilla** does crop up in sewing, woodwork or handicrafts you also find it wetting its feet at the seaside, as it generally means **shore** or **bank** (river, not finance). **Borde** has a couple of secondary, non-border type meanings: **a wild, uncultivated** or **ungrafted plant** (but not weed) as well as **a person who is uncouth and/or rude.**

Border appears as an adjective only when referring to **frontier,** and the Spanish version of the adjective **border** is **fronterizo: Ciudad-Rodrigo es una ciudad fronteriza – Ciudad-Rodrigo is a border town. Bordering** is another adjective but this one, despite its nice, neat translation of **limítrofe,** is used only in a territorial sense: **Toledo y Madrid son provincias limítrofes.**

As a verb, **to border** can be translated as **lindar, ribetear** and **orlar,** the last two once again referring to sewing and, in the case of **ribetear,** to knitting, too. **Lindar** relates to the **border** that marks a **limit** so **mi terreno linda con el suyo** means **my land limits with his** although what you've actually said is **my land and his have a common boundary.** This is why you come across **limitar** and **confinar** in the same circumstances: **su terreno limita con el mío – his land borders mine** as well as **su terreno confina en el este con el mío – his land borders mine to the east. Confinar** also coincides with an English-speaker's **confine** whose other translations range from **encerrar – to shut up, enclose** as well as **limitar** or **guardar: el médico le recomendó que guardara cama unos días – the doctor recommended that he stay in bed for a few days.**

When translating it is tempting to resort to lookalikes but **bordar** won't do you any favours as it means **to embroider.** On the other hand, **bordear** will come to your aid, but not in the sense of **to border.** This is a transitive verb –in other words someone or something is actually doing the **bordering,** either by actually **legging it** round a border, edge or shore or by **indicating** or **marking** it out. The articulate use **bordear** in cases where we use **to border/verge on: esa película bordea la obscenidad – that film borders/verges on obscenity.** Other translations **for verging on/bordering** are **rozar** and **rayar: esa película roza la obscenidad** and **esa película raya la obscenidad.**

Identical-looking English words with different meanings plus identical-sounding words with different meanings make learning English hard for Spaniards, so **border** and **boarder** provide their own quota of incomprehension. A school **boarder** is **un interno** while a **weekly boarder** would be **un medio-pensionista.** There are more **boarding schools** in Spain than there were, mainly due to the influence and needs of foreign residents but Spanish children were formerly educated near their homes or sent abroad. The name for **a boarding school** – an institutional-sounding **internado** – is revealing, as academically and materially they used to be pretty grim and had little in common with those of English-speaking countries. A **boarding house** – easier to come across and generally more comfortable to inhabit – is known as **una casa de huéspedes,** literally a **guest-house**, while a **boarder** there is **un/una huésped.**

There are several ways **to board,** of course, starting with the verb **to board – alojarse** or **entablar,** if **boarding-up,** not lodging. **Boards,** wooden or otherwise are **tablas** or **tableros** but a **board of directors** is **una junta directiva. Borda** is a tempting translation for **board** and for once it is possible to succumb, as **tirar por la borda** is what a Spaniard does when he decides to **throw something overboard** and, as in English, this is often more figurative than literal. An **outboard motor** can be translated as **un motor fuera de borda** or a muddling, **motor fuera-bordo.**

To be aboard/to be on board is again an easy one: **estar a bordo** but **to board a train** or **bus** is **subir al tren/subir al autobús. Abordar** is a different matter and when applied to a boat is positively piratical as it still means **to board,** but with hostile intentions. The same word is used for **ramming, colliding** in a nautical sense, together with **to come alongside** which isn't very far removed from **bordering** – because just as all roads lead to Rome, words lead to each other, too, if you try hard enough.

ON A ROLL

You might not have realised that a huckster's **roll up!** is **¡vengan!** in Spanish but there are no prizes for guessing that **enrollar, hacer un rollo** mean **to roll, to roll up** or that **un rollo** is **a roll**. They can often be used as in English: **andaba por la calle con un periódico enrollado en la mano** – he walked along the street with a rolled-up newspaper in his hand. That is merely an example of the past participle **enrollado** disguised as an adjective so it might be as well to give you a pure and simple verb: **preferiría que no enrollases así el periódico – I'd prefer you not to roll up the newspaper like that**.

Rollo isn't suitable for an edible **roll**, which is **un bocadillo** when it has a filling but **un panecillo** if it's a simple **bread roll**. Nevertheless, you buy anis-flavoured **rollitos de anís** at the baker's and can order **un rollo de primavera – a spring roll** at a Chinese restaurant.

A **roll** of banknotes is **un fajo de billetes,** literally a **bundle, sheaf of notes**. The **roll** that in the days of sailing ships was detectable in a sailor's walk and is still detectable in a drunk's is **tambaleo** or **balanceo. To be rolling drunk** is translated as **estar como una cuba** but **to be rolling in money** is **nadar en la abundancia – to swim in abundance –** or the idiomatic **estar forrado de dinero – to be stuffed with money.**

To roll is **rodar** when **rolling** involves **rolling down** or **rolling along,** while the preceding **ir (to go)** in **ir rodando** conveys **to roll away. To roll up one's sleeves** is **arremangarse**, an outstandingly specific word only used in these circumstances but **to roll out pastry** is a vague **extender con rodillo.**

Rolling countryside is **paisaje ondulado** but there is no equivalent for the **rolling of an R** that is so vital for adequate pronunciation of Spanish and which is described as **pronunciar bien la erre – to pronounce the R well**. The **roll of drums** is **el redoblar de tambores,** an example of a verb used as a noun. To **roll up a cigarette** is **liar un cigarillo, liar** meaning **to roll up, do up, wrap up** or **tie up** but also the popular **to confuse, embroil** or otherwise **subject someone to an annoying situation.**

The reflexive **enrollarse** is slang and **¡como se enrolla esa mujer!** means **how that woman does go on!** As well as **to go on, bore** it also conveys – occasionally rather euphemistically in **to get along with very well/to enjoy the company of:** **César y Fuensanta se enrollan bien. A Fuensanta le va el rollo** means **Fuensanta's easy to get on with** or even **easy to flirt with,** since **rollo** can sound lukewarm or ardent according to circumstances. Rather than a total bore, **un buen rollo** suggests something **satisfactory, amusing** or **nice,** while **un mal rollo** is the completely opposite, totally outdated **bad scene** which is the nearest, neatest translation.

Both **enrollarse** and **rollo** are amorphous words, acquiring the meaning you wish them to acquire, although the subtleties of the alternative culture are best understood by those who belong to it. The chasms and gorges of the generation gap are never bridged by misused slang, so be prepared for inappropriate or inaccurate use of **enrollarse** and **rollo** to be met by the young with a brusque **no te enrolles conmigo, tío.**

CHANCES ARE...

Some awkward words require translating via synonyms and this is what happens with **chance.** Thus, a **chance** that is **a risk** is **un riesgo** while anyone prepared to **take a chance** does so with the reflexive verb **arriesgarse.**

The **chance** that can be frustratingly random is translated as a hazardous-looking **azar** and a **game of chance** is **un juego de azar.** A slangy way to tell someone **you're chancing your luck** is **lo estás rifando,** making interesting use of **rifar – to raffle.** This verb's secondary, less-used meanings of **to quarrel, to fight for** tempt us into quasi-philosophy and reflections concerning chance, luck and all the unpredictable things we would like to be able to predict.

When **chance** is approximate to an English **possibility** you can use **posibilidad: no hay ninguna posibilidad de verle –** **there's no chance of seeing him. Le ví por casualidad el otro día** also sounds as though the meeting was casual: **I saw him by chance the other day. To meet by chance** is **topar con** and

Don Quijote is famously quoted as saying **con la iglesia hemos topado,** but contrary to what many of your Spanish friends may believe, he was not saying **we've come up against the Church** as an institution but literally **we've bumped into the church (building).**

If **chance** is an **opportunity** you are saved time and trouble with **una oportunidad: ¿a quién no le gustaría tener la oportunidad de viajar? –** who wouldn't like the chance to travel? or **todavía no he tenido la oportunidad de hablar con tu cuñado –** I've still not had the chance to speak to your brother-in-law.

Una oportunidad, as dedicated shoppers know, is not confined to wish-fulfilment because it does double duty as a Spanish **bargain, special offer** and the magic notice **¡oportunidades!** splashed over a shop front makes many a heart beat faster at the prospect of picking up **bargains.** A cynical saying used to warn the ingenuous that **nadie da duros por pesetas** – **nobody gives five-peseta pieces for peseta pieces** although that needs be modified to **nadie da euros por céntimos** now. Whatever the currency, this does not discourage some of us from deciding to **take a chance – probar suerte** and plunge into the fray.

The circumstances when you use **probar suerte –** literally **to try** or **to test your luck** involve rarely involve physical risk but can still be a toss-up: **¿probamos suerte echando una Loto? – Shall we chance our luck and do the Lotto?**

The temptingly lookalike **chanza** is a false lead, however, and means **a joke, piece of tomfoolery** or **lark** (a prank, not a bird). On second thoughts, though, perhaps **chanza** isn't so wide of the mark, bearing in mind the **chancy outcome – resultado dudoso** of some of the opportunities and chances most of us have been offered or taken at some stage in our lives.

I SAY! I SAY! I SAY!

Hablar means **to talk** or **to speak: Fausto habla mucho – Fausto talks a lot.** If you wish to go into more detail you can comment **Fausto habla a sus vecinos – Fausto talks to his neighbours**

or **Fausto habla con sus vecinos**. As well as supplying not entirely accurate information, since there are times when Fausto and I prefer not to converse, the preceding phrase illustrates how **hablar** can involve **con – with,** as well as **a – to.** The difference is subtle but **hablar con** suggests that Fausto is on speaking terms with his neighbours while **hablar a** can have a touch of harangue to it, which is usual where Fausto is concerned.

To talk to can be expressed as **dirigirse a** or the wordier **dirigirse la palabra,** which is often heard in negative circumstances: **Fausto y yo ya no nos dirigimos la palabra – Fausto and I aren't on speaking terms now**.

Tomar la palabra implies **to speak in public, to make a speech: Fausto nunca toma la palabra en las juntas de vecinos – Fausto never takes the floor during neighbourhood meetings**. A speech is **un discurso** and **a talk is una charla** but **charlar** is generally a cosy verb meaning **to chat.**

The noun **habladuría** means **talk** in the sense of **idle talk, gossip** and mainly exists in the plural. **Sólo son habladurías** is a Spanish dismissal of rumours, boasts or empty promises: **it's only talk. ¡Ni hablar!** is the same as **not on your life!** but **hablar por hablar** is **talking for talking's sake.**

Decir is an irregular verb that means **to say** or **to tell: Fausto dice que está contento – Fausto says he is happy.** Or you could say **dile a Fausto que se calle – tell Fausto to be   quiet** (you could but you wouldn't).

Decir que sí means **to say yes: Fausto dice que sí – Fausto says yes;** conversely **decir que no** is the same as **to say no.** As a noun, **un decir** is **a figure of speech, a saying** although you will also meet **a saying** translated as **un refrán.**

Es decir is equivalent to **that is to say,** so **no me entusiasman los rábanos, es decir que los aborrezco** means **I'm not keen on radishes, that is to say I loathe them. Querer decir** is closer to **to mean: si Fausto te habla, quiere decir que está contento – if Fausto talks to you, that means he's happy.**

Mejor dicho means **rather** or **in other words: no me chiflan los rábanos; mejor dicho, los odio – I'm not mad about radishes; in other words, I hate them. Dicho y hecho** is the same as **no sooner said than done.**

Dicha can be the feminine version of the past participle

dicho when used as an adjective: **me gusta Madrid y creo que dicha ciudad es la mejor del mundo** – I like Madrid and I think said city is the best in the word.

As a noun, **dicha** means **joy, happiness**. **Dichoso** has an attractively schizophrenic twist because it can be translated as **fortunate** or **happy** as well as **tiresome**. So when Fausto refers to **mi dichosa vecina inglesa**, it's easy to guess at the true – and not always fortunate – state of our neighbourly relations.

OUT AND OUT

Out (usually **fuera**) is absent from Spanish verbs like **averiguar** – **to find out**, as it is from **to throw out** – **tirar**, and **to put out** – **apagar** if it's a fire or a light but **molestar** if it's a person. **To go out** is **salir,** and this is why you find signs saying **salida** where in English-speaking countries you would see **way out** or **exit**.

An exhaustive list of ousted outs would be exhausting, but among the most usual are **to turn out/evict** – **desahuciar/echar: le desahuciarán si no paga el alquiler** and **le echarán si no paga el alquiler** mean **they will evict him/turn him out if he doesn't pay the rent**. When **to turn out** suggests **to happen**, use **acontecer, resultar** or all-purpose **pasar: al final resultó/aconteció/pasó que pudo pagar** – in the end it turned out that he could pay.

To be physically **out of touch with** is **no tener contacto con: no he tenido contacto con mi tío en tiempo** – I have been out of touch with my uncle for some time. **No estar en sintonía** refers to the **out of touch** that is due to lack of sensitivity or perception: **a veces los mayores no están en sintonía con los jóvenes** – older people are sometimes out of touch with the young.

To take out, remove is **sacar, quitar** or on some occasions, the reflexive **quitarse: quítate ese chicle de la boca** – take that chewing gum out of your mouth. With the negligible addition of the not-so-negligible preposition **de, sacar** may be used for people: **César sacará de paseo a su novia** – César will take his girlfriend out for a walk. And if César and

Fuensante was looking out of the window and saw César

Fuensanta are **going out together** in the sense of what used to be known as **going steady**, they are said to **salir juntos**.

To look out of requires the by-no-means negligible preposition **por,** which is less intimidating when you're not struggling to unravel it from **para**. On this occasion **por** isn't formidable because **to look out of** is conveniently near to **look through** – **mirar por: Fuensanta miraba por la ventana y vio a César** – **Fuensanta was looking out of the window and saw César.**

If **out** is preceded by some part of the verb **to be** and is followed by a pinpointing noun, you can sometimes use **fuera**, so to be **out of the range/reach of** is **estar fuera del alcance de: los soldados estaban fuera del alcance de la artillería** – **the soldiers were out of the range of the artillery.** The verb

alcanzar generally means **to reach/reach out** but has another function in a lazy request like **¿me alcanzas ese vaso?** literally **could you reach** (out for) **that glass for me?**

To be out of danger is **estar fuera de peligro** while an infuriated **out of my sight!** is an equally infuriated straight translation: **¡fuera de mi vista!** On the other hand, **the ship was out of sight** needs rearranging with the help of the verb **ver: no se veía el barco.** You can tack on **fuera** when you **eat out** – **comer fuera,** while to **hit, throw, kick the ball out** is **golpear/echar/tirar la pelota fuera.** Expect to hear **¡fuera!** for **out!** when a tennis ball doesn't go where it is meant to, although in less sporting circumstances **¡fuera!** will be understood as **get out!**

El equipo de fuera describes **the away team** and the parochial **de fuera** indicates **a stranger,** so a newcomer to a community is asked **¿usted es de fuera?** in the sense of **are you from other parts?**

Not surprisingly, **fuera** is used when you're **out** because you're not **in: fui a ver a Fuensanta pero estaba fuera – I went to see Fuensanta but she was out. Estar fuera** also means **to be away,** so **César ha estado fuera toda la semana** means **César has been away all week** and isn't a complaint that he has been out on the town every night. Unaccompanied, negative use of **estar** also gets across the idea of absence and that someone is **out/not in: fui a casa de Fuensanta pero no estaba – I went to Fuensanta's house but she was out.**

Something **out of this world** is invariably translated as **divino, fabuloso,** but **to be out of something** needs restructuring. You use **tener: no tengo tabaco/gasolina/azúcar** or opt for the reflexive **acabarse** or **terminarse: se me ha acabado el tabaco, gasolina, azúcar** or **se me ha terminado el tabaco, gasolina, azúcar** both mean **I am out of cigarettes/petrol/sugar.** To be **out** in one's calculations requires **faltar: contó el dinero pero le faltaban cien euros – he counted the money, but he was a hundred euros out,** literally **he lacked a hundred euros.**

To be out of breath is expressed as **quedarse sin aliento** and **to be out of fashion** is **no ir a la moda.** If the ornaments on your sideboard **are out of place** you might grumble **están fuera de sitio,** although this phrase does not describe a person who feels **out of place**. Instead of **sitio**, he or she would use **lugar**, another translation for **place: me siento fuera de lugar – I feel out of place** or complain **aquí desentono**, literally **I don't tone in here**.

English-speakers are so fond of **out** that they cram it into sentences like **the floor is made out of marble** but this is an occasion when Spanish is more concise: **el suelo es de mármol.** Flowers and blossom are also denied the **out** treatment, so **the almond blossom is out** becomes **los almendros están en flor – the almond trees are in flower**.

When **fuera** teams up with **por,** it gives you **outside, on/from the outside: la casa parece muy vieja por fuera – the house looks very old from the outside.** Another translation is **desde fuera: sólo he vista la casa desde fuera – I've only seen the house from the outside.** When the temperature drops, a Spaniard says **it's cold outside – hace frío fuera** or might enlarge on this with **hace frío allí fuera** and these phrases are repeated more often than you would expect. Spain is basically a warm country that can sometimes be very cold and must be one of the few places in Europe where a woman needs to keep both a pair of gloves and fan in her handbag.

POWERFUL

Poder – to be able is fitting for the vital but hard-to-pin down **can** and, as a noun, translates the strong-arm kind of **might.** Better still, you are spared the old **can/may** quandary and the reply to **can I have the last biscuit? – ¿puedo comer la última galleta?** does not prompt an irritating **you can but you may not** but an unequivocal **sí** or **no**. With the loquacious, this can be extended to **sí, puedes** or **no, no puedes.** The exquisite and super-polite might choose to ask **¿me permite usted comer la última galleta?** but anyone who uses **permitir** in this way wouldn't expect the last biscuit anyway.

You use **poder** much as you use **can** in English: **I can see the sea from the terrace – puedo ver el mar desde la terraza; can I help you? - ¿te puedo ayudar?** and **he could see that she was busy – podía ver que estaba ocupada.**

We habitually use **can, can't** to ask questions and so do the Spanish: **can't you go and buy biscuits – ¿no puedes ir a comprar galletas? – can't you go and buy biscuits** or **¿puedes bajar la radio? – can you turn the radio down?** You can tack it on tetchily, as in **quita ese rollo ¿puedes? – turn that rubbish off, can't you?** Our **I can't help thinking he's greedy** has a Spanish equivalent, although with a slightly reconstructed construction: **no puedo dejar de pensar que es glotón**.

Although **puede** means **he, she** or **it can,** when pronounced with sufficient doubt, boredom or reluctance **puede** also conveys **perhaps/could be.** The less laconic elongate this to **puede ser** or **puede que sí** and a hopeful **¿crees que traerá galletas? – do you think he'll bring biscuits** might be answered with **puede ser** or **puede que sí** or possibly an apprehensive **puede que no – perhaps not**.

Puede ser isn't limited to answering questions and you'll also hear it in statements: **puede ser que traerá galletas – it might be that he'll bring biscuits** together with the shorter **puede que traiga galletas** which eliminates **ser** but introduces the subjunctive. **¡No puede ser! – it can't be!** is a favourite Spanish exclamation and, as in English, can convey delight, horror or resignation.

¿Se puede? is a courteous little formula which corresponds to **may I?** It is used in Spain when wishing to eat your biscuits or read your newspaper but, and particularly with those you address as **tú,** is often reduced to **¿puedo?**

A serene **no puedo más** implies **I can't manage any more** and is said when offered more biscuits, for instance, but once **¡no puedo más!** incorporates an exclamation mark, even the least sensitive realise that you're shrieking **I can't take any more** and you're not referring to biscuits.

El niño no podía con su cartera means **the boy couldn't manage/was struggling with his satchel** while his mother might lament **mi hijo no puede con las mates – my son can't manage maths. ¡A que te puedo!** is the boast a child makes to friend or foe: **I can beat you!**

Estar en el poder de is a predictable **to be in the power of, to be in the hands of: el rehén estuvo tres meses en poder de sus captores – the hostage was in the hands of his captors**

for three months. El **poder** also infers **the powers that be,
political power: hay otro partido en el poder** – there is
another party in power.

The noun **poder** means **power, might** but **nuclear power**
is **energía nuclear. A power drill** omits **power** to become **un
taladro eléctrico** but **a power cut** is a technical **corte en el
suministro eléctrico** although it is popularly known as **un
apagón**, literally a **big turn-off**.

The **power** of an engine or a strong man is **potencia** while
the adjective **powerful** – **poderoso** applies to any animal,
vegetable or mineral in possession of literal or metaphorical
power. Potente is suitable for a **powerful motorbike** – **una
moto potente** or a **strong** (invariably alcoholic) **drink** – **una
bebida potente** and **impotente** describes the state of being
helpless, powerless in any type of situation. **Ser** and **estar**
are about to lugged out again, because **ser impotente** is the
macho nightmare while **estar impotente** applies to anything
or anyone who is **helpless, powerless**.

The plural noun **poderes** can indicate **mystic, magical
powers: cree que tiene poderes** could be loosely translated
as **he** or **she thinks he** or **she is psychic. Lo hizo por poderes**
is an unsupernatural **he** or **she did it by proxy/power of
attorney. Dar poderes a alguien** means **to give power of
attorney to someone**.

Our resigned **it can't be helped** can be transformed
into a fatalistic **no se puede hacer nada** – **there's nothing that
can be done** or the **poder**-less **¡que le vamos a hacer!**
Or the terminal **no hay remedio** – **there's no remedy**, all
of whichare incontrovertible indications of **tremendous
pessimism** – **pesimismo a más no poder**.

CHARGE SHEET

The nouns **cargo** and **carga** are annoyingly interchangeable
as both can mean **charge, load, burden** or **weight**. You find
that **un cargo** tends to be **a load, burden** of qualms or
reservations but not bricks. Thus **hacerse cargo** means **to take
charge of: yo me hago cargo de eso** – **I'll deal with that**.

Tener a su cargo is **to have something or someone in one's charge:** Blas tiene a su cargo cuidar la huertecita de Fausto – **Blas is in charge of Fausto's vegetable patch. Estar a cargo de...** allows you to put the previous statement a different way round: **la huerta de Fausto está a cargo de Blas.** Whichever way you put it, though, everyone is aware that Blas is doing Fausto's weeding while he's away on holiday.

In a business letter, **un cargo** might be the equivalent of **cargo, freight** although **un cargamento** or **un envío** are more popular terms these days. **Un cargo** can also be **a post, a duty** which means that **un alto cargo** isn't an elevated shipment but **a high-ranking official,** frequently gubernatorial and always endowed with bureaucratic clout. **Cargo** also indicates **a debit** and implies plural **costs: libre de cargos** refers to a sum of money **with no extra charges added to it** but this does not mean **free of charge** which is **gratis. Libre de cargos** is also a reassuring trial verdict as it implies **without charges** of a judicial, not financial, kind.

Carga is **a burden, weight** so a donkey is **un animal de carga – a beast of burden.** Less tangible but no less weighty is **una carga fiscal – a tax burden** and when you rejoice to find a parking space you are often confronted with a terse **sólo carga y descarga – loading and unloading only.** And **Fausto vuelve a la carga** doesn't mean my neighbour has gone back to loading lorries but is **up to his old tricks again** (in other words over-reacting when he finds Gilbert asleep amongst his tomato plants). **¡A la carga!** is the military command **charge!**

Una carga is the **charge** produced by electricity or gunpowder but **un muro de carga** is a **load-bearing wall** while **una carga de profundidad** is **a depth-charge. A charge** that is **an indictment** is closer to **una acusación** or, once it has been formalised, **un expediente.**

The adjective **cargado** means **charged, burdened, loaded** but when applied to the weather infers **overcast, sultry** although **café cargado** is **strong coffee.** Someone who is **loaded** with money is described formally as **adinerado** or slangily as **forrado,** literally **lined, stuffed.**

Cargar crops up in the slightly slangy **to break, to spoil** and the very colloquial **to kill. Lo vas a cargar** is a common reaction to meddling: **you're going to break it** or **you're going to spoil it. Le van a cargar** could mean **they're going to bump him off** but a student's **me van a cargar** means **they're going to fail me.**

Cargar is as appropriate to light brigades as lorries and also applies to the **weighing-down** produced by a physical or mental burden. **¿Tengo yo que cargar con esto?** is as likely to mean **have I got to carry all this?** as **have I got to assume responsibility for all this? Cargar** is not the right verb when **to charge** prompts the handing over of money, for which you use **cobrar: ¿cuánto me va a cobrar? – how much are you going to charge me?** You will find the magic phrase **¿me quiere cobrar?** is always the easiest way to attract the attention of an inattentive shop assistant or waiter.

Un cobrador is a **charger** insofar as he or she takes your money, so a **bus conductor** is **un cobrador.** A Spanish **conductor** is **a driver** and you will be met with polite incomprehension if you refer to Daniel Barenboim as **un conductor de orquesta** instead of **un director de orquesta.** Not that **an orchestra driver** sounds less bizarre than an **orchestra manager** – and besides, whichever way you look at him **he's the one in charge – quien manda es él.**

SPITTING DISTANCE

Wotcher was a classic greeting among Londoners who might have been unaware that it was a corruption of the quainter, more antiquated **what cheer?** Neither might those same Londoners have realised that the Elephant and Castle is the result of sixteenth century English-speakers' attempts to get their tongues round the foreignness of **Infanta de Castilla – Princess of Castile**, in other words poor mismatched Catherine of Aragón.

This kind of thing is not exclusive to English as you will discover if you ask a Spaniard the origin of **Carabanchel** in Madrid. It's a pound to a céntimo he'll shrug and look generally mystified, thereby affording you the pleasure of telling him it is a corruption of **garbanzal – a plot where** chickpeas are cultivated. Chickpeas – **garbanzos** are, of course, the inescapable, non-substitutable main ingredient of Madrid's mind-blowing, digestion-destroying contribution to international gastronomy: **cocido madrileño.**

Another English corruption is **spitting image**, a mutation of **spit and image**. This is a saying that has no Spanish counterpart, because when one Spaniard is **identical to another** saliva is dispensed with and nails used instead: **Nieves y Esperanza son clavadas**, literally **Nieves and Esperanza are nailed.** According to your preferences, **water** can be employed too: **son como dos gotas de agua – they are like two drops of water**, a variation on **like two peas in a pod**.

Spanish soldiers bestow as much **spit and polish** on their kit as English-speaking soldiers, but have no accepted phase for it. **Spit** is also absent from **a sand spit** which is **un banco de arena** although a **spit of land** is still orally-orientated: **una lengua de tierra – a tongue of land.** A roasting spit is **un asador** or the less-used **espetón;** few go to the bother of using the verb **espetar – to spit, to skewer** in connection with the housewife's mainstay, the **spit-roasted chicken,** that can be bought in bars, markets and supermarkets. Normally it is described simply as **pollo asado** or **pollo a l'ast,** a foreign-sounding term which Valenciano, Catalán or French speakers deny has anything to do with them.

When an infuriated cat **spits** a satisfyingly onomatopoeic noun translates its short, sharp warning: **un bufido.** Or you can use the verb **bufar: Gilbert bufaba cada vez que veía a Fausto – Gilbert used to spit every time he saw Fausto**. The **spitting** which is unpleasantly preceded by sonorous hawking and throat-clearing (this has its own verb, **carraspear**) is translated as **escupir.** That Spain was until comparatively recently a nation of spitters could be deduced from notices on buses and trains that sternly announced **prohibido escupir – spitting prohibited**.

The now non-existent **spittoon** is **una escupidera** while **spittle** can be a tactful **saliva** or a dribbly **baba. Baba** is what runs down a baby's chin but although **se le cae la baba** is one way to say an infant is **dribbling,** it can also mean that an adult **is drooling** and the phrase is equally appropriate when something or someone is appetising. Incidentally, it should be borne in mind by dribblers and droolers that **una babosa** is **a slug** (lettuce-eaters, not a shot of whisky).

When you **spit out something unpleasant or unkind** (words, not food) you can still use **escupir** but with its usual way of surprising you when least expected, Spanish also allows you to use **espetar,** the verb that means **to spit, skewer.** Little quirks like these can make you want to spit, but when a Spaniard wishes to express this sort of **irritation, chagrin** or **outrage,** he goes off at a hydrophobic tangent and while foaming at the mouth spits out **me da rabia**, literally **it gives me rabies**.

Eliza Doolittle learnt long ago that the rain in Spain falls mainly on the plain, but didn't suspect that periods of fraught drought alternated with tropical deluges on plain, coast and valley alike. Neither did she know that it can **drizzle** and **spit with rain** too; in fact there is a specific word for it – **chispear** – which means **to sparkle, scintillate,** just like those stray raindrops. It's easy to connect this verb with the noun **chispa** – **spark** and when a Spaniard **spits** with wrath and/or fury he is said to **echar chispas** – and there are no prizes for guessing whether he's producing sparks or raindrops.

COMFORTING THOUGHTS

That frequent target of music-hall scatology, **a commode**, can't be transformed into a Spanish **cómoda** because as a noun this is **a chest of drawers** – yet another butt of turn-of-the-century ribaldry. Although even a common or garden chest of drawers is now liable to turn up in lifestyle magazines as a **commode,** what English-speakers generally associate with this item is a Spanish **bacín** (sounding unappetisingly like our own *basin)* as well as **silleta** or **sillico**. These are merely variations on **silla** – **chair** and are further illustrations of how Spanish resorts to diminutives when wishing to gloss the unglossy. The **–ico** suffix, normally scorned by the urban inhabitants of central Spain, also indicates the rustic origins of this rudimentary portaloo.

As an adjective, **cómodo** or **cómoda** more often than not means **comfortable: esta silla es muy cómoda** – **this chair is very comfortable.** Not being **comfortable** is much the same as being **uncomfortable** and the Spanish version is easily arrived at: **incómodo.** When a chair is comfortable, you expect it to remain so until it falls apart, so conveying this characteristic obviously requires the verb **ser. Estar** is used to announce temporary comfort or discomfort: **estoy cómodo en esta silla** – **I'm comfortable in this chair** and **no estoy cómodo/estoy incómodo en esta silla** – **I'm not comfortable/I'm uncomfortable in this chair.**

An alternative **comfortable/uncomfortable** effect can be produced with **encontrar: me encuentro cómodo en este traje** – **I'm comfortable in this suit** and **no me encuentro cómodo/me encuentro incómodo en este traje** – **I don't feel comfortable/I'm uncomfortable in this suit.**

As usual, it's hard to prevent the multi-faceted reflexive verb, **ponerse,** from putting in an appearance and **se puso cómodo enseguida** means **he made himself comfortable straight away.** You can also use **acomodarse: el gatito se acomodó inmediatemente** – **the kitten immediately made itself comfortable** (when do they not?). A dictionary confirms that **acomodar** and **acomodarse** correspond to all aspects of **to accommodate** but as a rule they are limited to **get/make comfortable, adapt to, make room for** but **hotel accommodation** is **alojamiento.**

As an adjective, the past participle **acomodado** is a frequent synonym for **prosperous, well-off** but this covers finances that are somewhat more buoyant than an English **comfortable,** which in Spanish is **holgado.**

In spite of the adequate role of **cómodo** and **comodidad** – **comfort**, this doesn't prevent your meeting **confortable**, together with **confort,** both of which are variously attributed to French or English. Whatever their lineage, these wrong-side-of-the-blanket words are esteemed by shop assistants, publicists and the writers of hotel brochures whose clients are naturally keen to enjoy the advantages of **habitaciones a todo confort** and **habitaciones confortables** instead of **habitaciones cómodas** and **habitaciones muy cómodas.**

Comfortably is a logical **cómodamente**. Further words connected with **cómodo** are **comodín** – **the joker** in a pack of

Esta silla es muy cómoda

cards but not the joker who tells funny stories and plays the fool. He or she is more likely to be dubbed **un payaso** or the idiomatic **un cachondo mental. Comodín** is also a word for verbal tics like **know what I mean?** which become **¿sabes?** or the longer **¿sabes lo que quiero decir?**

Change the suffix and you get **un comodón,** a **person who**

171

habitually seeks comfort or **the easy way out.** Less passive are **un acomodador** and his female counterpart, **una acomodadora** – a cinema and theatre usher or **usherette**.

A very Spanish way **to feel** rather than to *be* **comfortable** again makes use of **encontrar** attached to **a gusto: ¡qué a gusto me encuentro aquí! – how comfortable I feel here!** (a common kitten reaction). As with **no estar cómodo, no estar a gusto** describes not only physical discomfort but the tacky sensation of **feeling out of place** or **awkward.** There is another option with **consolar: me consuela saber que la habitación no costó cara – it's a comfort** (literally it consoles me) **to know the room wasn't expensive.**

That's as an adjective, but used as a noun, **un consolador** brings to mind something more vibrant than sympathy for one's woes or a shoulder to cry on. In fact, using this at an inappropriate moment or in an ambiguous context could make the speaker **sentirse bastante violento,** which has no violent connotations but means **feeling** not only **uncomfortable, but red-faced with it.**

STRINGING YOU ALONG

Dictionaries overflow with words for **string**. Some correspond to the kind that is suitable for parcels: **cuerda, cordel, bramante** although **cordel** is on the rope-y side and **bramante** is more like twine. **Cuerda** isn't restricted to parcels, so **cuerdas** give clout to your tennis racquet **strings** and tone to **string instruments – instrumentos de cuerda.** The presence of **string** or **cord** has long been forgotten in the verb **dar cuerda,** which means to **wind up** watches, clocks or toys but is not apt for people you wish **to unnerve – poner nervioso/a** or matters you want **to finalise – finalizar.** The adjective **cuerdo** leads a separate existence that involves neither **string** nor **winding-up** but corresponds to **prudent, sane.**

Una ristra is the **string** associated with **sausages: una ristra de salchichas. Una reata** is the **rope** that ties **a string of animals** or **horses** together and – not always encountered in casual, inarticulate chat – **una retahíla** is another kind of string or series: Fausto nos soltó una retahíla de excusas – Fausto gave us a string of excuses.

Una hilera is a string, row: a lo lejos había una hilera de casas – there was a string/row of houses in the distance. A string of pearls is un collar de perlas, but to emphasise that it has one string, call it un collar de una vuelta; if it has two it is un collar de dos vueltas and so on. To string beads is ensartar in the sense of to thread and a little-used word for string is sarta, although you meet it still in una sarta de mentiras – a pack (string) of lies.

If your stringing-up does not involve necklace-making, use the less-specific colgar – to hang or, if things get really tough, ahorcar – to hang or the mis-spelt Anglicism, linchar.

The nearest translation to string along is a bald engañar – to deceive or tomarle el pelo a alguien – to pull someone's leg (literally to take someone's hair). No strings attached is sin compromiso and is less uncompromising than it looks since a Spanish compromiso generally implies an obligation, difficulty, embarrassment.

You occasionally find string translated as hilo although this crops up more often as cable, cotton or linen thread. Thus colgar de un hilo means to hang by a thread while un hilo de humo is a plume of smoke. Un hilo de voz is a faint, barely audible voice, while a slightly old-fashioned person might comment on picking up the telephone: Elena está al otro lado del hilo – Elena is on (the other end of) the line. Almost as disquieting as a phone call from Elena is hilo musical, the dreaded and dreadful musak or piped music.

More comfortable and comforting are un vestido de hilo, sábanas de hilo or calcetines de hilo - a linen/cotton dress, linen/cotton sheets and cotton socks (how often do you see linen socks?). Linen – lino, as the European Commission famously remarked regarding a subsidies scandal, isn't a typically Spanish product although cotton – algodón was once grown extensively in southeast and southern Spain. If you are sock-shopping and look aghast on glimpsing a price-tag, the assistant is likely to reprimand you with a reproving ¡pero si estos calcetines son de hilo! – but these socks are best quality cotton! because if an item made of hilo is not linen then it will still be very superior cotton.

Having rather **lost the thread – perdido el hilo** of our original examination of **string**, it's time pick it up again with a **string vest**, known here as **una camiseta de malla**. Not that Spanish men ever wear them, thank goodness – or any other kind of vest come to that – unless they are very, very cold or very, very old.

DARK DOINGS

Although a principal Spanish synonym for **oscuro** is **moreno (dark), un funcionario oscuro** will be **an obscure civil servant,** a personage to be found in any English- or Spanish-speaking country. If you want this character to have **dark hair** and/or **a dark complexion** instead of a lowly position in a government department, describe him as **un funcionario moreno** because **moreno** is the adjective to use for hair and skin. It's also appropriate for **brown sugar – azúcar moreno** as well as **brown eggs – huevos morenos.** However, as always in Spanish, eggs are good for a ribald laugh and if you can't avoid mentioning them at least be circumspect in your phrasing.

Dark eyes are invariably translated as **ojos oscuros** although they can also be described as **ojos pardos.** Usual translations for **pardo** are **dun, drab, dark grey** as this is an obliging adjective that takes on whatever dark tone is in the eye of the beholder. It also appears in **por la noche, todos los gatos son pardos – all cats are grey in the night.**

We occasionally have **insignificant** in mind when using **obscure** and this happens in Spanish, too, so your all-purpose civil servant might also be described as **un funcionario insignificante** or **un funcionario humilde,** since **oscuro, insignificante** and **humilde** are as much in line as **obscure, insignificant** and **humble** in English. In some circumstances though, you will encounter **humilde** where we would choose **simple, ordinary: viven en una casa humilde en un barrio obrero** is less unprivileged than it sounds: **they live in an ordinary house in a working-class neighbourhood.**

Usually, **oscuro** is less concerned with dark, insignificant civil servants than what is **dark, not light, dim, gloomy: le** sienta bien el azul oscuro – dark blue suits him/her; ¡qué cielo más oscuro! – what an overcast/lowering sky! ¡Qué noche más oscura! is an obvious what a dark night! but to translate it was a dark night you use the verb to be – ser: era una noche oscura. If you equate dark with gloomy or dull and decide to translate it quite correctly as triste – sad, use hacer: hacía un día triste. This is because fue un día triste implies a day that was sad because of something or someone – but not the weather. As well as triste, further dark, gloomy adjectives are the darker and gloomier lóbrego and tenebroso.

Oscuro forms part of the enigmatic, virtually untranslatable esto pasa del castaño oscuro, approximately this is too much or this has gone too far. Less mysterious is cámara oscura, the fascinating camera oscura where our great-great-great-grandparents enjoyed reflected projections of what went on outside, although a photographer's dark room is un cuarto oscuro. Being banished to el cuarto oscuro was a ploy to frighten children into behaving themselves and once there were sure to fall into the clutches of el coco – the bogeyman.

The feminine noun oscuridad is darkness, together with the similarly feminine tenebrosidad, penumbra. La oscuridad also implies the Dark which some people still fear but a cheerful don't sit there in the dark uses a oscuras: no te sientes allí a oscuras.

The verb oscurecer means to obscure, darken, but to keep something dark is translated by ocultar, literally to hide. When you are in the dark about something you would use ignorar: ignoro cuando llegará mi hija – I have no idea when my daughter will arrive. To get dark reverts to oscurecer although this time it is the reflexive oscurecerse. An alternative is anochecer: vente a casa antes de que se oscurezca/antes de que anochezca – come home before it gets dark. A further verb is hacerse de noche, literally to become night, which is appropriate for a country where twilight exists as the beautiful-sounding crepúsculo but is rarely observed, since day's journey into night is never noticeably long in Spain.

FIXATIVE

¡**Fíjate!** is a stock Spanish phrase and even those who maintain few Spanish conversations should be able to distinguish it in the flood and flow of overheard dialogue. It corresponds to **well I never! fancy that!** or **would you believe it!** and is the familiar, second-person imperative of the reflexive verb **fijarse**. There are also polite, third person **usted** versions: ¡**fíjese!** and ¡**fíjense!**

As in English, comments containing ¡**fíjate!** convey surprise, approbation or condemnation: **Nieves tiene veinte pares de zapatos ¡fíjate! – Nieves has twenty pairs of shoes – just imagine!** And despite the grammatically necessary accent on the first syllable, you'll often hear emphasis on the last: ¡**fíjaTE!**

Spanish gets its money's-worth out of **fíjate, fíjese** etc. as they occur in the same situations as our **I knew, I said so, I told you so** and the enigmatic-looking ¡**fíjate que sabía yo que ibas a caer!** is simply **didn't I just know you were going to fall!**

Like all verbal tics – sometimes known in Spanish as **muletillas** (little crutches) –**fíjate, fíjese** etc. mean what you'd like them to mean. On the other hand, **fijarse** has associations other than the obvious translation of **to fix.**

As well as **to fix, secure, stick, paste, determine, decide, settle,** you can add **to stare at, pay attention to,** when **fijarse** is followed by the preposition **en.** Starting with an appreciative **en el Prado, todo el mundo se fija en Las Meninas – at El Prado, everyone looks at Las Meninas** you progress to an equally appreciative **se fijó en sus piernas – he stared at her legs/fixed his gaze on her legs.** It is also possible to sound querulous, not appreciative: ¿**por qué te fijas en ella? – why are you looking at her?**

Fijar is a good translation for **to fix** when this means **to settle upon, decide, determine** but is less suitable for **fix** when it means **to repair, mend**, for which you need **reparar** or **arreglar.** Another verb, **remendar** which means **to fix, repair** is often used in connection with sewing, so **un remiendo** is **a patch, darn** while **un zapatero remendón** is **a cobbler.**

At El Prado everyone looks at Las Meninas

Reparar is used in the same way as **repair** in English but **arreglar** also pops up in connection with situations, hairstyles, clothing as well as objects that are broken or otherwise damaged. **Arreglar** is particularly suitable when **to fix** is on the shady side although you might use the even shadier **amañar,** which applies to the **fixing** of a game, competition or match. The individual who is good at fixing and repairing continues to be **handy** as **un manitas.**

The adjective **fixed, permanant** is **fijo: un empleo fijo – a permanent job; un domicilio fijo – a fixed abode; una mirada fija – a fixed stare** but the lack of a specific word for **to stare** and its usual substitution by **look** doesn't come as a surprise. In Spain, people always stared openly at anything or anyone that caught their eye although this has become less apparent with the implementation of trans-Pyrenean manners.

177

As a noun, there are many ever-changing cult words for a drug-taker's **fix** but the medical term is **una dosis.** A **fix** or **fiddle** is **un chanchullo** when it results in personal gain or profit but **un tongo, un amaño** or **un arreglo** when a match or competition is **fixed,** a circumstance that would once be greeted with outraged cries of ¡**tongo!** ¡**tongo!** An uncomfortable **fix** that is **a spot of bother** is **un aprieto,** a word closer to **a squeeze** than **a fix,** but still as unwelcome in Spain as anywhere else.

HANG IT ALL!

Most of the time, **colgar** means **to hang.** It is a moderately irregular verb as it fails to conform in the present tense of the indicative (**cuelgo, cuelgas, cuelga, colgamos, colgáis, cuelgan**) and subjunctive (**cuelgue, cuelgues, cuelgue, colguemos, colguéis, cuelguen**). Naturally, this also affects the imperative (¡**cuelga!** ¡**cuelgue!** ¡**colgad!** ¡**cuelguen!**). The first person of the preterite – **colgué** – needs a little thought, although it is modified on orthographic, not grammatical, grounds.

You encounter **colgar** in circumstances where something **hangs** or is **suspended** from something else: **hay un hilo colgando de tu chaqueta** – there's a thread hanging from your jacket; ¿**dónde cuelgo tu chaqueta?** – where do I hang your jacket? To **hang up the telephone** with good manners or a bad grace is also **colgar: me ha crispado tanto que le he colgado a Esperanza** – Esperanza annoyed me so much that I hung up on her or **me colgó la grosera de Esperanza** – rude Esperanza hung up on me. The preposition, **a,** appears and disappears because a proper name should be preceded by **a** in these circumstances, but is implicit in a pronoun like **me.** The totally unconnected **hang-up** or **problem** is a far more analytical **complejo.**

Dejar colgando is to leave **something hanging** – the telephone perhaps – but **dejar colgado** is **to leave in the lurch.** Instead of **colgar,** a Spaniard uses **ahorcar** for Judge Jeffreys-type activities, although **a hangman** is **un verdugo.**

Una horca is a gallows, gibbet as well as a less predictable pitchfork; there is nothing to prevent your regarding una horquilla as a small gallows or a small gibbet but you're more likely to find it in a woman's hair or on a bicycle, as it is a hairpin as well as the part of a bicycle frame that supports the front wheel.

Neither colgar nor ahorcar applies to hanging out washing which is tender, a verb whose principal meanings are to spread, lay out. English-speakers who grew up in rural surroundings without washing machines and driers will remember how sheets and towels were spread on the grass or laid over bushes to dry in the sun – when there was sun around, which wasn't often. Spanish housewives enjoy a more privileged climate and while few now spread out washing, hanging out laundry is still described as tender.

Use frecuentar if to hang out implies to frequent, but merodear or rondar for to hang around; when you want someone to hang on a moment you ask them to wait –esperar: espérate un momento. Hang is also mislaid in hang back – vacilar, quedarse atrás – while to get the hang of something is coger el tranquillo: montar en bici es fácil una vez que has cogido el tranquillo – riding a bike is easy once you've got the hang of it.

To hang onto is agarrarse, not only for material objects but also ideas, ideals, beliefs or notions, while aferrarse is mainly limited to the ideological. Should to hang on require endurance or resistance, choose between aguantar or resistir.

A hanging that isn't un ahorcamiento can be un tapíz – a tapestry but although in theory a hanging should also be un colgajo, this has come to mean a fussy adornment not in the best of taste. A hangnail is un padrastro, literally a stepfather, while a coathanger is una percha and a hanger-on who is a scrounger is un gorrón.

You may have noticed that ahorcar sounds almost the same as ahogar and loss of breath and life are involved in both, since ahogar means to drown, to choke. There is also another closely related verb, desahogar – to let off steam. Even though this looks more like UNchoking or UNdrowning this is about as near as uptight Spaniards get to that very Seventies exercise in self-indulgence: letting it all hang out.

GOING, GOING, GONE

Ni me va, ni me viene, combines **ir** and **venir** to convey **it's all the same to me.** This ambivalence may explain why a Spaniard calls out **voy – I'm going** when hurrying to answer the doorbell or some other call for attention. We, of course, say **I'm coming,** which sounds as odd to Spanish ears as **vengo** does to English, and possibly responds to profound questions of perspective, orientation and temperament.

Voy is the first person of the present tense of the verb **ir – to go.** It is frequently followed by the preposition **a,** so **I'm going home** is **voy a casa,** but if you were in something of a pet, you'd use the reflexive **irse – to go away** as you flounce off: **me voy a casa.**

When something goes well – for instance, a car or a business scheme – you proclaim **va bien – it's going well** or even **va de maravilla – it's going marvellously** (literally **as a marvel**). When things are less encouraging you're more likely to say **va mal – it's going badly,** but don't spend too much time puzzling over the presence or absence of **de** (but if you really want to know, it's because **maravilla** is a noun but **mal** is an adverb).

If your future tenses are shaky, circumnavigate them with the present tense of **ir,** plus the infinitive of your choice: **mañana vamos a comprar bígaros – tomorrow we're going to buy winkles; voy a verte – I'm going to see you.**

Ir also translates **go** when this implies **to work: este reloj no va – this clock isn't working.** While we say **it** *is* **fast/slow,** the Spanish often use **ir,** particularly if a clock or watch habitually *goes* **fast** or **slow: este reloj va adelantado/atrasado.** If you prefer *is* use **estar: este reloj está adelantado/atrasado.** On the other hand, if someone or something makes **slow progress,** you use **ir** plus **lentamente: va lentamente – he, she** or **it goes slowly.** When progress is particularly snail-like you encounter **ir a rastras: ella va a rastras – she's crawling along.**

Predictably, **ir** is occasionally unpredictable as one of its past tenses is indistinguishable from that of **ser. Fui, fuiste** etc. mean **I was, you were** etc. as well as **I went, you went** etc.

but what follows can be relied upon to reveal whether you are **being** or **going**. Besides, when **fui** means **was**, it won't be followed by the prepositions **a** or **de: fui feliz allí – I was happy there** but **fui a verle – I went to see him** and **fuimos de compras – we went shopping**.

Ir provides indispensable exclamations. **¡Ahí va!** is said roughly fifty times per day per Spaniard but although it means **there it goes!** this is a suitable reaction to anything that startles, surprises or confounds you. **¡Qué va!** expresses disbelief, cynicism or scepticism and can substitute a rejecting **not at all – de ningún modo. ¡Vaya!** is conveniently indefinite and suits eyebrow-raising situations as well as those when you are at a conversational loss.

Ido is the past participle of **ir** and as well as **gone**, it refers to someone who might – if your level of political correctness allows - be described as **not all there. Vamos** is perhaps the first Spanish word many of us learnt from childhood Westerns, when it was pronounced **vamoose**. It forms part of everyday Spanish, too, and means **let's go** although you meet **¡vamos!** as a succinct alternative to lengthier English phrases like **come on, you must be joking** and, once again, a Spanish **ir** is converted into an English **come**.

You will also meet the **vámonos** variation, as well as **nos vamos** which serves as a rather terse leave-taking often softened to **bueno, nos vamos** or its singular version: **¡bueno, me voy! – I'm off!**

DIFFERENT ASPECTS

Not only is **diferente** little different from an English **different** but unlike some other Spanish-English look-alikes, it often behaves predictably: **pareces diferente con ese peinado** is a no-hassle **you look different with that hairdo**. Further phrases are similarly free of surprise: **me gustaría probar esa camisa en un color diferente – I'd like to try that shirt in a different colour; la película era diferente de lo que yo esperaba – the film was different from what I was expecting; los hermanos son muy diferentes – the brothers are very different**.

So far, so good – and there's little difference to worry about. But you can obtain the same effect with a different word – **distinto: con ese peinado pareces distinto/a; me gustaría probar esa camisa en un color distinto; la película era distinta de lo que yo esperaba; los hermanos son muy distintos.**

There's not much to choose between **diferente** and **distinto**, but as they are adjectives the grammatically lazy may prefer to stick to **diferente**, as it has the same ending whether attached to a masculine or feminine noun. On the other hand, with **distinto**, in common with all adjectives ending in **-o**, you need to remember to turn this into an **-a** when joining it to a feminine noun.

Distinto looks and sounds very much like **distinct**, but definitions in the Diccionario de la Lengua Española start with **"not the same as, of a reality or existence different from, not similar to, having different qualities to."** Nit pickers with their own copies of the Diccionario will immediately point out that the entry for **distinto** does end up with **intelligible, clear, without confusion.** On the other hand, my neighbour Fausto rarely uses it or hears it used in these circumstances.

If you want to translate **distinct**, you will get the desired effect with **claro** or **marcado**, according to context: **esta letra no es muy clara – this writing isn't very clear; hablaba con un marcado acento andalúz – she spoke with a distinct Andalusian accent.**

It is also possible to translate **different** as **otro/otra: pareces otro/otra con ese peinado; me gustaría probar esa camisa en otro color** while the moan about the film remains much the same: **la película era otra de lo que yo esperaba.** Of course **otro/otra** actually means **other** – and although Spanish doesn't have an equivalent of **another**, what you are actually saying is **you look like another (person)** and **I'd like to try that shirt in another colour.**

To differ is a good example of a Spaniard's occasional preference for shades of grey rather than black or white. In the same way that Spanish has trouble expressing **to be wrong**, it is also impossible to translate **to differ** with a nice short, sharp word and you have to pussyfoot around with **ser distinto de, diferenciarse de, no estar de acuerdo con**. If you find these too tangential for your needs, you might prefer **discrepar,** although this is closer to **disagree,** which again could be described as another shade of grey. **Diferir** looks as though it might do the trick but in practice usually means **to defer, postpone** although, as with **distinto**, it is used by the super-articulate with the meaning of **to differ from, to differ in. Diferenciar** poses few problems and does a straight swap with **to differentiate, to make a difference between** or **to distinguish between.**

The nouns **difference** and **diferencia** are conveniently interchangeable between one language and another: **¿ves que diferencia hace un nuevo peinado? – see what a difference a new hairstyle makes? hay poca diferencia entre esa camisa y aquella – there's little difference between that shirt and the one over there.** And when, for one reason or another, you're lost for words regarding new hairstyles or shirt colours, **¡qué diferencia!** will let you off as many potential hooks as **what a difference!** in English.

SMALL WONDER

Pequeño means **small** or **little: un hombre pequeño – a small** or **little man; una población pequeña – a small town**. When the well intentioned insist on heaping plates with unwanted food you hear protests like **sólo quería una pequeña cantidad – I only wanted a small amount.** This can be rephrased with **poco,** which means **little, not much, not many, few;** it refers to quantity rather than size and can be used as noun or an adjective: **sólo quería un poco – I only wanted a little** or **sólo quería poca cantidad – I only wanted a little amount.** Someone who is **a small eater,** however, is known as **una persona de poco comer.**

As a noun, **un pequeño/una pequeña** is usually **a child: a los pequeños les gustan los videojuegos – children like video games; un pequeño** or **una pequeña** can be shortened to **peque** but is unappetisingly closer to **kiddy** than **kid. Pequeño/pequeña** used as a noun is an endearment between adults, regardless of size or mental age, but with these exceptions it is usually encountered as an adjective.

Poco is more versatile because it pops up as a noun, a pronoun, an adjective and an adverb but you can relax if parts of speech make you panicky, because it should be translatable without too much scrutiny. Nonetheless, you'll still have to remember that **poco** has masculine and feminine versions and can be singular or plural: **comeré unas pocas gambas – I'll eat a few prawns; conoce a poca gente – he knows few people; los pocos que sepan cocinar – the few who know how to cook; pocas piensan como nosotras – few (women) think as we do.**

Una pequeña paella means **a small paella** but **poca paella** means **not much/a little paella**. Un poco de paella also implies **a little (of) paella** and in this construction **un poco de** is always masculine whether you are eating paella, pease pudding or poppadums.

When **poco** is an adverb, remember not to make it agree with anything or anyone: **ella habla poco – she doesn't talk much; hablábamos poco – we spoke little; este coche corre poco – this car doesn't go very fast.** When **poco** qualifies an adjective, it will also remain unchanged: **¡qué poco fina eres!** – the classic, sanctimonious reaction of the classic sanctimonious male to female rowdiness: **how coarse you are!**

Dentro de poco means **shortly/soon/in a little while. Hace poco is a little while ago** but **poco tiempo** (which can be shortened to **poco**) isn't the opposite of the big time but means **not long: ¿Cuánto vas a tardar? Poco – How long are you going to take? Not long.**

No, ni poco is awkward to translate but simple to understand: **¿A que no te he hecho esperar? ¡No, ni poco! – I didn't keep you waiting long, did I? You must be joking!**

Small is sometimes omitted in translation, so **small change** is **calderilla**, the **small hours** are **la madrugada** and **smallpox** is **viruela**. Someone who is **small** or **petty** is described as **mezquino** and if you meet someone you know far from home you might exclaim **¡el mundo es un pañuelo! – the world's a handkerchief!** instead of **it's a small world!**

Menudo is another adjective that's on the small side. It's not appropriate for quantity but does nicely for size, and the same people who refer to kids as **los peques** also refer to them as **gente menuda** – **small people. Mi abuela era una mujer menuda** means **my grandmother was a small woman** but **¡menuda era mi abuela!** conveys **what a woman my grandmother was!** regardless of stature.

Menuda is conveniently ambiguous and handy during potentially controversial discussions, so if you are unsure whether your neighbour roots for Barcelona or supports Madrid, play safe after matches and exclaim: **¡menudo partido!** – **what a game!** He'll realise that not only do you speak Spanish, but you also understand a lot about football.

LIES, LIES, LIES

Not telling the truth is **mentir** in Spanish and this is a straightforward, quirkless verb except for the present participle, **mintiendo: creo que estás mintiendo** – **I believe you're lying.**

Acostarse and **echarse** are the closest to **lying down, lying abed: Pareces cansado. ¿Por qué no te acuestas?** – **You look tired, why don't you lie down?** The other translation most often associated with **acostarse** is **to go to bed,** which amounts to the same thing, of course, but whose literal meaning is to **lie on one's side**.

Echarse is different, but only because this modest-looking word has an immodest number of translations. For the present it's enough to know that **You look tired, why don't you lie down?** can also be expressed as **Pareces cansado. ¿Por qué no te echas? Lying down** in Spain isn't confined to nighttime or illness but few choose the little-used verb **sestar** when they take an afternoon nap and refer instead to **echarse la siesta** as well as **dormir la siesta.** Whichever you choose, both mean **to sleep the siesta.**

Tumbarse, tenderse and **yacer** are other ways to **lie. Tumbarse** and **tenderse** convey the actual act of **lying down,** while **yacer** is almost exclusively reserved for **lying in our final resting place. Aquí yace Santos Campos** is what Elena sees on her grandfather's grave although modern epitaphs in Spanish cemeteries tend to be less explicatory. **Yacer con alguien** corresponds to the old-fashioned **to lie with someone,**

to sleep with someone when sleep is the last thing on anyone's mind.

Estar is frequently used for **to lie, to be situated: Madrid está en el mismo camino que Alcalá** – Madrid lies on the same road as Alcalá or **el libro estaba sobre la mesa** – the book was lying on the table. You are not limited to **estar** as you could also use **encontrarse: Madrid se encuentra en el mismo camino que Alcalá** and **el libro se encontraba sobre la mesa.**

There is no specific translation for our luxuriously lazy **to lie in** which is austerely explained as **quedarse en la cama** and consequently there is no corresponding noun for **a lie-in**.

A lie, falsehood is **una mentira**. Strangely enough in a language which favours plurals, enlargements and superlatives, our reaction of **lies!** to something or someone we don't believe is a singular **¡mentira! A pack of lies** turns into **a string: una sarta de mentiras.** Not all lies are big trouble or deep deception, so **a white lie, fib** is a diminutivised **mentirilla** while **a liar** is a logical **mentiroso/mentirosa**. This noun leads a dual existence as an adjective: **Angelines siempre me parecía mentirosa** – Angelines always looked like a liar to me.

The glorious **desmentir** means **to deny, refute, give the lie to** but the prefix **des-** (a cross between the English prefixes **de-** and **un-** as in **decompose** and **undo**) makes it irresistibly tempting to translate this as **unlie**. But this is the type of verb that could only exist in a nation of strong contrasts where so much is nevertheless defined in differing shades of grey.

NO, CORPORAL

If you feel like walking up a linguistic one-way street, just translate **no corporal** as **no cabo**. Not only will this phrase prove to be of little use in either language, but you could be misled into believing that the Spanish version is also the first person singular of the verb **caber – to fit into, to be contained in, to have room enough**. Don't take this wrong turning, though, as it is a verbal no-no.

You might suspect that **I fit** and **I don't fit** aren't going to be your two most-used Spanish phrases, but you'd be wrong. When you want to squash onto a crowded bus or worm your way into a full lift, you could find yourself insisting **sí quepo** – literally **yes, I fit** but implying **yes there is room for me.**

Other than this, the verb **caber** behaves with regular monotony, apart from its need to retain a sound that does not grate upon Spanish ears in the preterite tense **cupe, cupiste etc.** – **I fitted** etc. and those praiseworthy occasions when you venture into the subjunctive: **parece mentira que quepa tanta gente en un coche tan pequeño – it's unbelievable that so many people should fit into such a small car.** You will also encounter another side to **caber,** when it is used negatively but means **to be beside oneself with happiness, joy** or any other of those states of euphoria that are hard to achieve and harder to maintain. **Nieves no cupo en sí cuando supo que Blas iba a comprar un coche nuevo – Nieves was beside herself when she learnt that Blas was going to buy a new car.**

Your father will have a fit when he sees what you have done

Caber usually conveys physical **fitting** but **to be appropriate, to be apt** is translated as **ser** plus **apto, apropriado, adecuado, conveniente** or **digno**. So if house proud Nieves wants to boast **my house is fit for a queen** she says **mi casa es digna de una reina**.

When translating **to fit in** or **find room for** the Spanish often use two quite different words: **encontrar – to find** and **buscar – to look for, to seek. Te encontraré un hueco a mi lado** states **I'll find you a space beside me** but really means **I'll fit you in beside me** and you'll also hear **te buscaré un hueco a mi lado**, literally **I'll look for a space for you beside me.**

Another way **to fit** or **fit in** both in a physical and abstract sense is with **encajar,** so a social climber might pronounce **Nieves no encaja en mi círculo de amistades – Nieves doesn't fit in my circle of friends**. On the other hand, a handyman might announce **me resultó difícil encajar el cristal en el marco de la ventana – I found it hard to fit the glass in the window frame** although the verb **colocar** is equally suitable for do-it-yourself struggles: **me resultó difícil colocar el cristal en el marco de la ventana**

To fit up with is **proveer** but **to fit together** is **unir** and **to fit out** is **equipar**. When a skirt or a pair of trousers doesn't fit because it is too small or too big, you return to **caber** and rephrase: **esta falda no me cabe – this skirt doesn't fit me**. Likewise, **si sigues comiendo así, no vas a caber en ese pantalón – if you go on eating like that, those trousers won't fit you.**

When **fit** is an adjective that bounces with health it is described as **en forma** or **sano,** a word that does not correspond to **sane** in English but means **healthy**. The **fit** that is a noun as well as definitely unhealthy is **un ataque** or **un acceso,** often accompanied by the verb **dar – to give: a Blas le dio un ataque de tos – Blas had a coughing fit**.

Ataque also describes the **fit** experienced by the furious, impatient and/or flabbergasted: **le va a dar un ataque a tu padre cuando ve lo que has hecho**. The sentence is worded differently, but the sentiment of this ominous statement will be recognised instantly by mothers and children everywhere: **your father will have a fit when he sees what you've done.**

PLAIN AND SIMPLE

Plain, as in Jane, gets us off on the wrong foot because although **plain** Spanish girls and women do exist, there is no specific word for a female who is neither **pretty – bonita** nor **ugly – fea**. You have to beat around the bush instead and describe her as **no muy bonita – not very pretty, poco atractiva** or the discreet **poco agraciada** which is the most uncomplimentary of all in its discretion. As always, it won't hurt to remember that the adjectives **atractiva, agraciada** are preceded by an immutable **poco – little** or, in this case, **not very**. So don't overdo things and succumb to the temptation to turn **poco** into the feminine adjective **poca**. Returning to plainness and unkindness, **a really plain girl or women** can be described – preferably not to her face – as **un callo,** which is **a corn.**

Translations for the **plain stitch** in knitting include the political-sounding **punto a la derecha**, literally **right stitch** with continuous **plain knitting** described as a sternly totalitarian **todo a la derecha – all to the right**. Some prefer **punto espuma,** which means **foam stitch** or **punto bobo. Bobo** means **silly** and crops up in the name of that nicest non-flying bird, the **penguin – pájaro bobo.**

The **plainclothes police force** used to be called **la secreta** and a plainclothes policeman was **un secreta**. They were less sinister than their name suggests but nowadays the force is known as **el cuerpo de policía no uniformada** and an officer belonging to it is a non-specific **un policía**. The Guardia Civil also has a plainclothes branch, which is known as **la Policía Judicial,** while one of its agents is **un policía judicial.**

On the occasions when **plain** means **unadorned**, use a predictable but plural **sin adornos – without adornment** or **sencillo – simple** as well as **llano**. These last two are appropriate for someone whose manner is **plain**, although **a plain** of the Salisbury variety is also **un llano.**

Plain speaking is **hablar sin rodeos** or **hablar francamente. Llamar al pan, pan y al vino, vino** is the way the **plain speaker** gets down to brass tacks and **calls a spade a spade** by **calling bread, bread and wine, wine.** Someone who wants to know **am I making myself plain?** asks **¿me explico? – do I**

explain myself? As well as **¿me entiende?** or **¿me entiendes?** depending on the degree of intimacy between the speakers.

On the whole, the Spanish are not very adventurous about any food that they have not eaten from an early age. They are willing to eat **fried lamb's intestines wound round a stick – zarajos,** but a Spaniard, particularly of the older generation, can be as set in his or her culinary ways as the most conventional English-speaker. **Plain cooking** is at a premium and sounds simple: **cocina sencilla** or there is **cocina casera** – closer to **home cooking** but which, depending on the home in question, need not be identifiably plain.

When looking for an equivalent to the **plain** that is **evident** you can use **evidente: es evidente que no sabe cantar – it's plain that he can't sing.** **Obvio** is another obvious choice together with the eternally popular **claro: está claro que no debe cantar – it's plain that he shouldn't sing. Claro** will crop up again in a further version of **am I making myself plain?,** which is **¿está claro?**

Our **plain as a pikestaff** for something that is **plain to see** lacks alliteration in Spanish and makes reference to elements that can be pretty murky in English-speaking climates: **tan claro como la luz de día – as clear as daylight** and **tan claro como el agua – as clear as water.**

Viento en popa, literally a **following wind,** is sufficiently nautical to translate **plain sailing** although this unstressful state of affairs is also considered a question of **coser y cantar – to sew and sing.** This might be a piece of cake for good needlewomen or singers but doesn't make allowances for the difficulty many us find in doing either, let alone both at the same time.

PLUMBING THE DEPTHS

Deep generally descends into **profundo: el estanque en El Retiro no es muy profundo – the pool in the Retiro park isn't very deep** (it isn't very big either, but what can you expect in a city like Madrid where a stream like the Manzanares is called a river?). When needing to ascertain something's depth, you ask **¿cómo es de profundo?** and, although this is recognisable as **how deep is it?,** adding the preposition **de** makes a totally foreign, completely Spanish construction. Things can also be put another way by using the noun **profundidad – depth: ¿qué profundidad tiene?**

Nearly always, however, **profundo** is the word you need to translate **deep: una voz profunda – a deep voice; un sueño profundo – a deep sleep; un respeto profundo – deep respect; un pensador profundo – a deep thinker; un suspiro profundo – a deep sigh** and even **un odio profundo – a deep hate.**

We use **deep** to describe people, but to do so in Spanish you will have first to assess whether the **depth** you have in mind is closer to **penetrating – penetrante, astute – astuto, reserved – reservado, mysterious – misterioso, enigmático** or possibly **sly – taimado.**

It's easy to link **profundo** to our **profound: a profound book – un libro profundo.** We often use **profound** to describe **heartfelt, intense** emotions and so do the Spanish. Thus a heartfelt phrase like **anhelo a Madrid desde lo más profundo de mi ser** translates into **I long for Madrid from the depths of my** (literally **deep of my**) **being** and **una profunda afinidad para con los gatos** means **a tremendous affinity with cats.** Neither profundity nor intensity is reserved exclusively for emotion in either English or Spanish, so **deep blue** is **azul profundo** or **azul intenso.**

The obvious definitions of **to deepen, make deeper** for the verb **profundizar** don't make this the word a navvy chooses when he deepens a ditch, which he would convey as **hacer más profundo – to make deeper (more deep).** Normally, **profundizar** is followed by the preposition **en** and means **to go into deeply, to make a thorough study of** or **to get to the bottom of: el libro profundizó en la poesía de Lorca – the book made a thorough study of Lorca's poetry.**

Other translations for **deep** start with **hondo: una respiración honda – a deep breath, un lago hondo – a deep lake** or **el pueblo está situado en el hondo del valle – the village is situated deep in the valley.** Quite often **hondo** implies **bottom** which, when non-anatomical, can be translated as **fondo.** This is logical when you remember that the **F** of early Spanish frequently metamorphosed into **H: facer/hacer –**

to do and **farina/harina – flour**. This explains the two versions of some names and surnames – **Fernando/Hernando** and **Fernández/Hernández** for instance.

The verb **ahondar** means **to deepen, make deeper** as well a **to dig out**, and although it's still not exactly a navvy-friendly term, it's used more readily than **profundizar**. As with **profundizar,** it also has the **deeper** meaning of **to study thoroughly, examine in depth**.

You'll find the verb **sumir** used for **being in the depths of misery or despair**. It means **to plunge, sink** and although the word **deep** is not mentioned, it is inferred: **sus deudas le han sumido en la ruina – his debts have plunged him into (the depths of) ruin**.

To be deep in a book is **estar absorto/a en un libro** while someone who lives in **the depths of the country** would probably use the adjective **isolated** and say **vivo en lo más aislado del campo**. **To be out of your depth** because you are in unfamiliar surroundings or an uncomfortable situation is **estar incómodo, estar fuera de lugar**. This last phrase is particularly appropriate for being out of depth socially, while **no saber estar** is a scornful phrase applied to someone who is conspicuously lacking in social graces.

To be **out of one's depth** while swimming is the hard-to-translate **no hacer pie** which refers to not being able to touch the bottom with one's foot. **Deep-sea diving** is a contradictory-sounding **bucear en alta mar** but although **deep** changes to **high** in this instance, it still means you are a long way out. On the other hand height, rather than depth of water, is involved when fury makes you **go off the deep end** and the Spanish use **subirse por las paredes – to go up the walls** instead.

PURPOSELY

There is no Spanish equivalent to our all-purpose **purpose**, so **what was your purpose in coming here to-day?** needs to be translated with **propósito, intención, motivo, fin, objeto**.

Oscar Wilde said that answers, rather than questions, were

indiscreet but whether you put your foot in it with a question or an answer, it is indisputable that **what was your purpose in coming here today?** sounds faintly pompous in English. Nevertheless, **¿cuál era tu propósito al venir aquí hoy?** together with **¿cuál era tu intención al venir aquí hoy?** and **¿cuál era tu motivo al venir aquí hoy?** not to mention **¿cuál era tu objeto al venir aquí hoy?** or **¿cuál era tu fin al venir aquí hoy?** are all common-or-garden, more or less street-level Spanish.

If you want to express a more crusading **purpose,** use **meta: tengo una meta en la vida – I have a purpose in life.** You might meet the less fervent **propósito** in the same circumstances or possibly **fin,** but be careful of **fin** preposition-wise because **un fin en la vida** corresponds to **a purpose in life** but **el fin de la vida** is considerably more terminal because **fin** plus **de** always signifies **the end of something,** whether it's life, wine or the biscuits.

Plural **purposes** translates better as **fines: propaganda purposes – fines publicitarios** and note that, cynical as ever, the Spanish view **propaganda** as **publicity** and are also sufficiently sceptical to regard **publicity** as **propaganda.**

Because they mean the same thing, **on purpose** and **purposely** get the same translation treatment to become **adrede, a propósito, aposta, deliberadamente, intencionadamente, expresamente.** Thus **you did that on purpose!** could be **¡hiciste eso adrede!** or **¡hiciste eso a propósito!** and so on and so on accusingly down the remainder of the list. **A propósito** makes another appearance in **a propósito, ¿hiciste eso adrede? – by the way, did you do that on purpose?**

Purposely-built is slightly different from **purpose-built** and the difference in the volume of their translations speaks volumes about Spanish volubility: **edificado adrede, edificado a propósito** etc. but **edificado con fines específicos.**

Similarly subtle is the misleading resemblance of **adrede** to **alrededor** (which means **around**) and **aposta** to both **apostar** and **apuesta. Apuesta** is the feminine version of the adjective **apuesto – good-looking, attractive** as well as a noun meaning a **bet** or a **bid at cards** but not at **an auction**, where it is **una puja. Apostar – to bet, bid** appears to be irregular in the present tense but in fact it is modified to soothe Spanish ears: **apuesto, apuestas, apuesta, apostamos, apostáis, apuestan – I bet, you bet, he bets** etc. This verb also has the further definition of the almost obvious **to take up a post/position/station**.

As in English, **purpose** is often inferred, not spoken: **what's (the purpose of) all this for? – ¿para qué es todo esto?** or **this should be sufficient for (the) present (purpose) – esto debe ser suficiente por ahora.** **Purpose** may also be eliminated in **to serve a purpose/to answer a purpose**, which is simply **servir.** Continuing to be economical with words, **to put to good purpose** is **aprovechar** and its opposite, **to put to no good purpose** is **desaprovechar** if implying **not to take advantage of** but **malgastar** when waste is feckless or careless.

Purposefully becomes **resueltamente** or **decididamente, determinadamente** while **purposeful** is **determinado, decidido, resuelto** or **empeñado,** the past participle of the verb **empeñar – to pawn, pledge.** Admirable but occasionally wearying **strength of purpose** allows itself to be compressed into **resolución,** which is also the word for tongue-twisting **purposefulness. Resolución** has close political links when it means **motion, proposal** and politics inevitably bring to mind the last definition of all: **purposeless – irresoluto, indeciso, vacilante, perplejo.**

RIGHTLY SO

Right has several English meanings and various Spanish translations of which **derecho, derecha, recto, correcto, oportuno, adecuado, justo, indicado, debido** are the most usual.

It's right to do that is translated as **es correcto hacer eso,** although both **es oportuno hacer eso** and **es indicado hacer eso** suggest that something is **right** because it is **convenient.** Something that is **right** because it is deemed **fitting** is expressed as **adecuado** but **es justo hacer eso** implies that something is **right** because it is **fair.** On the other hand, although you lose out on articulacy, in each case it's possible to save time and bother by resorting to **bien: está bien hacer eso.**

Recto refers to rightness of an upright variety, so **un hombre recto** is **a right-minded man. Debido** corresponds to **proper: hace las cosas como es debido – he does things the right/the proper way.** Again it's possible to substitute both words with **bien** although you add the preposition **de** for the **good guy: es un hombre de bien.** For the perfectionist, you rearrange things slightly: **hace las cosas bien – he or she does things well.**

Right sometimes becomes **bien** in connection with the **right** time. Someone whose watch is unreliable might ask someone with a Rolex, **¿tienes la hora bien? – do you have the right time?** But the subtly different **¿tienes la hora buena?** suggests you are asking for the Greenwich, atomic-clock, spot-on **right time.** You'll use neither if you want to **put the clock right** and instead use **poner en hora: por favor, pon el reloj en hora – put the clock right, please.**

Nevertheless, if something needs **to be put right, repaired** use **reparar, arreglar.** This last is also suitable if you need **to put a situation right: ¿me puedes arreglar las cosas con Fausto? – can you put things right with Fausto for me?** To be **right** is **tener razón** but **to have right of way** when driving is **tener preferencia.**

There are occasions when **mejor – better** is the right word for **right** and **la mejor persona para la tarea** is our **the right (best) person for the task. Correcto** fits the bill when something does or doesn't **look right: esta cuenta no me parece correcta** although yet again, you can use **bien: esta cuenta no me parece bien.** If something seems a bit fishy, stay with **bien: dice mi marido que este pescado no sabe bien – my husband says this fish doesn't taste right.** You will find that **all right** also requires **bien** while dispensing with **all: pregúntale si está bien comerlo – ask him if it's all right to eat it.**

For an affirmative **all right** there are **de acuerdo** or **conforme** but as nearly always happens, **bien** is equally suitable. Dependant on requirements of vehemence, consensus or resignation you can go for **bien**, the repetitive **bien, bien** or the somewhat tetchy **¡está bien!**

The **right** that is the opposite of **left** is **derecha: el castillo está a tu derecha – the castle is on your right.** In politics,

My husband says that this fish doesn´t taste right

la derecha is the **right wing** but **right-hand, right-handed** is **diestro,** a word that is also used for a **bullfighter.** The English **right, left and centre** that implies **all over the place** loses its centrepiece in Spanish, which prefers **a diestro y siniestro – left and right. Derecho** can be used for **recto** when it means **upright** but not in a **right angle – un ángulo recto** or when it is – ahem – **a rectum.**

The masculine noun, **derecho,** means **law,** especially in connection with studies but **tener el derecho** followed by **de** means **to have the right to: cree que tiene el derecho de hacer lo que le da la gana – he believes he has the right to do what he wants.** Plural **derechos** are **dues, taxes, royalties** and crop up in **derechos reales** as **death duties or tax paid on a property transfer.**

Right is not mentioned in **right there – allí mismo** and **right away** has several versions, the most common being **ahora mismo** and **enseguida.** Be wary of **ahora después** as this deceptive little phrase really means **now afterwards** although some Spanish-speakers would have you believe that this, too, means **right away.** For those who have learnt to understand Spanish ambivalence regarding time, this comes as no surprise but any innocents who may still be abroad might react with a resentful **they've no right! – ¡no hay derecho!**

SHORTLISTED

Short can indicate **not long** as well as **not tall,** which not only eliminates Sally in the first round but also indicates that there will be at least two translations for **short.**

The most frequent are **corto** and **bajo: a short story – un cuento corto, a short woman – una mujer baja.** Lack of height is always conveyed by **bajo, which** is synonymous with **low** rather than **short: una temperatura baja – a low temperature.** As well as an adjective, **bajo** can be a noun, so **un bajo** is as likely to be one of the Seven Dwarfs as a bass singing Old Man River.

Since **una baja** is **a short woman,** the sentence **los expertos temen una baja en Bolsa** could be translated as **experts fear a short lady in the Stock Exchange** as well as **financiers fear a slump on the Stock Exchange. Jugar a la baja** is less fun than it sounds unless you're a financier, as it means **Stock Exchange speculation on a fall in prices. Baja** on its own is also **a recession, slump, drop: una baja del diez por cien en el precio de esmeraldas – a ten per cent fall in the price of emeralds.**

That's not all, though, since **una baja** can be **a casualty** in the military sense: **la unidad sufrió serias bajas – the unit suffered heavy casualties. Estar de baja** means **to be absent from work or school** for most reasons excluding holidays. **Dar de baja** is stressful because absence is imposed, not sought, by a doctor, perhaps, or an employer: **a César le dieron de baja la semana pasada – César was laid off last week.** The **dar de baja** formula is used when a member is obliged to resign from a club or association but the reflexive **darse de baja** means that withdrawal, retirement, resignation, dropping or opting out is voluntary: **César se dará de baja en el club de ajedrez – César will resign from the chess club.**

When **short** is translated as **corto** this is as suitable for **a dress – un vestido corto** – as **a conversation** which becomes **una conversación corta** or **a short-term solution – una solución a corto plazo.** This adjective will also ensure you are served with **weak coffee – un café corto de café** which sounds repetitive but keeps your caffeine level low. Don't ask for **un cortado** unless you can cope with a normal-sized amount of coffee with very little milk, served in a smallish cup or glass.

Un traje is a **man's suit** as well as a **woman's suit, dress** and **un traje corto** could turn out to be **a woman's short dress** or **suit.** Normally, though, **traje corto** is traditional male Andalusian dress and also worn by **un rejoneador – a mounted bullfighter** or **un matador – bullfighter** at an informal bullfight or one that is held outside the official bullfighting season.

Short-legged is **paticorto** while **short-sighted** is **corto de vista** or **míope. A short-cut** is **un atajo**, the nearly extinct **shorthand** is **taquigrafía** and **a short-list** is **una terna**, not to be confused with **un terno – a man's three-piece suit with waistcoat.**

To shorten is **acortar** but not **cortar – to cut**, although in popular speech **cortar** can signify **to cut another person short.** In popular speech, the reflexive **cortarse** suggests **to feel embarrassed, awkward** or **tongue-tied** while **to fall short** is similarly reflexive: **quedarse corto** which also implies **not to do enough** or **say enough** as well as **to fail to speak up for oneself.** More adequate is **ni corto ni perezoso** – literally **neither hesitant nor lazy** although the phrase amounts to immediately, decisively: **cuando le despidieron a César, ni corto ni perezoso buscó otro empleo – when they sacked César, he looked for another job without delay.**

Shortage is **escasez** or **falta** but because the Spanish tend to link shortage with crisis they will often refer to a **water shortage** as **una crisis de agua**, suggesting both lack of water and the consequences of its absence.

With the exception of **bajo** there is no empathetic word for **short,** apart from **de poca estatura** but there *are* alternative ways to convey brevity, starting with close-to-hand **breve: una carta breve – a short letter or un mandato breve – a short term in office**. Use another lookalike, **sucinto,** or **seco – dry** for someone whose **short manner** remains this side of politeness but **brusco** when it doesn't. When **shortly** refers to manner it is translated as **bruscamente, secamente** but in connection with time it is translated by untrustworthy phrases like **dentro de poco, en breve, luego**. The Spanish are well aware that **enseguida** means **straight away** but tend to use it when **shortly** suggests **before long – dentro de poco,** a short-sounding phrase that can still herald a lengthy wait.

DARESAY

Spanish comes up with two verbs, **osar** and **atreverse** as translations for **to dare: No me atrevo a decirle a Fausto que los gatos han estado en su huertecita – I don't dare tell Fausto that the cats have been in his vegetable patch.**

Only confirmed feline risk-takers could be so reckless and ignore uncompromising bellows of **¡que ni os atreváis a hacer eso otra vez! – don't you dare do that again!** This could be expressed with the reflexive **ocurrirse: ¡que ni se os ocurra hacer eso otra vez!** (literally **don't even let it occur to you to do that again**) as it implies exactly the same thing and is particularly useful when the recriminator knows the recriminated hasn't a leg to stand on.

When daring induces wonder, not wrath, you stick to **atreverse: ¿cómo os habéis atrevido a hacer eso? – how did you dare do that?** On the other hand, when **to dare** implies **to defy, desafiar** is better: **te desafío decirle a Fausto que los gatos han pisoteado sus habas – I dare you to tell Fausto that the cats have trodden down his broad beans.** The Spanish will often use **ser capaz** when we prefer **dare: ¿a que no eres capaz de decirle a Fausto que han pisoteado sus habas?** although still more colloquial would be **¿a que no le dices a Fausto que han pisoteado sus habas?,** where **dare** isn't mentioned but is implicit.

In less fraught circumstances, after copious amounts of food and drink for instance, the Spanish will likewise turn a harmless invitation into a challenge: **¿te atreves con un postre? – do you dare manage a pudding?**

A dictionary might not always offer the verb **retar** with its accepted meaning of **to defy, to challenge** but you often find it disguised as **to dare**, so at the time of the nerve-racking broad bean episode, any member of our family might have been heard to say **te reto decirle a Fausto que los gatos han pisoteado sus habas – I dare you to tell Fausto that the cats have trodden down his broad beans.**

It's not easy to find an equivalent to the English **daresay** that incorporates doubt tempered with hope: **I daresay he won't even notice** can be variously translated as **acaso no se dará cuenta; quizás no se dará cuenta** as well as the optimistic but self-deluding **me figuro que no se dará cuenta.** Meanwhile, the gentleman in question was heard to say **me imagino que a algunas personas les importa un pepino lo que hagan sus gatos – I daresay that some people don't give two hoots** (but literally **a cucumber**) **what their cats get up to.**

You'll soon realise that the verb **osar** is used less in conversation than **atreverse,** which doesn't mean you'll never hear it, but it is more of a written, not a spoken verb. There is not so much of a gulf between **osado** and **atrevido** but **atrevido** still seems to be preferable when describing a person who is daring in manner or dress. Female entertainers are no longer required to fill in **a low neckline – un escote** with a chaste wisp of tulle or lace as in the days of the former regime, but it is still possible to encounter elderly black-clad ladies who refer to less reticent women as **atrevidas** or **osadas.** This word is also applied half-admiringly to women who are energetic enough to undertake something others would shirk – coal-mining or plumbing, perhaps. The kind of daring person who doesn't aim to shock with necklines or out-of-character activities but likes to amaze with action, is labelled **temerario, imprudente** or **arriesgado.**

All these adjectives are easily turned into nouns and someone who is **daring** in any sense of the word can be described as **un temerario, un imprudente, un atrevido, un osado** or **un arriesgado. Arriesgado** is interesting in these circumstances because it is the past participle of **arriesgarse – to risk,** but is synonymous with **dare.** This explains why, when asked to explain to Fausto what had happened to his broad beans, my husband shook his head and declared **no me quiero arriesgar.**

UP TO SOMETHING

A phrase that is guaranteed to irritate finicky speakers is the increasingly frequent extension of **subir – to go up** into **subir arriba.** As the same finicky speaker would be quick to point out, it is impossible to **subir abajo,** as anyone who ever tried to walk up a down-escalator is well aware. Its incorrectness has no bearing on the phrase's popularity, nor that of its opposite number, **bajar por abajo** instead of **bajar.** Nevertheless you will hear both the offending phrases in all situations from all kinds of people – except finicky speakers.

Subir means **to raise, lift up, go up, get up** plus a lengthy entourage of similarly uplifted verbs, so you might hear or say **los sueldos han subido – wages have risen.** Latterly, wages go up less often than prices and you are more likely to hear or say **los precios están subiendo horrorosamente – prices are going up horrendously.** If the grumbler were on the articulate side you might hear instead **los precios están subiendo vertiginosamente – prices are rising dizzyingly**. Doubtless because of the dizzying heights of some bills, **subir** often corresponds to **to amount to: la cuenta subirá a unos doscientos euros – the bill will come to some two hundred euros.**

Subir appears in circumstances where someone or something ends up in a higher position than he, she or it started off and applies equally to status and physical situation: **le han subido a director – they've promoted him to manager**.

The **rising** of water is also translated by **subir: en el Mediterráneo, sube poco la marea – in the Mediterranean, the tide rises very little** although the **source** where a river **rises** is **el nacimiento**. Unrelated to the gentle babble of river or brook, **subir** also means to **turn up** the sound of a babbling radio or television.

All the preceding elevating effects can be taken care of with **subir** but second thoughts will sometimes be required when translating from Spanish. **El ascensor sube al quinto piso** means **the lift goes up to the fifth floor** but, depending on the speaker's location, **ella está subiendo** means both **she is coming up** and **she is going up**.

Indirect objects, which bring a third party into the proceedings, also give clues as to who is where or who wants something done on his or her behalf. Accordingly, the **me** that is tacked on to the imperative in **súbame los periódicos al quinto** is a request to **bring the newspapers up to me on the fifth** (floor) but **súbale los periódicos al quinto** is an order to a newspaper boy on the ground to **go up to the fifth floor with newspapers** for someone.

Subir is also a reminder of earlier days when **getting on** a vehicle or even an animal required a climb. It is now also used for **getting on** aeroplanes, boats, trains and horses and is generally followed by the preposition **a: subimos al tren justo cuando salía – we got on to the train just as it was going**. Sometimes **subir** goes reflexive on you, particularly when used by drivers or givers of lifts: **súbanse rapido – get in quickly**. The reflexive **subirse** can refer to clothing, too: **súbete los calcetines – pull your socks up** although, unlike English, this phrase is not an exhortation to pull your self together.

Still reflexive, **subirse los humos a la cabeza** describes a person who lets real or imagined importance to go to his or her head. Likewise, the best way to take someone down a peg is **bajarle los humos** and in both instances, **humos** resemble **vapours** more than smoke.

Alcohol often goes to the head in English but in Spanish it rises: **ella dice que el cava le sube a la cabeza – she says cava goes to her head**. After too much cava, some tend to look flushed and have a **high** colour which is regarded in Spanish as **risen** colour – **tener el color subido** and which uses the past participle of **subir** as an adjective.

The noun **subida** is a financial **increase** or **rise** as well as the **ascent** of a hill or mountain, but the adjective **subido** acquires the meaning of **strong,** and more so when coupled with **tone** as in **un discurso subido de tono – an impassioned, inflammatory speech.** On the other hand, if applied to a book or film, **subido de tono** invariably implies that the censorious feel its content – inevitably erotic – calls for censure as well as a censor.

LET'S CALL IT QUITS

Whatever you may decide to call **quitar,** you can't call it **quits. Quitar** has little connection with an English-speaker's **to quit** which in any case is more of an Americanism. When **calling quits** because of **settling differences** the Spanish use a conciliatory **hacer las paces – to make peace.** If it is more a question of **settling up an account** he or she would use the verb **pagar – to pay** or **liquidar.**

As for **quitar,** both this and the reflexive **quitarse** resemble chameleons because their translations are coloured by circumstances and include **to take off, take away, stop, leave, leave off** and **remove.** You encounter **quitarse** in **undressing** situations: **quítate la ropa – take your clothes off; ¿por qué no te has quitado los zapatos? – why haven't you taken your shoes off?** It also figures in the Spanish version of **ne'er cast a clout till May be out: hasta el cuarenta de mayo no te quites el sayo,** although **un sayo** is **a smock, a tunic** and one is advised not to remove it until the **40th May** – in other words, the first week of June.

Objects to be removed with **quitar** are limitless, and **haz el favor de quitar ese gatito de la mesa** means **kindly remove that kitten from the table.** The similar-sounding **quitar la mesa** suggests furniture removal, but is the Spanish way **to clear the table** during the aftermath of a meal. **To clear a room** or **to clear a runway** are translated by **despejar** although when someone in an uncouth, anti-kitten mood bellows **¡quítate de allí!** a kitten gets the **clear off!** message.

A gentle **quita, quita** is common between people who share some degree of intimacy and is a prime example of the way Spanish still dispenses with *please* on home ground.

When the kitten sat in the paella

Accompanied by a gentle, non-violent little shove it removes someone from your path or deters him or her from reading the newspaper over your shoulder. **Quita, quita** plus the same little shove is also a sulky response to unwelcome attention or an untimely demonstration of affection – but, again, only to someone you are close to.

Quita is built into some words: **quitaesmalte – nail varnish remover; quitapinturas – paintstripper; quitamanchas – stain remover** and the graphic **quitamiedos** for a **handrail.** The past participle **quitando** means **except** in phrases like **quitando el último capítulo, me gustó el libro – apart from the last chapter, I liked the book.**

Maths teachers favour **restar** for arithmetical **taking away** but **quitar** is equally serviceable, although less numerate: **si de once quitas tres, quedan ocho – if you take three from eleven, you are left with eight.** Occasionally **quitar** implies **to steal: me quitaron el monedero en el mercadillo – the took away (stole) my purse at the market.** As in English, an anonymous, unidentified, faintly paranoid **they** will be used.

The literal translation of **que me quiten lo bailao** (a

corruption of **bailado**) is **let them take away what I've danced** but it doesn't convey the cocky, almost nostalgic defiance that is missing from an English **they can't take that away from me.**

Quitar sueño is an obvious **to take away sleep: el café quita el sueño – coffee stops you sleeping.** It also implies **to lose sleep** in the sense of **being upset** or **bothered: tus amenazas no me quitan el sueño – your threats don't worry me.** **Quitar,** followed by **importancia** resembles **to diminish** and, in some situations, **to laugh off: cuando se sentó el gatito en la paella, sonreí y intenté quitar importancia al asunto – when the kitten sat in the paella, I smiled and tried to laugh the matter off.**

Quitar/quitarse un peso de encima is the same as **to relieve of a burden/to relieve oneself of a burden.** **Quitar/quitarse las ganas** is what happens when something or someone **spoils your fun** or **enthusiasm: casi se me quitaron las ganas de quedarnos con el gatito – I almost stopped wanting to keep the kitten.** You can continue with **quitarse las ganas** or substitute **ganas** with **apetito** to translate **to lose one's appetite: se le quitó el apetito a mi marido cuando se cayó el gatito en la sopera – my husband lost his appetite when the kitten fell in the tureen.**

Verb-spotters will by now have spotted the way that **quitar** often becomes a reflexive **quitarse,** which is less of a big deal than it looks, even if you aren't verb-friendly. It all boils down to whether you initiate the action yourself, or have it forced upon you – like a husband faced with a fifth feline addition to what was formerly a happy home.

PART THREE
THERE'S NO PLACE LIKE IT

There's no place like Spain and there never has been. While the rest of Europe was muddling miserably through the grim Dark Ages, Spain was enlightened, learned and tolerant and its vastly dissimilar inhabitants managed to live together in a harmony that puts today's world to shame. With mutual Anglo-Spanish hostility consigned to the past, modern Spain beguiles English-speakers not only because of its climate and way of life, but because it is still rewardingly different from the rest of Europe. A lot of what makes it so different often surfaces in the Spanish language, which like the country itself, is attractive, individualist, occasionally irritating but always fascinating.

SPAIN IS STILL DIFFERENT

The Spanish are more self-contained than formerly but retain their reputation for hospitality, so a host will still tell a first-time guest **aquí tienes tu casa – here is your home**. This selflessness extends to food and if you interrupt the meal of a perfect stranger, if he or she is middle-aged or over, you may be asked **¿si quiere comer? – would you like to eat?** Despite the apparent generosity of these formulae, they are polite formalities, not invitations to collapse on the sofa and kick off your shoes or mop up the remains of someone's lunch.

The usual translation for **house** is **casa,** which is synonymous with **home** and used in this sense for **an apartment, flat – un apartamento** (small) or **un piso** (less small). This is why you hear **Nieves está limpiando su casa – Nieves is cleaning her house** whether she inhabits a house, bungalow, palace or apartment. You hear **nuestra casa**

está en la sexta planta – our house is on the sixth floor when the abode is clearly an English-speaker's apartment but this is because although it may not be a house it is unquestionably a home. **Hogar** is another homely word, but unlike **casa** its meanings are restricted to **home and hearth.**

The verb **casar,** which is intimately connected to **casa,** means **to marry, to wed, to unite** and a **married man** was described as **un casado** because he lived with his wife in their own dwelling. Further translations for **casar** include **to annul, repeal, abolish, abrogate** – none of which bodes well marriage-wise until you delve deeper and discover that despite their superficial similarity, the verbs have reassuringly different Latin roots.

The adjective **casero** means **homemade** and also **home-loving** but context should indicate whether reference is being made to a tea-cosy or a human. As a noun, **casero** is variously **a landlord, administrator** or **caretaker** but, once again, context makes it clear whether a boss or employee is alluded to. The phrase **César es de la casa** means **César is one of us or belongs,** but **de la casa** describes **a speciality, something made on the premises** when found on a restaurant menu, at a grocer's or a butcher's. Translated word for word, **como una casa** means **like a house** but also emphasises quality or size: **tengo una resaca como una casa – I have a tremendous hangover.**

Like most Spanish nouns, **casa** can be made to expand, contract or change meaning depending on the suffix used. Predictably, **una casita** is **a little house** while the almost-identical **caseta** is a **booth, fairground booth** or **beach hut. Una casilla** is **a forest-ranger's hut, a gatehouse** or **level crossing-keeper's shelter** as well as a **pigeon hole** (for letters or keys, not pigeons), a **blank space on a form** or a **square on square-ruled paper. Una casona** is a **large house** but as well as **large** you often find that **un caserón** is dilapidated, too, and as is usual with this kind of suffix, there has been a disparaging gender change, in this case from feminine to masculine.

Certain houses and buildings are found in specific regions and the **barraca** found in Valencia or Murcia is **a house with a steeply pitched roof. Barraca** is also the name given to temporary constructions where people eat and dance – but mainly drink – during local fiestas anywhere in Spain. Asturias is blessed, or cursed, with heavy rainfall and the typical **hórreo – house, barn, granary** is built on stilts or columns to keep its contents dry and beyond the reach of rats and scavenging animals.

A country house, its outbuildings and surrounding land is **un cortijo** in Andalusia or Extremadura, **un caserío** in the Basque region and **una masía** in Catalonia. The most frequent translation for **una villa** is **a town** and although a Spanish English dictionary defines it as a dwelling, what an English-speaker regards as a **villa** used to be **un palacete**. Now **a villa** tends to be smaller and cheaper and is known as **un chalé** while a **semi-detached** or **terraced house** is **una casa adosada** and, particularly on English-speaking coasts, **un bungalow**.

Casa crops up where it doesn't in English, beginning with **una casa de empeño – a pawnshop**. Villages and small towns without a hospital have **una casa de salud – a health centre,** towns of all sizes have **una casa consistorial – town hall** and even small villages boast **una casa de cultura – a cultural centre. Una casa-cuna** is **a crèche** and at the other end of the scale **una casa solariega** is a **family seat**.

Literal translations seldom turn out as you expect, but **una casa de huéspedes** does turn out to be **a guest house** although the now-outdated **casa pública** never did correspond to a **public house** but was **a brothel**. This institution was also known as **una casa de citas – a house of appointments**, a euphemism that puts a **well-appointed house** in a much more intriguing light.

C FOR YOURSELF

When spelling out words, especially over the telephone, confusion arises from the fact that so many letters sound similar – for instance **B, C, D, E, G, P, T** and **V**, also **S** and **F**, likewise **M** and **N**.

To solve this problem, people resort to some sort of identifying alphabet and those who have seen military service – or war-films – will remember **ABLE, BAKER,**

CHARLIE, DOG, EASY etc. while some favour the American **ACK, BEER, CHARLIE, DON...**

Civilians tend to use Christian names: **M** for **Molly, R** for **Robert,** but foreign residents in Spain may have noticed that the Spanish – military, civilian, pacifist or otherwise – favour place-names when spelling out words likely to cause confusion. A certain amount of leeway is tolerated by *Telefónica* employees, who know how to improvise with surprising empathy when a caller is stuck for an example.

Unlike English, the majority of Spanish letters have individual spellings and for those who may be unfamiliar with it, here is the whole alphabet – not that familiarity with it is guaranteed to clear up all spelling doubts: **A** (pronounced AH), **Be, Ce, De, E** (pronounced EH), **Efe, Ge, Hache** (silent H), **I** (pronounced EE), **Jota, Ka, Ele, Eme, Ene, Eñe, O** (pronounced OH), **Pe, Qu, Erre, Ese, Te, U** (pronounced OOH), **Uve, Uve doble, Equis, Y-griega, Zeta.** No longer there, but present in the minds of all but the youngest, are **Che – CH** and **Elle – LL** which are being eradicated as separate letters in recent Royal Academy-approved attempts to line up Spanish with everything else.

English seems to have missed out on the idea of making letters into words and the only English letters that can actually be spelled out are **H – Aitch** and **Z – Zed.** In any case, phonic – and especially telephonic – confusion reigns in Spanish, too, except over **I** and **Y** with their specific labels of **I-latina** and **Y-griega,** as well as the not legitimately Spanish **W – uve doble.**

Nevertheless, a bad speller will invariably trip up on and juxtapose **I-latina** and **Y-griega.** To English-speakers, **Ge** and **Jota** are totally different but these, too, succeed in muddling the unwary Spanish speller and their identical sound when they appear before **E** and **I** explains why there are two versions of the same surname: **Jiménez** and **Giménez** and why you encounter **paisaje – landscape** incorrectly written as **paisage.**

L and **R** present more home grown difficulties in words like **alto – high** and **escuchar –to listen,** which in the badly-spoken will emerge as **arto** and **escuchal.** **M** and **N** are as easy to confuse as they are in English but the Spanish sometimes ignore an **M** when it appears at the end of a word. Thus **Benidorm** can be pronounced and written as **Benidor** and tuna fish – **atún** is sometimes misspelled as **atúm**. English **rum** turns into correctly spelled Spanish **ron** and an umm... er... **a condom** is a correctly spelled **condón**.

Like an English **F**, **Efe** sounds a lot like **S** – **Ese**, while a Spanish **P** easily metamorphoses into **T**. To overcome potential misunderstanding, the Spanish opt for a phonetic alphabet based on the names of towns, provinces or countries: **A de Alicante, B de Barcelona, C de Cáceres** etc. This still doesn't guarantee immediate comprehension but bad spellers in any language can be remarkably tenacious and doggedly determined not to get it right. In practice, Spanish does not recognise a spoken difference between **V** and **B** and small children refer inaccurately to **uve bajo** – **low V** and **uve alto** – **high V** (**V** and **B** respectively) without modifying the sound of either. This does nothing at all to dispel spelling quandaries and as a result, many adult Spaniards see nothing incongruous in saying **V de Barcelona** and **B de Valencia**, so the word-for-letter is neither foolproof nor consistently reliable.

FOOTAGE

Uses for **un pie** in Spanish are largely pedestrian, as a foot isn't used as a rough and ready measure, unlike **a finger – un dedo** or **a palm – un palmo**. Despite being as arbitrary as a piece of string, **dedo** and **palmo** are still much-used by the Spanish especially when specifying non-precision measurements for drinks or textiles: **ponme dos dedos de whisky – pour me two fingers of whisky** or **córteme un palmo de tela – cut me a palm's width of material.**

An animal's **leg** is always **una pata**, but the word can be used none too elegantly for a human **leg,** too. Like an English-speaker who recognises that to err is human, a Spanish-speaker uses **pata** when careless enough to **put a foot in it: meter la pata.** As well as the **leg, foot** or **paw** of an animal, **una pata** is the **leg of a piece of furniture** or **clothing,** so **a table leg** is **una pata de mesa** while **a trouser leg** is **una pata de pantalón.** The weave we know as **hound's tooth check** is **pata de gallo,** literally **cockerel's foot. Pata** also applies to edible legs: **pata de cordero** is **leg of lamb** and **pata negra** is truly superior cured Spanish ham.

Because people occasionally have **patas,** a person who is bandy is **patizambo. Andar a la pata coja** could be interpreted as **lame** but is generally limited to children's games when it means **to hop** but the less amusing **estirar la pata – to stretch a leg** is an idiomatic **to kick the bucket. Patas arriba** sounds similarly terminal but means **upside down, untidy: cuando está en casa mi hija, todo está patas arriba – when my daughter's home, everything is untidy. Tener mala pata** has nothing to do with a bad foot or leg, but is a colloquial way **to have bad luck.**

Pie is usually fitting for phrases involving **foot: at the foot of the mountain – al pie de la montaña; at the foot of page two – al pie de la página dos; at the foot of the bed – al pie de la cama; flat feet – pies planos**.

The Spanish equivalent of **Shank's pony is el coche de San Fernando** and when **to go on foot** involves wearisome tramping or trudging, **patear** can be used, although it also means **to trample. Ir a pie** is more usual but there is a subtle difference between **estar de pie – to be standing up** and **estar a pie – to be on foot. Estar en pie** normally refers to something, rather than someone, which is **still standing** or **upright** while **ponerse en pie** infers **to stand up after having being seated.**

Apparently similar but not directly connected to standing or feet, **de a pie** describes your average man in the street, often as a deprecating diminutive: **un españolito de a pie.** Some phrases have no direct English equivalent, for instance **andar con pies de plomo – to walk with leaden feet** which has less to do with **dragging one's feet** than a metaphorical **to go carefully, warily.**

Entrar con buen pie and **entrar con el pie derecho** are virtually self-explanatory: **to get off to a good start. Levantarse con el pie izquierdo – to get up with the left foot** is held responsible for days when everything goes wrong, The Spanish tend to disapprove of superstition but are as superstitious as we are, although different traditions and beliefs govern good or bad luck and what attracts or repels it. Many take great care to ensure that the first foot to touch the floor each morning is the **right foot – el pie derecho** and not **el pie izquierdo.**

To be born lucky, to be born with a silver spoon in one's mouth is **nacer de pie – to be born standing up.** As in English, **caer de pie** is a fortunate **to fall on one's feet** but the only English phrase that corresponds to **creer a pies juntilllos** is **to believe blindly.** Something that **doesn't make sense or has neither head nor tail to it** isn't very different: **no tener ni pies ni cabeza – to have neither feet nor head. Pararle los pies a uno – to stop someone's feet** is closer to **clip someone's wings, take someone down a peg or two.**

The enigmatic **buscar tres pies al gato – to look for three legs on the cat** is the Spanish version of **hair-splitting** or **quibbling** and keeps even the Spanish guessing, since most cats have four. It has been suggested that the **pie** in question is the **metre** or **foot** in poetry and the saying refers to the futility of trying to locate three syllables in a two-syllable word like **gato** – which in itself is a rather clever piece of hair-splitting.

A LITTLE PEACE AND QUIET

The first translation that comes to mind for **peace** is **paz,** a word which as well as being the opposite to **war – guerra,** also applies to personal peace. **¡Qué paz!** is the stock exclamation (but not necessarily sincere praise) of urban Spaniards when removed from their unpeaceful cities.

Dejar en paz means **to leave in peace** and acquires different shades of meaning depending on the addition or subtraction of the preposition **a.** Thus, **te dejo leer en paz** is a thoughtful **I'll let you read in peace. Te dejo a leer en paz** is even better as far as bookworms are concerned because it implies **I'll leave you and let you read in peace.**

Déjame/déjale/déjanos/déjales en paz – leave me/him/ us/me/him/us/them in peace is the Spanish version of **leave me/him/us/them alone** and if you use the obvious-looking **solo** you'll be saying something rather different: **déjale solo – leave him on his own.**

Paz turns up on gravestones but instead of **R.I.P.** – the

My aunt Angela, may she rest in peace, used to have a budgerigar

internationally recognised **Requiescat in Pace** or **Rest in Peace** – you also see **D.E.P. – Descanse en Paz.** When referring to someone no longer alive, an older person is liable to say **mi tía Angela, que en paz descanse, tenía un periquito** – my Aunt Angela, may she rest in peace, used to have a budgerigar.

There are other words for **peace: tranquilidad, sosiego, calma, placidez** and **concordia.** You are less likely to encounter **sosiego** and **concordia** in casual chat but although they are conspicuously missing from contemporary events, you read or hear them in the media.

Tranquilidad, calma, placidez, concordia are used in the same circumstances as **tranquillity, calmness, placidity, concord/harmony** in English. For adjectives you have **apacible, plácido** as well as **tranquilo,** which is a favourite calming-down, smoothing-over word and you find a hypnotically repetitive **tranquilo, tranquilo** will often insulate you from the wrath of others.

Peace is eagerly sought by the Spanish, despite the unpeaceful surroundings with which they like to surround themselves. For a Spaniard, the presence of **paz, tranquilidad, calma etc.** does not necessarily entail an absence of **noise – ruido** and in fact an absence of noise is a vacuum so abhorred by Spanish natures that somebody invariably attempts to fill it.

This usually comes in the form of television, radio or some kind of background music, the volume of which makes it nearer to foreground music. Spanish voices are similarly **loud,** a quality that is translated by **fuerte – strong,** so **to speak loudly** is translated as **hablar fuerte.** Another translation is **hablar alto**, literally to **speak high** regardless of sex or whether a voice is high or low, soprano or bass. To **speak softly** is **hablar bajo** while to **read out loud** is a falsetto **leer en voz alta – to read in a high voice.** The contradictory **reading out loud in a low voice** is still hard to hear, but marginally more logical: **leer en voz baja.** To **think out loud, voice thoughts** is **pensar en voz alta** while **hablar por lo bajo** is **to speak under one's breath, mutter. Hablar por lo bajinis** is the same thing in outdated slang now heard only from the middle-aged or older. Although they have some of the noisiest cities in the world, the Spanish can be very **quiet** when the mood takes them. Usually a person of a **quiet** nature is termed **reservado, callado. Callado** is the past participle of **callar – to keep quiet, to say nothing** and is often applied to a habitually noisy person who is temporarily silent. **Estaba muy callada** means **she was very** (possibly unnaturally) **quiet** and calls for temporary **estar,** although your close-lipped, monosyllabic type gets the **ser** treatment: **era muy callado – he was the quiet type**.

You can use **silencioso** for **quiet** but more than quietness of speech it infers quietness of movement. On the other hand, don't use **quieto** because this adjective means **motionless, immobile, still** and **¡quieto!** is the **down!** addressed to overenthusiastic animals or the **stop it!** to someone who whips away the newspaper before you've finished with it.

If you want someone **to be quiet**, you make a request: **¿te puedes callar – can't you be quiet?** Despite its apparent civility, this phrase is tetchy, and anti-social newspaper readers who use it too frequently often find themselves having **to make up - hacer las paces** afterwards.

STRICTLY FOR THE BIRDS

The Spanish still tend to be unenthusiastic about cats, but many families have a dog, which they like to be as big and expensive as possible or as small and expensive as possible. Until prosperity was evenly distributed, an animal here was regarded as a source of food or an auxiliary member of the workforce although songbirds and racing pigeons were always exceptions to the unsentimental rule. This was because songbirds provided background music, needed little attention and ate next to nothing while a champion racing pigeon could turn out to be a nice little earner thanks to competitions and side bets.

A canary – un canario or **a linnet – un jilguero** still throbs its heart out and trills and tweets and scatters its **seed – alpiste** in Spanish apartments while **racing pigeons – palomos de competición** can still change hands for unbelievable amounts of money in some parts of the country.

A pigeon-fancier is **un colombófilo** and the **fancy** itself is **colombofilia**. Spanish pigeon racing bears more resemblance to **a chase – una caza** than a **race – carrera** as a **female pigeon – una paloma** is set loose and the first male bird to reach her and escort her back to its own **palomar – pigeon loft/dovecote** is the winner. **A young pigeon – un pichón** grows into **un palomo** whether it is intended for the pot or competition but **pichón** and **pichona** are also endearments. **A turtledove** is **un tórtolo/una tórtola** and **enamoured couples who bill and coo** are compared, as in English, to **two turtledoves - dos tórtolos.**

Despite their specific names, city-dwellers who are non-fanciers will refer to a pigeon, dove or turtle dove as **una paloma** but, with a capital letter, Paloma is a popular name for a girl, particularly in Madrid since **La Virgen de la Paloma** is the capital's patroness. **Soy como Juan Palomo, yo me lo guiso y yo me lo como – I'm like Juan Palomo, I cook it myself and I eat it myself** is said of self-sufficient, independent people who neither seek nor want assistance and tend to say, "I'm all right, Jack."

When translating **bird**, you can choose between **ave** and **pájaro**. Of the two, **ave** can sound pedantic and too poetic if used where the common or garden **pájaro** will do. When edible, however, **una ave** corresponds to **a fowl** and **aves** to **poultry** while **a game-bird** is **una ave de caza**.

To call another person **un pájaro** or **una pájara** isn't the worst of insults, but it's no compliment and can sound woundingly contemptuous. **Bird** never applies to the **young woman** that nostalgic middle-aged English-speakers would recognise as a *dolly* sort of bird. Instead, if she is pretty, a young Spanish girl is given a label of a more edible kind – **un bombón,** a masculine-gender word that describes someone who is nevertheless very feminine. Even before the advent of sexual equality, though, a girl was quite prepared to refer to an attractive young man as **un bombón**. Although it is an old term, an **attractive girl** or **woman** is still **una tía buena** but if she is not pretty she will, as in the past, be dismissed as an adjective-less **tía**.

Long before the arrival of dollybirds it was common to describe a man as **a bird**, as in **he's a rum old bird.** The Spanish would refer to him as **un tipo raro** but **something or someone out of the ordinary** is **un mirlo blanco,** a super-contradictory **white blackbird**. It is still possible to hear the Latin **rara avis** which is just the same as the **rum bird** or **white blackbird** already mentioned. Equally out of the ornithological ordinary, though, is **el AVE**, the acronym for the Spanish **High Speed Train – tren de Alta Velocidad**.

Birds turn up in as many Spanish proverbs and sayings as ours, but we have none that corresponds to the martyred **cría curvos y te sacarán los ojos**. This means **hatch crows and they'll peck out your eyes** and is regularly sighed by a resigned parent, generally the mother. The saying is so wellknown and so often-repeated that with **cría cuervos...** enough has been said.

The **bird-brained** are accused of having **una cabeza de chorlito – a plover's head** and the **featherbrained** are told **tienes pájaros en la cabeza – you have birds in your head**. Less flighty and more down to earth are those who are convinced **that a bird in the hand is worth two in the bush**. The Spanish agree with this sentiment but are of the opinion that **más vale pájaro en mano que ciento volando** and they characteristically multiply our two in the bush to an even more unattainable **hundred flying**.

ON SUFFERANCE

Sufrir – to suffer is one of those verbs that not only trails a preposition in its wake, but requires a different preposition from the one you are used to in English. If you are unacquainted with prepositions and propose to ignore them, don't rush away too soon. There are people who like and are happy with grammar the way other people like and are happy with billiards or cactus-growing, but even those who think they don't know a noun from a noodle instinctively know a lot more about grammar than most of us know about billiards or cactus-growing.

Prepositions have to be mentioned because you're going to translate boh **to suffer from** and **to suffer with** as **sufrir de**. **De** does mean **from**, but never **with**, and its principal meaning as far as most English-speakers are concerned is **of.**

He suffers from indigestion is translated as **sufre de indigestión. Padecer** can substitute **sufrir** so **padezco de callos – I suffer from corns** conveys something unpleasant in the region of the feet that is not sufficiently serious to require dramatic medical attention. Nevertheless, **padecer** shares the honours with **sufrir** in translating big league indisposition too: **el suegro de Nieves padece del hígado** and **el suegro de Nieves sufre del hígado** both mean **Nieves's father-in-law suffers with his liver**.

The past-participle **sufrido** doubles as an adjective corresponding to **long-suffering: ¡qué hombre más sufrido**

es el suegro de Nieves! – what a long-suffering man Nieves's father-in-law is! There is another aspect to **sufrido** when applied to a colour, finish or material: **el color crema es más sufrido que el blanco – the colour cream shows the dirt less than white**.

Sufrimiento is appropriate not only to physical **suffering** but to the **misery, anguish** and **unhappiness** caused by mental or emotional suffering. There is no equivalent to a **fellow-sufferer** although you'll get across the idea of shared distress with **te acompaño en el sentimiento – I accompany you in sentiment.** This solicitous expression is also the stock phrase of Spanish condolence known as **el pésame. A sufferer** exists in Spanish as **un enfermo** if health is involved, a pessimistic translation since **enfermo** means **ill. Un sufridor** is reserved for your miserable, anguished, unhappy but basically healthy **sufferer**.

To suffer in silence is not a Spanish trait, but **sufrir** is no longer popular for the **suffer** that signifies **to tolerate** or **put up with** although you still hear **sufrir un cambio** for **to suffer** or **undergo a change. Sufrir las consecuencias** hardly needs translation and **si como en casa de mi nuera, sé que sufriré las consecuencias después** is a gloomy prophecy often made by Nieves's father-in-law: **if I eat at my daughter-in-law's I know I shall suffer the consequences afterwards**. In fact he knows he stands a good chance of suffering that most Spanish of ailments, **a liver attack – un ataque al hígado.**

Preposition-avoiders will be gratified to note that **sufrir** in the previous circumstances is preposition-less, although the preposition that crops up in **ataque al hígado** (which is **a**) might not be the one you were expecting and in any case immediately combines with **el** to form **al**.

When **suffering** involves insult as well as injury, your encounter **inri: y para más inri, a Nieves no le hace gracia si dejo algo en mi plato – and to add to my sufferings, Nieves doesn't like it if I leave something on my plate. INRI** was the inscription nailed to the Cross, but older, less ecumenical Spaniards still feel they have direct access to the Almighty and do not question the propriety, let alone the piety, of this phrase.

There is no equivalent to **on sufferance**. For **I'm here on**

sufferance you'll have to turn things round and sniff **sólo me aguantan – they only put up with me** or **me están tolerando – they're tolerating me**. The often-heard **no sufras** and **no padezcas** have a sympathetic ring when conveying **don't worry**. As often as not they are classic examples of Spanish irony and stand you in good stead when what you really want to say is **don't overdo that show of counterfeit anguish, misery and unhappiness as I haven't been taken in for one moment**.

SAD TO SAY

It cannot be accidental that one of Spain's national heroes, Don Alonso Quijano, a.k.a. Don Quijote, should be characterised by his doleful, soulful countenance. And although Spanish only by adoption, Domenikos Theotokopoulos a.k.a. El Greco painted a lot of Spanish people who didn't look as though they'd just won **La Primitiva**.

When not laughing, talking, shouting or eating, many Spaniards look **sad – triste** regardless of mood, making Anglo-Saxons and Celts look manically jolly by comparison. The Spanish are much given to **sadness – tristeza** as well as **melancholy – melancolía** and some know how to make an art form out of depression. In fact, they are on such good terms with **depresión** that it has a pet name: **la depre**.

Sadness here tends to be genuine, or at least for as long as it lasts. Naturally there is a risk of misinterpreting Spanish sadness as Mediterranean **moroseness** but don't fall into the trap of translating **morose** as **moroso**. At best this adjective describes someone who is a **bad payer** and at worst **a debtor** – a type who might nontheless correspond to a Spanish-English dictionary's translations for **morose: taciturno, hosco, malhumorado**. However, none of these adjectives quite succeeds in conveying what we understand as **moroseness** and although this isn't necessarily synonymous with **sadness** the two are interchangeable for a Spaniard, who identifies both as **tristeza**.

These are circumstances where the terrible twins rear their alarming heads but it's a fact of grammar as well as a fact of life that **estar triste** means **to be sad** but **ser triste** generally

Three sad tigers in a wheatfield

describes **a sad circumstance: estoy triste porque he perdido la sortija que me regaló mi hermana – I'm sad because I've lost the ring my sister gave me**. On the other hand you would say **es triste que haya perdido la sortija que me regaló mi hermana – it's sad that I should have lost the ring my sister gave me**. Sorry to throw in the subjunctive like that, but **ser** plus **an adjective** plus **que** usually heralds an immediately following subjunctive verb.

There's nothing to prevent your connecting feeling **sad** with being **unhappy – infeliz** even though the presence or absence of happiness does not always entail the absence or presence of sadness. **A sad person** is usually described as **un tristón** or **un infeliz** but as well as being **a sad, unhappy** or **wretched individual, un infeliz** also defines someone who is **slow-witted**. He or she might well be held to exude good

221

nature accompanied by an ingenuous disposition, so **pobre Fausto es un infeliz** can mean **dear Fausto's such a simple soul** as well as **poor Fausto is an unhappy sort.**

Mustio is another **sad** adjective, redolent of the unsunny, the shut-up and musty. **Lamentable** rarely applies to emotion or state of mind and can be as pompous and critical in Spanish as in English: **hablar así demuestra una lamentable falta de comprehensión – talking like that displays a sad lack of understanding.**

The adverbs **tristemente** and **lamentablemente** provide you with **sadly** and, needless to say, there is also a wide choice of sad-making verbs: **entristecer** and **entristecerse; hacer triste** and **hacerse triste; poner** and **ponerse triste.** The reflexive versions are apt for those occasions when you're submerging yourself in the depths of misery rather than dragging down someone else.

It would be a pity to leave out **three sad tigers in a wheatfield.** This isn't an attempt to draw your attention to down-in-the-mouth felines, though, as **tres tristes tigres en un trigal** is a Spanish tongue-twister that makes **the Leith police dismisseth us** look like a **sad imitation – una burda imitación...**

MY CUP RUNNETH OVER

Optimistic sheep can always be sorted from pessimistic goats by the **glass that is half-full** or **half-empty.** Spaniards who view the bright side of life with rose-coloured spectacles refer to **un vaso casi lleno – an almost-full glass** while the gloom merchants see the same thing as **un vaso casi vacío.**

Lleno is the principal adjective that comes to mind for **full: luna llena – full moon; una tienda llena de clientes – a shop full of people; un cenicero lleno de colillas – an ashtray full of cigarette ends.** Then there is the credo of overweight ladies of certain age: **a los hombres les gustan las mujeres llenitas – men like plump women,** although in this situation a diminutive unfortunately doesn't diminish size.

Lleno is used when you're **full up** – or the more modern stuffed – after eating: **estoy lleno/estoy llena**. If you are uncomfortably **full** you might even groan **estoy harto/estoy harta** which, away from the table, is another way to say **I'm browned off/brassed off/cheesed off**. Tone, expression and degree of flatulent discomfort will dispel uncertainties surrounding the set of circumstances you are complaining about.

Spanish is mainly Latin-based but modifications crept in along the way, so there is another, more Latinised version – **pleno** which is still blood-brother to **lleno**. **Pleno** sounds posher than **lleno** but isn't generally a substitute for it and is used by the slightly more articulate for comments like: **robaron al banco en pleno día** – they robbed the bank in broad daylight or **¿por qué mi marido siempre pregunta dónde están las llaves cuando están a plena vista** – why does my husband always ask where the keys are when they are in full view?

Un pleno is a recognisable **plenary session** as well as everyone's wildest, dearest dream: **un pleno de La Primitiva** – a lottery coupon with six correct numbers.

Llenar nearly always translates the verb **to fill**. It is suitable for stomachs, dustbins and petrol tanks although when you **fill the car with petrol** you can say **repostar** while eliminating mention of petrol: **paremos en Albacete para repostar – let's stop in Albacete for petrol**.

Llenar has a very Spanish function to imply that something doesn't fill you with joy, admiration or pleasure: **a pesar de lo que decían las críticas, el libro no me llenó – despite what the reviews said, the book didn't impress me**. There are other **filling** verbs including **rellenar** when **filling** or **stuffing** (cushions or chicken, but not over-eating): **a Blas le entusiasman los pimientos rellenos – Blas is very keen on stuffed peppers**.

Rebosar indicates **brimming** fullness: **dice Nieves que Blas rebosa salud – Nieves says Blas brims with health**. She could put it differently and boast **Blas está rebosante de salud** – **rebosante** being another of those ever-so-slightly more articulate adjectives sometimes preferred to **lleno**.

Colmar is over-generous both physically and figuratively and means **to fill, to heap: sus palabras me colmaron de**

felicidad – his words filled me with happiness. Or la receta especifica dos cucharadas colmadas de ajonjolí – the recipe specifies two heaped spoonfuls of sesame seeds.

La gota que colmó el vaso is literally the drop that made the glass overflow, recalling our own cup that runs over with happiness. This is yet another example of the difference between sunny Mediterranean gloom and cloudy northern cheerfulness, because it is equivalent to the straw that broke the camel's back.

BROAD BEANS AND GYPSIES' ARMS

An English-speaker would be forgiven for assuming that French beans were judías francesas but this translation would put an ethnic, religious complexion on matters as this phrase means French Jewesses. You'll be more likely to track down the vegetable by requesting judías verdes – green beans despite the fact that all fresh beans are green. Neither will you acquire broad beans by requesting a logical judías anchas as you will be offered what we know as runner beans: if you've truly set your heart on broad beans you'll get them by asking for habas.

You might raise an amazed eyebrow to learn that the Spanish version of a Swiss roll is un brazo de gitano – a gypsy's arm although you will still find un suizo at the baker's, in the form of a bun which is vaguely rhomboid in shape and has the texture and taste of a teacake. You don't have to look far to find una palmera – palm tree swaying above you in Spain, but you'll also find one nestling beside the suizo at the baker's, where it is what we know as a pig's ear. You might find yourself eating either of these at una mesa de té, but it will be what we regard as a coffee table rather than a tea table.

An apple is una manzana as well as a block or group of buildings although a man's Adam's apple isn't Eve's fault at all, but la nuez - walnut instead. You will find una alcachofa - artichoke not only in a field or on your plate but in the bathroom where it is a showerhead. Un tomate – tomato is slang for a mess, a complication and instead of saying "cheese" to produce a cheesy grin for a photograph, a Spaniard pronounces a mouth-widening **patata**. **Una criba** turns out to be **a sieve**, not **a crib** although a cheat's **crib** is a meaty-sounding **chuleta,** which in turn is **a chop**. **Rape,** a nastily stark word in English, is **anglerfish** and **al rape** describes a **close-cropped** or even **shaved haircut**

Obvious translations for less edible items prove similarly unreliable and, rather than losing something in translation, some terms defy it, kicking off with **court shoes - zapatos de salón.** These are literally **drawing-room shoes** but both terms convey the idea of rather posh footwear. **Un sombrero** is any type of **hat** in Spain, and not an English-speaker's **Mexican hat,** since an adjective must be added for headgear to acquire geographical associations, as in **un sombrero mejicano** or **un sombrero cordobés** – **a Cordovan hat.** The Spanish describe **a bowler hat** as **un sombrero hongo,** literally **a mushroom hat** or, alluding to its rather **convex – abombado -** shape, **un bombín.**

You might have assumed that **a helmet – un casco** would involve few ambiguities, and you're probably prepared to accept **el casco polar** as **the polar ice-helmet** and not **ice-cap.** But you might find it harder to regard **un casco** as **a layer** (of an onion, not an egg-producer) as well as **hoof, hull, hulk** (boats, not brawn), **cask, barrel** or an **empty bottle** that might once contained have beer or Coca Cola. You also find it in a **town centre – casco urbano,** while the plural **cascos** is slang for **brains.**

Un panty looks as though Spanish has got the wrong end of the stick, because the term is almost devoid of knicker-imagery and is how girls and women describe **tights.** On the other hand, the **tights** worn by **dancers** are **un leotardo** although this is yet another motive for muddle since our **leotard** is expressed as a French **maillot.**

A **slip** is revealed as **men's underpants** instead of an expected petticoat; the original name for **a petticoat** was **una enagua** but copywriters, department stores and would-be smart talkers have decreed this sounds nicer when described as **una combinación,** blissfully unaware of the word's ludicrous proximity to **combinations.** Still, this notoriously old-fashioned undergarment does bear a legless resemblance to that now indispensable feature of many wardrobes, an item with a name which is as misleading in English as it is in Spanish: **un body**...

PAINT BOX

To **paint** is **pintar**, a **painter** is **un pintor** and **paint** is **pintura**, three translations posing few problems. Less predictable is a **paint box** – **una caja de pinturas** or **una caja de colores**, a term less childish or amateurish than it sounds, as adults and professionals use it, too. An English **layer of paint** is described as **a coat of paint**, a logical association since a coat is also a covering, but the Spanish equivalent is harder to fathom since it is **una mano de pintura** – **a hand of paint**.

Un pintor can be any kind of **painter** but some differentiate a **house-painter** by calling him **un pintor de brocha gorda**, or **a painter with a fat brush**, since the **paintbrush** used by an artist is **un pincel**.

Pintar fits the bill in situations where colour is added to something or deliberately changed: **Blas pasó las vacaciones pintando el salón** – **Blas spent his holidays painting the parlour**. **Pintar** is the Spanish way **to put on makeup**: **anda, píntate y vámonos** – **come on, put your makeup on and let's go** is the perennial injunction of impatient partners, Spanish or otherwise. **Pintar** is also used for the more specific **to put on lipstick** – **pintarse los labios** and **pintalabios** is the most customary translation for **lipstick**, although older Spaniards continue to refer to it as **carmín**. The word **paint** reappears in **nail varnish** – **pintauñas** although this is also known as **laca de uñas**.

Pintar does not necessarily imply that an artist needs to wield a brush to get something down on paper or canvas, as a Spanish artist tends to use **pintar** for anything involving colour. At the same time, you encounter **pintar** with the popular meaning of **to matter, to be important,** so **Nieves no pinta nada** need not mean **Nieves doesn't paint anything** but also **Nieves is of no importance**. So if Nieves bursts into the parlour while Blas is painting it and he doesn't pay enough attention to her suggestions, she is liable to stalk out muttering, **se ve que aquí no pinto nada – it's plain that I don't count for anything around here.**

Una pintura is understood to be **a painting** but a person who heartily dislikes someone or something will declare **no le quiero ver ni en pintura – I don't want to see him/her even in a painting,** in other words, **I can't bear the sight of him/her**.

The past participle **pintado** obviously means **painted** but it also conveys **perfection, something that is absolutely right: ganar la lotería me vendría que ni pintado – winning the lottery would suit me down to the ground.** When turned into a noun, **una pintada** has separate definitions of **a guinea fowl** in the kitchen and **a graffito** on a wall.

Blas spent his holidays painting the parlour

Pintoresco is easy to pinpoint as **picturesque** but **pinta-rrajeada** is apt for a **badly made-up** or **over made-up woman** and **pintarrajeado** for a **badly-painted** or **garish picture**.

The **painter** that is used to tie up a boat is **una amarra. Una pinta** is **a spot, dot** of the type that appears on material or the wall-paper in Blas's parlour although it can also refer to the way a person looks. Exasperated parents say **¡vaya pinta que tienes!** to teenagers getting ready to go out for the evening and teenagers say the same thing when their parents are all tricked out to go to a wedding. In both instances it means **what on earth do you look like!**

La Pinta, as well as being the name of one of the trio of ships that Columbus took the New World, is an old card game, also known as **La Brisca** although you find the verb **pintar** figures in all card games and indicates the **leading suit** or **palo**.

LUCKY FOR SOME

Luck is **suerte** but its further translations of **fate, destiny, chance** and **fortune** also say something about Spanish feelings about luck. This is emphasised by the way an English-speaker's **to be lucky** becomes **to have luck – tener suerte** although **to be in luck** is **estar de suerte** and the presence of impermanent **estar** should not be lost upon you.

When **luck** is scandalously conspicuous, you meet unexpected words in familiar speech: **tener potra** and **tener chorra**, neither of which lends itself to coherent translation since **potra** means **filly** and **hernia** as well as **luck,** while **chorra** is an **idiot** as well as slang for a male's anatomic unmentionable. On the other hand, something dismissed as **una chorrada** is a slangy **rubbish** or **nonsense,** instead.

To try one's luck is **probar suerte** but **echar suertes** is **to draw lots** while the warning **don't chance your luck** would be translated with the verb **pasar: no te pases. Traer suerte** is easy to identify as **to bring luck,** a construction that is used in preference to our **to be lucky: dicen que el ambar trae buena suerte – they say amber is lucky (brings good luck).**

A transitory **to be in luck** is **estar de enhorabuena:** César está de enhorabuena, pues Fuensanta ha ido a Madrid – **César's in luck because Fuensanta has gone to Madrid.** Really **bad luck** is often described as **suerte de perros – dogs' luck** but if you **are down on your luck** you would use **estar pasándolo mal** or simply **estar mal** which, tellingly, also means **to be ill**. Further down-on-your-luck phrases include **ir mal** or a more explanatory **ir mal las cosas: Fuensanta dice que las cosas le van mal a César últimamente – Fuensanta says things are going badly for César lately.**

On referring to something best not referred-to, a Spaniard might now use our imported superstition and **touch wood** although it used to be more customary to cross one's fingers while intoning **lagarto, lagarto – lizard, lizard to ward off bad luck – quitar el gafe. To be habitually unlucky** is **ser gafe,** as **gafe** is a word that serves as noun or adjective, so **es un gafe** and **es gafe** mean **he's an unlucky person** and **he's unlucky/jinxed** respectively. Both are doom-laden pronouncements guaranteed to ensure that those in the immediate vicinity sidle away, subtly but surely.

Use of **gafe** with permanent, immutable **ser** instead of temporary, mutable **estar** indicates the alleged durability of Spanish bad luck although to make matters really cosy, there's a verb thrown in for good measure: **engafar – to bring bad luck to, to put a jinx on, to put the mockers on. Estar engafado – to be jinxed/cursed** provides a gleam of light at the end of the tunnel, however, by latching itself onto **estar.**

On a more optimistic note, **a stroke of luck** is **un golpe de suerte** but instead of **third time lucky** the Spanish say **a la tercera va la vencida – third time won.** The ironic **just my luck** has no equivalent but this lament is conveyed by the equally resigned **¡vaya suerte! – what luck!** or the considerably more fatalistic **ya lo sabía yo – I just knew it.** The adverb **luckily** becomes the phrase **por suerte: por suerte, mañana tengo el día libre – luckily, I have the day off tomorrow.**

Although **salud** was more usual as a pre-Civil War leave-taking, **suerte** was also used by those averse to the religious implications of **adiós** and many of the middle-aged and elderly still use it unthinkingly. It is also what a bullfighter says to his **cuadrilla – team** when he goes out to fight the bull. The bullfight itself is divided into different phases, each of which is called **una suerte,** as in **la suerte de varas, la suerte de banderillas** and **la suerte de matar** – although no doubt the bull fails to appreciate that luck comes into it at all.

AN EVERYDAY STORY
OF COUNTRY FOLK

Peasant! is a tried and true insult amongst English-speakers and although **¡campesino!** is not a tried and true Spanish insult, some urban Spaniards might not regard it as a compliment. Others would probably look puzzled and explain that they aren't from the country as it happens.

Un campesino is a person who lives in, on or off **the countryside – el campo**, a word that is so popular with foreign residents that they use it when speaking English, too. A Spanish **campesino** often owns the land he cultivates and although in the less visited parts of deepest Spain a chicken or two may still scratch around back doors, there is no shame and a fair amount of pride in being a **countryman**.

The alternative description, **labrador**, can still be a matter of pride in older people and, once again, it provides little in the way of insults. **Un paisano** is another peasant-sounding word you'd be forgiven for translating as **countryman,** although in practice it is nearer to **fellow countryman** and is used by a Spaniard for anyone who comes from his own neck of the woods. **Paisano** also indicates **mufti, plain clothes,** so **un militar vestido de paisano** is an **out-of-uniform soldier** although **un policía de paisano** is **a plainclothes policeman**.

Intended barbs have more chance of hitting home if you use **gañan, paleto, cateto** or **hortera**. The original meaning of **gañan** was **farmhand**, an employee who probably prefers to be known as **un trabajador agrícola** these days. As an exclamation, **¡gañan!** suggests exactly the same mild scorn that an English-speaker conveys with **peasant!**

The first entry in the Diccionario de la Lengua Española for **un cateto** comes straight from a geometry lesson: **either of the sides enclosing the right-angle in a right-angled triangle.** The second is a noncommittal **villager** followed by **yokel,** another favourite insult favoured by city-dwellers. To be called **un paleto** is equally unflattering, as this implies a **yokel** or **bumpkin** who earns a living digging fields or shovelling manure with **una pala – a spade.**

Hortera is an adjective that can accompany a masculine or feminine noun; it can also be used as a noun and nominally describes anything or anyone originating in **la huerta – cultivated land, a market garden. La Huerta** with capital letters refers to the strip of intermittently fertile land stretching from Valencia to Murcia which was responsible for much of that area's affluence before tourism. To the urban poor as well as more austere, less prosperous, inland farmers this affluence was too often manifested by ostentatious bad taste.

In the past when a Spaniard succeeded in making large amounts of money he – it was always a male – immediately tried to merge himself and his family into the landscape and lived and behaved like the established, unostentatious gentry. In our present egalitarian society, wealth is more widely distributed and good taste is no longer a privilege of the privileged – but being labelled **un hortera** or **una hortera** hurts not for being termed **a peasant** but for being considered a **vulgar peasant.**

CHIEF CONCERN

Not only the Spanish but also foreign Spanish-speakers can be unenthusiastic about the way the language is increasingly affected, and sometimes infected, by words of foreign origin – usually English. However, time endows earlier borrowings with a patina of respectability, so a French-influenced word like **jefe** is not only accepted but has a pedigree, too.

You encounter **jefe** in the tribal, clannish sense of **chief, chieftain: el jefe de una tribu india – the chief of an Indian tribe.** Your dictionary may tug eagerly at your sleeve and try to convince you that **a chief, chieftain** is **un cacique** and so he was in the past. The word comes from the Caribbean where it meant **a provincial overlord of vassals**, or the **superior of an Indian tribe or province.** It is now something of an insult in European Spanish when denoting **someone whose position in a town or village has allowed him** (it is rarely a "her") **to accumulate and exercise excessive power in politics or the Administration.** In short, **un cacique** is not inevitably an employer, but still a **Boss** with a capital **B**.

Caciques apart, a Spanish **jefe** also corresponds to a **boss** or **employer** although there still exists the kind of Spanish man who, particularly when occupying a lowly position at work and/or in society, tells wife and children **soy el jefe.** To be fair, his English counterpart would be equally inclined to proclaim **I'm the boss.**

The **leader** or **head** of a non-sporting team is usually described as a **chief: el jefe de los bomberos – the chief of the fire brigade.** A Spaniard often uses **jefe** where we choose **head,** especially when referring to **el Jefe de Estado - the Head of State** who, as in England, is the monarch. The country's political leader is referred to as **el Jefe del Gobierno** or **el Presidente** rather than the **Primer Ministro** which was still common at the beginning of the Transition following Franco's death.

A department head is **un jefe de departamento** and by natural progression, **un jefe** can also be **a manager** as these titles often imply much the same status: **jefe de ventas – sales manager.**

A military **Chief of Staff** is **Jefe de Estado Mayor** while **Commander in Chief** could be translated as **Comandante en Jefe.** Nevertheless, it does not figure in Spanish military usage and **Jefe Supremo** might be nearer the mark although you'll meet **Capitán General,** the head of all three armed forces. This is reserved for the Head of State, so a **General** whose seniority would make him eligible for the rank is **Teniente General – Lieutenant General** instead.

In English we resort to French for another kind of **chief,** the marginally less bellicose but still highly respected and often-feared **chef** whose job description in Spanish is **jefe de cocina.**

Jefe is not used for **chief** when this implies **main: my chief concern is that he won't be able to see her – mi preocupación principal es que no la podrá ver.** In this context not much differentiates **chief** and **principal** in either language, but it is characteristically and pessimistically Spanish that **a concern**

should also be a **worry**. More telling still, **principal** can be substituted by **major** – **mayor: mi mayor preocupación es que no la podrá ver.**

The adjective **chiefly** is unrelated to **jefe** and again makes use of **principal: principalmente, un jefe de cocina sabe que puede hacer exactamente lo que le da la gana – chiefly, a chef knows that he can do exactly what he wants. Principalmente** can also be expressed as **sobre todo – above all.**

Unfortunately, those who dislike being addressed as **chief** still run the risk of being called **jefe** in Spain. Some Spaniards maintain that using **jefe** this way is a relic of the Falange, when this party, also known as El Movimiento and organised on para-military lines, was Spain's one and only. **Jefe**, old Republicans grumble, is what younger members called their immediate superiors in the hierarchy. Regardless of whether **jefe** was in use before the Civil War, a certain type of Spanish-speaker uses it in exactly the same way that a certain type of English-speaker uses **chief** – at a petrol station perhaps, or an ironmonger's: **is that everything, chief? – ¿es todo, jefe?**

BOTHERING YOU

Molestar is an unattractive word. Basically it means nothing more unappetising than **to subject to intentional annoyance** but at best it has an importunate sound and at worst conjures up lurking perverts.

The principal associations of **molestar** and **molestia** are with **bother, irritation: ¿sería mucha molestia dejarme el periódico? – would it be a lot of bother to let me have the newspaper? Molestia** is also used by doctors and their patients to mean a painful symptom, a health problem. Spanish being the way it is and Spaniards being the way they are, **molestias** are frequently suffered in the plural.

The verb **molestar** and the reflexive **molestarse** invariably mean **to bother, annoy, upset** and an inoffensive reaction when someone reads the newspaper over your shoulder or eats with his mouth open would almost certainly be **me estás molestando**. This plaintive but firm little phrase conveys differing shades of displeasure without straying too far from the nominal politeness so necessary to trouble-free relations in Spain, whether domestic or otherwise.

¿Le molesta? ¿te molesta? or simply **¿molesta?** is a Spanish solution to doing what you want while insinuating that the merest hint of protest will make you stop. Nonetheless they are rhetorical questions and the last thing anyone expects is an answer of **sí, me molesta**.

No se moleste and **no te molestes** can be interpreted as a kindly **don't take it to heart, don't upset yourself**. These phrases are often pronounced with a genuine desire to make life easier for others but are also uttered sarcastically when it looks as though a resentful gut will have to be busted on someone else's unappreciative behalf.

Whatever the circumstances, **molestar** succeeds in giving a solicitous impression: **¿te molestaría dejarme el periódico cuando hayas acabado con él?** An English-speaker hoping for a shufti at the Guardian or the Sun would say **can I see the newspaper when you've finished?** but word-for-word translation of the Spanish version is a prolix **would it bother you to let me have the newspaper when you've finished with it?** The length of this sentence is inevitable because Spanish rarely uses one word where three can fit in and Spanish verbs require constant shoring-up by prepositions. But it might also be due to a Spaniard's inborn dislike of having to ask – or answer – an outright question. Consequently, in casual conversation or requests to strangers, **molestia** and **molestar** occur all the time and in the case of the verb, you will commonly encounter the tentative conditional tense.

When a Spaniard can't be bothered to do something he might use **molestarse: no me quiero molestar – I can't be bothered** but he may choose instead to say **me da pereza – it makes me feel lazy; no me apetece – it doesn't appeal to me** or the slightly defiant **no me da la gana**. Each is rather different from our own **not being bothered** but they convey much the same thing to a Spanish-speaker. **Dignarse** means **to deign** and when it crops up negatively this, too, gives the impression of **not bothering: César no se dignó contestar la** carta de Fuensanta – César didn't bother to/deign to anwer Fuensanta's letter.

A person who does not **bother** about what he or she either does, or looks like, is decribed as **descuidado/a, dejado/a** – yet another facet of that many-faceted verb, **dejar – to leave**. At the same time, the pains taken when the painstaking go to **a lot of bother** are expressed by the verb **esmerar**, literally **to polish, brighten** and the adjective, **esmerado**.

That leaves the **bother!** we exclaim in mildly stressful situations. As in English, you have a choice of unprintable exclamations but of the printable, the most satisfying and nearest to **bother!** is **¡maldito sea!** This is as near as dammit to **damn it!** and while it doesn't involve **molestar**, it gets across roughly the same degree of **bother**.

SWEET NOTHINGS

Una rosca is two separate things in Spanish. It is the **thread** of a screw or screw top as well as a **round, biscuity sort of cake with a hole in the middle** – not particularly exotic but more interesting than its distant English relation, **a rusk**. A young male who is not over-successful with the opposite sex might complain to a friend, **no me como ni una rosca**. This sad admission means literally, **I don't even get a biscuity sort of cake etc.** but implies (for want of a better way of putting it) **it's been a long time since I've been intimately involved with a woman.**

It's curious that such an austere turn of phrase should be chosen for such an unaustere activity, especially on pondering the euphemistic possibilities of the cakes, tarts and biscuits on view at a Spanish baker's. Spaniards visiting England sometimes voice surprise at finding so many churches in a protestant country. Britons exploring inland Spanish cities react in much the same way to the many **panaderías – bakeries, pastelerías, reposterías and confiterías – cake shops** that jostle establishments selling the expected **vino, tapas, paella** and **turrón**.

Resort towns and villages have bakeries and cake shops,

What a sweet little home

too, but souvenir shops, estate agencies, travel agencies, bars and restaurants overshadow them. It is necessary to leave the coast behind to sample the calorie-laden plurality of **pastelerías** and discover just how sweet Spain's tooth is. Ask for a **café bombón** (a shot of black coffee poured over an enormous slug of sweetened condensed milk) and it will invariably be served with a packet of sugar in the saucer.

There is no exact Spanish equivalent of **sweet-toothed** but someone who likes sweet things is known as **goloso**, a pretty-sounding word that sounds less pretty when translated as **greedy**. **Una golosina** is one translation for **a sweet** and **un caramelo** is another. This looks as though it should be a caramel and sometimes it will be, but the word applies to any kind of sweet not involving **chocolate** or **turrón**.

A **pudding** or **dessert** is **un postre** although the Spanish are apt to stick to fruit, yoghourt or milk puddings such as **cuajada – junket, flan – caramel cream, natillas – custard** (always cold) and **rice pudding – arroz con leche** (similarly cold and usually flavoured with cinnamon, not nutmeg). There is a pudding called **budín** but don't look forward to apple crumble and steel yourself for something like blancmange, instead. Away from the table, you meet **postre** in the phrase **a la postre – after all: a la postre nos siguen gustando los postres – when all's said and done we still like puddings.**

Despite coddling their digestions and their livers during and after enormous digestion-ruining, liver-blasting meals, the Spanish spoil everything by dashing out and eating cakes with their coffee before they start work or at mid-morning, not forgetting the mighty **merienda** (eaten at approximately our tea-time) which they wedge between **lunch – comida** or **almuerzo** and **dinner – cena**.

A cake, whether individual or big enough to slice is **un pastel** while **tart** is simply **tarta**. A favourite at breakfast and tea-time are **magdalenas**, rather leaden but agreeable **fairy cakes,** although both meals can also feature **bollos – buns and/or substantial, unfancy cakes. Pastas de té** suggest a combination of tea and spaghetti but are **biscuits** a.k.a. **galletas** while **bizcocho**, whose name looks as though it should be related to a biscuit, is nearer in appearance and texture to **plain cake**.

Much that is sweet and Spanish has a religious name or connection, possibly because so many convents maintained (and still maintain) themselves by producing and selling cakes and confectionary. **Huesos de santo**, literally **saints' bones** are **small rolls of marzipan with a sugar and yolk-based filling;** delicious, cholesterol-rich **yemas de Santa Teresa** are again made from egg yolks and sugar but **cabello de angel** or **angels' hair** is a type of **jam** made from the malabar gourd. **Tarta de Santiago** is **almond cake** from Galicia while **Tarta de San Jorge** is a Catalonian speciality.

The sweetest thing of all – **sugar** or **azúcar** – can't make up its mind whether to be masculine or feminine. Described as ambiguous because it is as correct to say **el azúcar** as **la azúcar**, European Spanish-speakers choose the masculine version as it is easier to say. **Azucarar** means **to sugar, sweeten** and the adjective **azucarado – sweetened, sugared** also conveys a **sugary** person or sentiment. **Empalagoso** is appropriate for both food and people who are **oversweet, saccharine, cloying**.

The adjective **sweet** is normally translated as **dulce: hogar,** dulce hogar – home, sweet home; este pastel es demasiado dulce – this cake is too sweet. Dulce turns up in agua dulce – fresh water and is coupled to pimentón – paprika to differentiate from pimentón picante – hot paprika. A Spaniard would probably substitute amable, agradable for an English-speaker's sweet person, reserving dulce for someone who is not only sweet but also gentle and charming and possessed of genuine, not synthetic, dulzura – sweetness.

Un mono is a monkey but as an adjective is synonymous with sweet, nice when applied to females of any age and children of either sex. It can also refer to the disposition or attractiveness of objects of all kinds: ¡qué cuadro más mono! – what a sweet picture! Nevertheless you could just as easily exclaim ¡qué cuadro más salado! and although you're saying what a salty picure! no-one will doubt that you find it sweet.

FANDANGO

When a fan is not an enthusiast it is un abanico, a formerly flirty little item which despite the advent of air-conditioning still fulfils a vital role during Spain's long, hot summers, especially out of doors. The slightly more newfangled electric fan goes off in a different direction to become un ventilador and a car's fan belt is la correa del ventilador.

Returning to abanico, you encounter this in both commercialise and journalese in the sense of selection, range or other similarly vague collective nouns, and un abanico de propuestas is the raft of proposals found in modern English.

As you'd expect, there is an associated verb, abanicar which, as you'd also expect, means to fan, but only in the sense of flapping said fan in order to cool down. When it's a flame you're aiming to fan, the handiest verb is atizar, a word that is also apposite to fanning the flames of passion. Inappositely, ¡atiza! is one of the politer manifestations of Spanish surprise and equivalent to a squeaky-clean golly!

To fan out is usually expressed as desplegar, diseminar, dispersar or, in a military context, avanzar en abanico. All of these turn reflexive as the occasion demands: **desplegó las cartas – he fanned out the cards** or **los policías se desplegaron por las calles de la ciudad – the policemen fanned out through the streets of the city.**

A **fan** who admires **rock** or **pop** is happy to be referred to as **un fan** and is equally happy to join **un club de fans. Un forofo** is another enthusiastic word for **an enthusiast** although the more articulate might prefer to be described as **un/una entusiasta** or **un admirador/una admiradora.** Other options are **un hincha** (feminine-sounding but seldom feminine-looking) and **un aficionado/una aficionada.**

A bullfighting fan is always **un aficionado** while **la afición** is rather like the **fancy** with bulls instead of pigeons. **Una afición** is understood to be **liking, fondness** as well as **a hobby** although an increasing number of people use the English term preceded by a Spanish definite or indefinite article: **un hobby** with **hobbys** as its plural.

Un aficionado can be translated as **an enthusiast, someone who is keen on** or is **a dedicated follower of** something or someone. This word also represents **an amateur** as well as **a person who dedicates a lot of his or her time to sports without financial gain.** The reflexive verb **aficionarse** usually signifies **to become fond of** (something rather than someone) but also hints **at becoming hooked on something** in both an innocuous and less innocuous sense.

A **football fan** might be, but rarely is, described as **un aficionado** and is known as **un hincha.** This above all is the word you meet in connection with a **male football fan,** despite ending in **-a.** Other translations for **hincha** include **ill will, animosity** and **bad blood,** none of which is overwhelmingly reassuring but not surprising when you consider the amount of ill will, animosity and bad blood sometimes stirred up by football. This brings to mind the close relationship between **a fan** and **a fanatic,** which you will have no difficulty in identifying as **un fanático.** To progress from **fanático** to **a fan** doesn't require excessive mental gymnastics and this is the cue to ask when is **a fan not a fan?** When it is **afán,** of course: a noun whose various meanings range from **industry** to **anxiety** and from **urge** to **zeal.**

IT`S ONLY NATURAL

La naturaleza isn't a bad translation for **nature**, particularly the woods, trees, birds and bees Nature that comes equipped with a capital letter, but although you find references to **Mother Nature – Madre Naturaleza** this pagan old lady is basically a foreign migrant. The Spanish are as fond as we are of citing **human nature – la naturaleza humana** as an explanation for weakness, self-indulgence and downright nastiness but **naturaleza** also describes the **nature** that is a **quality: debido a la naturaleza del problema, no sera fácil resolverlo – owing to the nature of the problem it won't by easy to solve.**

When **nature** implies **character** the Spanish prefer **carácter,** so our **he's ill-natured** becomes **tiene mal carácter** but on the more pleasant side, **he's good-natured** is **tiene buen carácter.** As so often happens with Spanish mood and mien, it is necessary to **have** your nature and not **be** it, so you find yourself using **tener – to have.**

Naturaleza combines with **muerta – dead** for a grim **naturaleza muerta** or **still life** which is more likely to be called **un bodegón**, since a classic Spanish **still life** seldom featured Constance Spry flower arrangements. Instead it concentrated on utensils, edibles and other unremarkable objects found in a kitchen or **eating place where ordinary food was prepared in an ordinary way** – in other words, **un bodegón.**

The identical-twin appearance of **natural** looks as though it should pose few translation problems and sometimes it co-operates, so a **natural blonde** is **una rubia natural.** But **leche natural** and **agua natural** mean that **milk** or **water** are at **room temperature** regardless of their purity while food is described as **al natural** if it has been prepared without flavourings or additions. **Zumo natural** is **fresh, pure fruit juice** and this usage has entered the speech of English-speakers in Spain who now ask for **natural fruit juice** in English too.

Natural also means **originating** or **born in: mi suegra es natural de Cuenca – my mother-in-law comes from Cuenca. Es natural que le guste Cuenca** means **it is natural that she should like Cuenca.**

Natural does not appear in a natural dancer which is una bailarina nata, literally a born dancer, but turns up in the princess seemed very natural – la princesa parecía muy natural although a Spaniard would just as soon say la princesa parecía muy sencilla, literally easy, normal. Another option is la princesa parecía muy llana. As with food, when natural is applied to looks, make-up or dress it conveys simplicity and lack of pretension. Unnatural used to be a popular verdict for anything that went against the grain and in Spanish you can choose between anti-natural, no natural, perverso, anormal or afectado.

The adverb naturalmente corresponds to naturally: naturalmente le gusta Cuenca – naturally she likes Cuenca. It also helps to keep you afloat during uninspiring conversations and naturalmente... naturalmente... interspersed with the occasional claro... claro... allows you to sound not only sympathetic and empathetic but fluent, too.

Un naturalista is a nudist and natura looks as though it should fit in somewhere but curiously never crops up in day-to-day conversation. A quick flip though a Spanish-English dictionary may explain why, since the sole definition for natura is nothing more and nothing less than genitals. Oh well, live and learn...

BRIEFLY SPEAKING

English-speakers use verbal shorthand and so do Swedes and Swahilis, but until recently Spanish seemed to prefer the long way round. A truncated hang on a sec' or half a mo' are requests for forbearance when time is short but the Spanish forego brevity with un momento while some tack on a lengthening diminutive and many now add please: un momentito, por favor. The use of -ito is deliberate because Spanish is basically an austere language which resorts to diminutive suffixes to soften plain speaking or the suggestion of discourtesy.

The Spanish still have a horror of being thought bad mannered which, together with a tendency to associate formality with verborrhoea, gave rise in the past to letters which routinely ended with a compassionate **...que Dios le guarde muchos años – may God grant you long life.** Sometimes, for lack of space, solicitous leave-takings were abbreviated to a tangle of initials: **S.S.B.S.M. – Servidor seguro besa su mano: a trusted servant kisses your hand.** These days, of course, **servidor** has an entirely new take on a trusted servant and is your **Internet server.**

Public speakers in Spain are notoriously long-winded and writers often portentously prolix but the sporadic conciseness of Spanish can break through like a ray of sunshine piercing fog. **S.M.** stands for **Su Majestad – His** or **Her Majesty** but **SS.MM.** is an admirably economical **Their Majesties.** This plurality is also responsible for the apparently mystifying abbreviation of **EE.UU.** for **Estados Unidos (United States)** and **CC.OO.** for the trade union, **Comisiones Obreras.**

Less a question of economy and more a matter of laziness and/or convenience is the shortening of **señorita** to **seño**, a popular way of addressing a **female schoolteacher,** whether single or married: **hoy se enfadó la seño conmigo – today Miss got cross with me. El director** is frequently shortened to **el dire**, particularly by schoolchildren in which case it means **headmaster.** Outside school, and particularly in the hotel and catering industry, **director** refers to a **manager** despite the preference of English-speakers for translating this as a not-quite appropriate **director.**

Children's abbreviations have infiltrated adult conversation, so adults say **el super** for **supermercado, la pelu** for **la peluquería** or **hairdresser's, el frigo** for **el frigorífico - refrigerator** and **el cole** instead of **colegio (school)**. Few would shorten **por favor** to **porfa** when speaking to the butcher, a policeman or doctor but wouldn't hesitate to use it with family or friends.

Christian names are shortened or modified, too. **Jesús** becomes **Chus, Concepción** gets contracted to **Concha, Conchi** or **Conchita** and **Merche** is **Mercedes.** Shortening can be minimal and consist of merely dropping a final *a* to turn **María** into **Mari** or the familiar-looking **Mary.** A **Joaquín** of your acquaintance will often be known as **Chimo** while **José María** can be **Josema** or **Chema;** many a **Manuel** is called

Manolo although some answer to **Lolo**, too.

There are **Josés** who prefer to remain **José** but others are happy enough with **Pepe**. **Pepe** is held to be the spoken version of the letters **P.P.** which in more pious times were written after the name of **San José – St. Joseph** and stood for **Padre Putativo – substitute** or **stand-in father**. It's simple enough to trace **Maite** to **María Teresa** and **Toñi** to **Antonio** or **Antonia** but once you realise that the cut-off point in a Spanish name doesn't necessarily come where you'd expect, it's easier to see why **Asunción** answers to **Asun** and **Sebastián** to **Sebas**.

No-one has come up with a convincing explanation for cutting down **Francisco** to **Paco** but it's easy to see the connection between **Enrique, Quique** and **Quico**. Now accepted by the Spanish Royal Academy, **k** was not a Spanish letter, but long before post-modern youth substituted the **c** in **bacalao – cod** and **ocupa** with a **k** to change them into **bakalao – synthesised disco music** or **okupa – squatter**, even the staidest **Quico** would occasionally spell his name as **Kiko**.

ALL AT SEA

A life on the ocean wave is fine for those with sea-legs inside their sea-boots but landlubbers would agree that the Spanish show imagination by translating **the sea** as **el mar** and defining **marear** not only as **to sail** and **to navigate** but also **to be seasick, to make ill, to annoy, to disturb** or **to bother.**

Perhaps the occasional sailor employs the verb **marear** to describe the risky business of **going to sea** but this verb is mostly used in the circumstances already mentioned, which are generally anything but plain sailing.

¡Me estás mareando! is a stock reaction to someone who is being a nuisance: **you're bothering me/getting on my nerves/getting me down** while **¡no me marees!** is the stock injunction: **don't hassle me!** The announcement **estoy mareado** or **estoy mareada** is generally understood to refer to physical discomfort rather than state of mind and covers a wide range of queasiness: **I feel sick, I feel seasick, I feel giddy, I feel**

dizzy or simply **I don't feel too good.** This could also be interpreted as **I've had rather too much to drink** so, as often happens with Spanish diminutives which can herald excess and not moderation, **César estaba un poco mareadito** could easily mean **César was drunk**.

Marear is a prime candidate for reflexiveness, so **me mareo** means **I am seasick, giddy, dizzy etc.** So what's the difference between **estoy mareado** and **me mareo?** There's not a lot in it but there is more urgency when the latter becomes an exclamation, so on hearing ¡**me mareo!** it is advisable to have a brandy or, if the worst comes to the worst, a paper-bag at the ready.

In some circumstances the associated noun, **mareo** means **a nuisance** and complaining **esto es mucho mareo** informs someone that you are put out by his or her demand or request. A questioning ¿**es mucho marear?** – **is it too much of a nuisance?** is an apologetic, much-favoured way of indicating that you are aware of being a nuisance but have no intention of modifying or withdrawing the request that prompted the

When the water is licking around your ankles

question. A self-deprecating **sé que estoy mareando mucho, pero...** followed by your request will generally ensure co-operation and dispel resentment.

Living on the Mediterranean coast it is easy to forget that there are tidal, Atlantic coasts as well. The noun **marea** means **tide: marea alta - high tide; marea baja - low tide**. There are more erudite terms, too: **pleamar** when the water is lapping round your neck, and **bajamar** when it's licking round your ankles.

Marea is used metaphorically in English, but Spanish individualists who **go against the tide** are said to **ir contra la corriente** and fight the **current** instead. Conformists who **go with the tide** let themselves be carried along with it: **ir con la corriente**. Fine phrases like **a rising tide of indignation** exists in Spain too, and retain marine connections: **una oleada de indignación**, literally **a swell of indignation**.

Un maremoto is **a tidal wave** although a spot of straight translation reveals this to be **a sea-quake**. **Marejada** sounds slightly seasick and produces its own quota of wooziness, since it is **a heavy sea** and the diminutive **marejadilla** indicates the same state of affairs, only less so. A word that a certain sort of Spaniard has lately become attached to is **maremagno**, meaning **ocean, abundance** although it is increasingly used to denote **a lot of irritating details** or even **too much work.**

The English slang, **drink,** for **sea** has no Spanish counterpart but if we return to **marear** and scrutinise the word's associations with having drunk more than is advisable you might be interested to learn that a Spanish hangover is **una resaca.** The principal translations for **resaca** are **undercurrent, undertow,** plus the additional but magnificent definitions of **reaction, backlash.** Absolutely no-one would question their aptness on those awful mornings when you've celebrated too well the night before, when you're all at sea, shipwrecked too, and the only words you're capable of uttering are **¡vaya mareo!**

THE QUALITY OF MERCY

You was originally translated as **tú** in the singular and **vos** in the plural, but when wishing to be outstandingly courteous, **vos**

would also be used in the singular as **vous** still is by the French.

To avoid confusion and to differentiate between plural and singular, people started to say **vosotros**, literally **you others** – obviously a forerunner to **you lot.** Unfortunately, once every Tom and Dick was addressed as **vos** by Harry, the word lost much of its tone, and **Vuestra Merced** and **Vuestras Mercedes** began to sound a better way to designate those who were unknown to, or not on familiar terms with, the speaker but merited polite handling.

Meaning **Your Mercy** and **Your Mercies,** they were soon slurred into **Usted** and **Ustedes** when spoken and abbreviated to **Vd.** and **Vds.** when written. When you use them, you are employing the third, not the second, person of a verb: **¿ustedes quieren las sardinas a la plancha o fritas? – do your mercies want their sardines grilled or fried?** Nowadays they are no more than a routine formula, so when somebody in the bus queue complains **perdone usted, pero me está pisando el pie - I'm sorry, but your mercy is treading on my foot –** this conveys contained exasperation and not exquisite reluctance to offend a respected stranger.

Family, close friends, children and animals are addressed as **tú** and **vosotros** while strangers, those who are old and / or possess more authority than the speaker, are addressed as **usted** and **ustedes. Usted** or **ustedes** are used for formal business letters although routine business 'phone calls between people who never meet but carry out the same sort of duties – secretaries for instance – often assume a long distance camaraderie and call each other **tú**.

Young people expect to be called **tú** but address adults who are not relations as **usted** and you realise that middle-age is approaching and encroaching when more and more people refer to you as **usted** but you refer to more and more people as **tú.** In the past, royalty and the clergy addressed subjects or flocks with the singular **tú** and the plural **vosotros.** The unroyal, the unholy and even the holy, answered the priest as **usted** but the King as **vos,** while between themselves the unacquainted laity and commoners settled for **usted** until some degree of acquaintance had been established.

Nowadays it is possible to detect a touch of inverted snobbery attached to **usted.** A person who would previously have considered himself every inch an **usted** tends from the very beginning to **tutear** (the Spanish verb meaning **to use the second person**) those he identifies as equals, but continues ostentatiously to address the cleaning lady or a waiter as **usted.** There is a recent tendency for civil servants who deal with the public as well as doctors and nurses to **tutear** even those who double them in age, presumably to set them at ease.

If someone feels miffed at being called **tú** instead of **your mercy,** he or she will tell you so by not missing a beat but pointedly calling you **usted** in return. However, few are offended when over-democratically addressed as **tú** and still less when the person who gets it wrong is foreign and therefore entitled to a little indulgence when it comes to the intricacies of **you** and **non-you.**

FIRE DRILL

Fire – **fuego** is important in celebrations throughout Mediterranean Spain. Valencia burns **Fallas** on 19th March and the word **falla** even sounds like **fire**, although the link is tenuous, since it is Valencian for **torch, brand**. Ostensibly the **Fallas** celebrations commemorate St. Joseph's day but are also a throwback to equinox festivals. Alicante has superimposed the St. John's Night **Hogueras – Bonfires** on the summer solstice and further south Murcia still has a post-Easter bonfire, **El Entierro de la Sardina**, which is when the faithful would thankfully **Bury the Sardine** after having lived off fish during **Lent – Cuaresma.**

A focal – or should that be aural point? – of all these fiestas as well as smaller, humbler local fiestas in the provinces of Castellón, Valencia and Alicante are **fireworks**. Although you occasionally hear the more antiquated **fuegos de artificio,** collectively they are **fuegos artificiales** while **a set-piece** is **un castillo de fuegos artificiales.**

Fuego is the most common translation for **fire**, but **a fire** that requires extinguishing is **un incendio** and the man who puts it out is **un bombero.** Despite recalling a bomber, the word refers to a fireman's use of **una bomba** which existed as **a pump** long before people started dropping bombs on each other. As for the **fire engine**, this involves neither fire nor engine and is **el coche de bomberos**.

The questions **¿tienes fuego?** and **¿me das fuego?** are the usual way for a smoker to ask **have you got a light?** and **can you give me a light? Fuego** regularly and popularly describes **the burner** or **hob** on a gas or electric cooker and is also encountered in sentences like **Elena dice que el estofado se hace mejor a fuego lento – Elena says stew cooks better on a low** (literally **slow**) **flame**.

Me gusta sentarme al calor del fuego – I like to sit by the warmth of the fire can apply to any sort of fire, indoors or out. Where we might say **they liked to sit round the fire** when it's cold, the Spanish instead refer to the fireplace itself: **les gustaba sentarse alrededor de la chimenea** (and no pats of the back for linking **chimney** to **chimenea**).

Chimenea can also be translated as **hogar**, literally **hearth**, a word which discloses its connections with **hoguera – bonfire**. Both are close in origin to **fuego** since around the 16th century, the f at the beginning of many Spanish words evolved into h, although others, like **fuego**, hung on to it.

To set on fire, to set fire to is **pegar fuego** or **prender fuego. To set fire to** can be translated as **incendiar** whether unintentional or criminal, but **encender** when deliberate and controlled. **Encender** also appears in the non-inflammatory **encender la luz – to put the light on** and the reflexive **incendiarse, encenderse** which both mean **to catch fire**. With relation to pottery, **to fire** is **cocer – to cook,** although **to fire the imagination** is an easy **excitar** or the still-fiery **enardecer**.

To open fire on someone or something is **abrir fuego,** but **to fire a shot – disparar** and **a firing squad – pelotón de fusilamiento** both dispense with fire. **To fire, dismiss** is **despedir**, a verb which in more pleasant circumstances becomes reflexive and has the further meaning of **to say goodbye to.**

The **fire** of passion can be translated as **pasión** or **ardor**. The latter describes **heartburn**, too and it is a toss-up which of these conditions has the greatest impact on the average Spanish male. **Picante** is appropriate for **fiery, spicy food** and as an innuendo this adjective corresponds to an English **spicy, saucy** which is not restricted to food.

Other **fiery** adjectives are **ardiente, apasionado, vehemente** and **fogoso** – a damp, dismal-sounding word that is understood to convey Spanish fire at its most ardent but which these days seems to be aroused only by damp, dismal topics like football or politics.

UTTER BALLS

To **have a ball** in Spanish is an explosive **pasarlo bomba** and you'll have a ball, and possibly bomb now and again, when deciding whether to use **bola, globo, pelota** or **balón** to translate **ball**.

The first definition for **bola** en the Diccionario de la Lengua Española is **a spherical body of any material** and in practice the materials can be poles apart: **una bola de nieve** – a **snowball, una bola de helado** – a **scoop of ice-cream, una bola de fuego** – a **fireball, una bola de billar** – a **billiard ball** as well as a diminutive **bolita de alcánfor** – **mothball**.

Estar hecho una bola would be received as a mild insult by those who are **overweight, plump, well-built** or any of the other euphemisms we substitute for **fat**. Whether you are thin or not, **estar en bolas** refers to state of undress, not size, and means **to be naked**. You sometimes meet **una bola** as a **marble** – what children play with, not what sculptors sculpt with – although **canica** is more popular. **Meter bolas** is slang for **to tell fibs, tall stories**.

Estar hecho un ovillo is to **be curled up into a ball** and is applicable to things, people and animals. The oval-sounding **ovillo** is also **a ball of wool: un ovillo de lana** as well as **cotton** or **linen thread: un ovillo de hilo.**

Not all **balls** are **bolas** and in sport and play they are frequently **pelotas,** although in the kitchen or on the table **una pelota** is an outsize **meatball** sometimes wrapped in a cabbage leaf. **Una pelota de tennis** is **a tennis ball** and **pelota vasca** is familiar even to those who do not speak Spanish as **Pelota,** although there is a Mediterranean version too, **pelota valenciana** or **trinquete. Jugar a la pelota,** as well as a literal and sporting **to play ball,** is also a figurative **co-operate** but **hacer la pelota** is the Spanish way **to suck up to somebody** while **peloteo** is **the act of sucking up. El pelotón** has inched its way into English amongst cycling fans as **the main group of riders in a race** but **estar en pelotas is** yet another way **to be stark naked**.

Un balón is the type of **ball** used in **football – fútbol,** whose original name was a faithfully translated **balompié** with an **m** replacing the **n** of **balón** since Spanish spelling rules do not like an **n** before a **p. Un balón** can also be any kind of **large ball** but not **a balloon,** which is **un globo.**

It doesn't require much imagination to link **a bale** and **una bala** but it's less easy to pin this word down as **a bullet** and almost impossible to pin down the verb **balar** as **to bleat** but not **to bale**. Should you ever need or wish **to bale** this is **embalar,** a word that can be used in the sense of **to pack up, make a parcel** but a nautical **to bale out** is **achicar.**

A **ball-bearing** is **un rodamiento** but an English-speaker's response of **balls!** when in disagreement is an un-anatomical and totally anodyne **¡tonterías!** The Spanish epithet **¡huevos!** - literally **eggs!** tends to be an exclamation and not a contradiction as it is in English although the singular **¡y un huevo!** conveys disagreement and/or scepticism.

The little-used **ballar** is an all-singing, all-dancing **to sing and dance**. The **ball** that's a rather grand **dance** is **un baile** but hardly conjures up tiaras, tails and metres of tulle since this means any and every kind of dance. **Ballroom dancing,** on the other hand, is a less elite kind of ballgame and becomes **bailes de salón**. And there's no need to suffer **drawing room, parlour** or **lounge** qualms as on this occasion at least, **salón** can legitimately be translated as a public **lounge.**

COMPLETE RUBBISH

In Europe, English-speakers refer to **rubbish** while the transatlantic and antipodean favour **garbage** and/or **trash,** but whichever your preference or speech patterns, both are translated as **basura** in Spain.

The **rubbish bin** that moulders noisomely away in the corner of many a kitchen is **el cubo de la basura (un cubo** being a **bucket** and not a geometric figure in this instance). It is a popular ex-pat misconception that the big **rubbish container** to be found on rural roads and urban streets is **una basura** – no doubt because this often bears the legend **"basura"** on its side – but the correct name is **el contenedor de basura.**

The dustman is **el basurero,** and he empties bins into **el camión de la basura** – which ferries the proceeds to the **rubbish dump** or **vertedero**, literally **a tip,** and derived from the verb **verter – to tip, pour.**

A house or room that is dirty and/or untidy is often described as **a tip**, but a Spaniard, and particularly a house-proud Spanish lady, refers to squalid living quarters as **una pocilga** or **pigsty.** Continuing on the piggy theme, much of what we dub **rubbish** because it is useless, substandard or unworthy of consideration can be dubbed **basura,** although it might also be dismissed as **una porquería,** even when not recognisably mucky or unsavoury. This is a favourite with those who feel obliged to combine criticism of the sexually explicit with censure, so it is not unusual to hear a book or film described as **una porquería.** Another rubbishy word is **un bodrio** which strictly speaking doesn't mean **rubbish** but is nonetheless suitable for describing a **trashy, badly-made object.**

Leftovers that find their way into your rubbish bin or dustbin are variously described as **desperdicios, deshechos** or **despojos** and are generally used in the plural when referring to food. **Desperdicios** refer to what can't be made further use of while **deshechos** and **despojos** often describe the kind of **offal** that is so awful it never reaches the table.

When **food** is such **rubbish** that it is inedible, it is **una bazofia,** which is how many older people regard **junk food,** and although this is usually termed **comida rápida**, the younger generation are undiscouraged by the translation of **comida basura.** Not every English-speaker is fond of that junky-sounding pudding, **junket,** but it is popular here and eaten by old and young alike, who know it as **cuajada.** A **junky** or **drug addict** is invariably identified phonetically as **un** or **una yonki.**

A piece of **junk jewellery** as well as a would-be **objet d'art** lacking in quality is **una baratija** but something too

El cubo de basura

quaint or potentially useful to end up in the dustbin is **un trasto.** It's tricky to decide on a word for **junk shop** because although the occasional proprietor insists on referring to it as **una tienda de antigüedades,** most dealers are sufficiently down-to-earth to admit to ownership of **un rastro** or **un rastrillo;** both words mean **a rake,** presumably because these establishments allow a good rake round. Despite week-long competition from nationwide car-boot sales – often expat inspired –Madrid's famous open-air market, **El Rastro**, still sells a marvellous variety of junk each Sunday morning.

As well as a negative verdict on entertainment, food or an objection, **rubbish!** is also a normal if intolerant dismissal of another's views in English. A Spaniard's **¡basura!** or **¡es una basura!** could also be a judgement on entertainment, food or an objection but it isn't the way he habitually expresses disagreement. An everyday reaction could be **¡es una chorrada!** although this refers to something that is **rubbish** because it is absurd.

An earthier reaction is **¡una mierda!** – a retort that would be offensive in English but offends the Spanish considerably less. It is exclaimed far more than its scatological meaning would lead you to believe but nonetheless it is wiser to restrict this to those you know reasonably well, resorting to the less aggressive **¡pamplinas! ¡tonterías!** or **¡bobadas!** for nodding acquaintances. What these words lose in punch they gain in diplomacy and their use protects you from that modern process known as **to rubbish – ponerle verde a alguien,** an inexplicable **to make someone green** or the even more inexplicable **ponerle a parir – make him (or her) give birth.**

THE PAIN IN SPAIN

The noun **dolor** describes **pain: tengo dolor de cabeza – I have a headache** and unlike English where we have *a* pain, the indefinite article is usually omitted. Yet again unlike English, **earache** and **toothache** tend to be described in the plural regardless of how many ears or teeth are bothering you: **tengo dolor de oídos** or **tengo dolor de muelas. Backache** is **dolor de espalda** and **a stomach ache** is **dolor de estómago,** although **stomach** can also be translated as a popular **tripa** or **barriga** so you will meet **dolor de tripa** as well as **dolor de barriga.**

Use of the verb **doler,** followed by the name of the offending organ or member also indicates that things are not in perfect working order: **me duelen los riñones – my kidneys ache/hurt; le duele el dedo gordo – his big toe hurts.** Resist the temptation to use **pena,** which conveys **pain** only in a phrase like **bajo pena de muerte – on pain of death;** otherwise it implies **mental pain, a pity** or **shame.**

Molestar has little in common with its English version but is much-used in medical matters: **me molesta el oído – my ear is bothering me.** A doctor might ask: **¿cuándo empezó usted a notar las molestias? – when did you first notice the trouble?**

As well as hurting or aching, it is possible to be afflicted with **an itch – un picor,** derived from the verb **picar. To smart** is **escocer** but **smarting** is **un escozor, to swell** is **hinchar** and **a swelling** is **un hinchazón,** a word far-removed from **un hincha**

– **a fan** (football, not Lady Windermere's). **Encontrarse mal** or **no encontrarse bien** both get across the idea that you don't have a localised, identifiable pain but still **don't feel well**.

Una enfermedad – **a disease, una dolencia** – **an ailment** and **un trastorno** – **a disorder** are inescapably international and usually recognisable by their medical, Latin-based names. Childhood maladies are labelled differently: **sarampión** – **measles, paperas** – **mumps, varicela** – **chicken pox** although **rubéola** is close to **rubella (German measles)**.

A **stiff neck** is **tortículis** and someone with **indigestion** has it in Spanish, too: **indigestión**. In addition, he or she might complain **estoy empachado/a** – similar to **I'm stuffed** – or suffer the classic Spanish reaction to a blow-out, **tengo angustias**, literally **anguishes**. Inevitably the sufferer will also be writhing with **heart-burn** – **ardor** and **wind** – **aire**.

Those who shy away from the starkness of **diarrhoea** – **diarrea** often prefer **descomposición**, which sounds a hundred times worse. **Piles** are posher when called **haemorrhoids** in English, and **almorranas** are classier when described as **hemorroides** in Spanish. **An abscess** is **un abceso** or **un furúnculo** but non-medical people generally refer to either as **un quiste**, similar to **a cyst**. **A spot** is **un grano** and **a rash** is **una erupción** or **una erupción cutánea** for those who like to be specific.

A **general practitioner** is **un médico de medicina general** and a **family doctor** becomes **un médico de cabecera** – a **bedhead doctor** whatever his bedside manner. Specialists' names tend to correspond in both languages although **un tocólogo is an obstetrician, un traumatólogo** is **an orthopaedic surgeon** and every schoolchild's favourite is the tongue-twisting **otorrinolaringólogo** whose translation is still long, but easier to say: **an ear, nose and throat specialist. Un cardiólogo** is a **heart specialist** and **un estomatólogo** is **a dental surgeon**.

A **pill** is usually **un comprimido** or **una grágea** when sugar-coated; **una cápsula** needs no translation while **pomada** and **crema** aren't too hard to recognise as **ointment**. Spanish doctors are less keen than they were on prescribing **suppositories** – **supositorios** for just about everything but the older ones still prescribe them for **tonsillitis** – **anginas** or **amigdalitis** in what they obviously consider a rearguard attack. Second best is **an injection – una inyección** administered by **un practicante** or **una practicante,** the equivalent of a **state-registered nurse**.

The Spanish are often accused of being a race of hypochondriacs – but who could blame them in a country where women's names include **Angustias** and **Dolores**? On the other hand, at least they are far-sighted, because daughters can also be named **Socorro – Help, Salud – Health** and **Remedios – Remedies**.

ONLY JOKING

What used to raise a laugh in Spain rarely had much in common with what amused an English-speaker although the gap between the two senses of humour is closing noticeably. Mirth here belonged to a less benevolent society and placed uncharitable emphasis on mocking the tribulations of others, perhaps because the Spanish used to find it easier to laugh at others than at themselves. Things began to change when they realised that other nationalities disapproved of the way they were entertained by the weak, the susceptible or the defenceless. Privately if not collectively, though, older people continue to laugh at the same things. Ingrained, inherited habits die hard and it is no coincidence that Spain is the home of black humour.

A sideways look at a country's **sayings – refranes** and **proverbs** – sheds light on its awareness of the absurd, however, and gives a tangential hint or two about how and why people are amused. Not that there's much to provoke a smile in the sayings that exactly match ours: **buscar una aguja en un pajar – to look for a needle in a haystack; perro ladrador, poco mordedor – his bark is worse than his bite** and **escoba nueva barre bien – a new broom sweeps clean.**

Others are more revealing, though: **buen abogado, mal vecino – a good lawyer makes a bad neighbour; gato con guantes no caza ratones – a cat with gloves catches no mice** and, finally, the supremely cynical **del agua mansa me libre**

Dios, que de la brava me guardaré yo. It corresponds to **still waters run deep,** but its literal translation is **God protect me from the calm water, from the turbulent I'll protect myself.**

These tell slightly more about Spanish humour but it is more instructive to ponder on **éramos pocos y parió la abuela; si no te gusta el caldo, pues dos tazas** or **monta un circo y le crecen los enanos.** The first explains the melancholy Spanish sense of the ridiculous, the second illustrates the melancholy Spanish tendency to expect the worst and the third demonstrates the melancholy Spanish acceptance that the worst will happen.

The literal translation of **éramos pocos y parió la abuela** is **there weren't many of us and Grandma gave birth.** This is a variation on **the straw that broke the camel's back** but the joke is that the phrase means precisely the opposite to what it says. With not enough room to swing a cat, Grandma – not supposed to be of childbearing age – complicates things by adding another occupant.

Si no te gusta el caldo, pues dos tazas means **if you don't like soup, you get two bowls** and implies that aversion to something dooms you to having it shoved down your throat. The quite modern **monta un circo y le crecen los enanos** conjures up someone who has such bad luck **that if he put on a circus, the dwarfs would grow.**

If you still can't see that any of these illustrate the Spanish sense of humour, it hardly matters. The Spanish themselves don't always understand or appreciate each other's jokes, especially those who live in regions separated not only by geography but also language. Understanding the punch line of Spanish jokes entails more than vocabulary and never guarantees that you will split your sides with laughter.

All would agree, however, that the Spanish for **a joke** is **un chiste** which means any kind of funny story: **Nieves me contó un chiste muy gracioso – Nieves told me a very funny joke.** Also capable of raising a laugh is **una broma,** together with the verb **bromear.** These convey the joke one person plays on another or something not to be taken seriously: **Fuensanta dijo que César le gastó una broma muy pesada ayer – Fuensanta said that César played a stupid joke on her yesterday** as well as **César estaba bromeando cuando dijo** que se iba a casar con Fuensanta – César was joking/wasn't serious when he said he was going to marry Fuensanta.

When you can't see the funny side of something, mutter **no veo el chiste** - I don't get the joke and **no veo la gracia - I don't see what's funny** but if you're stony-faced because you haven't understood it, use **entender – to understand** or **caer – to fall: no entiendo el chiste; no caigo en el chiste,** or simply **no caigo. No veo la broma** or **no caigo en la broma** are closer to what you say when other people are laughing – at worst you, and at best something you are not privy to.

Jokey verbs are **bromear** and **gastar una broma** when playing a joke, but telling one is **contar un chiste** – not **chistar.** One definition of **chistar** is **to draw attention to** but **César lo hizo sin chistar** means **César did it without saying a word.** This doesn't necessarily signify that he did it silently but that he did it without complaining, confirming that there's nothing funny about **chistar** – or many a **chiste español** for that matter.

NAMESAKES

Although Spanish society used to be irredeemably male-orientated, women never lost their surnames on marriage as they did in English-speaking countries and a child here inherits not only the father's but also the mother's surname. In earlier times when children tended to be born – if not always conceived - in wedlock, those who were not and whose fathers declined to acknowledge them would be saddled with the additional burden of going through life with only his mother's surname.

Nevertheless, although Spain was paralytically rigid on the surface and the rules were never openly flouted, they were often bent. In the days before divorce, couples did occasionally separate and many a baby from the second relationship was registered in the **local records – registro** and **Libro de Familia – Family Book** (a small personal register issued on marriage) as though born to its father's legal wife. Any man who could afford the expense (and many who could not) had a **mistress,** who would be referred to as his **querida – loved one.** Less-loved by his wife, she would unlovingly describe

la querida as **la otra – the other**.

Surnames, whether contributed by husbands, wives, lovers or mistresses, are usually derived from occupations, place-names or nationalities as well as parents' and family names or nicknames. In a world where most people need to earn a living, many are tied to occupations old and new: **Mayordomo – Butler, Tejero – Tiler, Pastor – Shepherd, Panadero – Baker, Escribano – Scrivener, Tornero/Torner – Turner, Batanero – Fuller, Sastre – Tailor**.

Christian names appear as surnames, too: **María/Marías, Elvira, Elena, Ricardo, Bautista.** They can also bear a built-in **–ez**, the equivalent of an English **–son: González – son of Gonzálo; Benítez – son of Benito; Álvarez – son of Álvaro; Giménez – son of Giméno; Estebánez – son of Esteban.**

Towns, cities, provinces, countries or nationalities account for many Spanish surnames: **Soler, Ocaña, Castilla, España, Catalán/Catalá, Toledo, Madrid, Sevilla, Bilbao, Inglés, Francés, Alemán/Alemany** and so on and so on from one end of Spain to the other, and half-way across Europe, too.

The prefixes **Ben-** and **Ab-** usually denote Jewish or Moslem origin, but city surnames – **Madrid, Toledo** etc. – often indicate Jewish or Moorish ancestry too. This is due to the determination of the **Reyes Católicos – Catholic Monarchs** to deport all Jews and Moslems. Those who stayed were obliged to convert to Christianity and many changed their names, adopting the name of the city where they lived. Others chose a saint's name: **San Juan/Sanjuan, Santamaría, San Pedro/ Sampedro** (the **–n** becoming an **–m** because Spanish usage decrees it must).

When a first name is used as a surname, it is often preceded by **de: Pepito de Juan, Fausto de Andrés**. The same thing happens when a surname is a noun, either proper or common: **Alicia de España, Genoveva de la Rosa** (also spelt **Delarrosa**), **Margarita del Pozo** (well).

Some are obvious nicknames: **Rubio – Blond, Blanco – White, Valiente – Valiant** for instance, that echo English surnames, while others like **Mago – Magician, Regatero – Bargainer, Izquierdo – Left**, do not. Others recall an employer or landmark: **Conde – Count, Barón – Baron, Molino – Mill, Castillo – Castle, Sala – Hall**.

Possibly out of misplaced gentility or the erratic spelling of earlier times, trade surnames were modified in English, giving **Tyler, Shephard, Taylor**. In Spanish this tends to happen with surnames derived from nicknames and landmarks, often in the form of a gender change. **Rizo – Curl** becomes **Riza** while **Ribera/Ribero/Rivera/Rivero** must all have been associated with a **riverbank** at some stage. Spanish surnames are often plural where ours aren't and vice-versa: **Tapias – Wall, Prado – Meadows**; occasionally they correspond exactly: **Campos – Fields, Arenas – Sands**.

Before migrations and emigration, the prefixes in **Macdonald, Fitzgerald, Tremayne** were instant geographic markers for British surnames. Similarly, **Ll** at the beginning or end of a name indicated Valencian, Catalonian or Balearic origin, as did surnames ending in –á: **Llinares, Ripoll, Durá**. **-Uru, -egui, -echea, -alday** are classic Basque endings and **González, Hernández** and **Fernández** were originally Asturian surnames while you find **Márquez, Marín** or **Carrasco** in Andalusia. Other surnames traditionally – but not exclusively – belonged to gypsies: **Carmona, Cortés, Montés, Montoya, Correa, Giménez/Jiménez, Reyes, Heredia**.

Every language possesses surnames that defy categorisation and sometimes their owners must regret that legal name-changing in Spain is such a palaver. Like the gentleman overheard spelling out his name to a doctor's receptionist. With the weary air of one who knows what to expect because it has happened so often before, he reluctantly spelt out **J-o-d-a-s**. The startled young woman looked up. **¡No Jodas!** she exclaimed, a favourite but extremely rude phrase approximate to **You don't say!**

MOTHERS AND FATHERS

In the bad old, sexist, pre-video game days, Mothers and Fathers was perhaps the only game where very small girls could play with very small boys on something approaching equal terms. Spanish children playing at **mothers and fathers** used to call it **jugar a las mamás y los papás**, an oddity in itself, because a Spaniard always referred to **my mother and father** as a collective, comprehensive **padres**, literally **fathers**. Outside influences have recently introduced the concept of a couple formed by a separate **madre y padre** but in the meantime a collective **mother and father,** as well as **parents,** remain **padres**, particularly in the minds of the middle-aged and over.

Look up the entry for **father** in the Spanish Royal Academy's Diccionario de la Lengua Española and you will see that the entry for the word **padre** is about 56 lines long, give or take a line or so to allow for the point half-way down where your eyes cross and you lose your place. The entry for **madre** – again making the same allowances for inaccuracy – is about ten lines shorter. Not surprisingly, apart from the biological definitions of **a man who has fathered a child**, the word **padre** or others involving it, all concern authority, leadership and dominance. Celibacy does not prevent a priest from being considered a **padre**, although he will be a **padre espiritual** thanks to his authority over parishioners or patrons.

The male and female heads of religious communities also receive the title of **padre** and **madre** although when addressing them or members of the priesthood it is more usual to use their names, preceded by a respectful **don: nuestro párroco, don Felipe – our parish priest, don Felipe** or **doña: la abadesa, doña Inés – the abbess, doña Inés.**

As well as **a woman who has borne a child**, terms incorporating **madre** in Spanish embrace **networks, frameworks** and **ramifications** so **the principal canal in an irrigation system** is **la acequía madre**. A **main drain** is **una alcantarilla madre** while the **principal beam** or **column** in a building, structure or mechanical object will be described as **la madre**.

When the habitually emphatic Spanish wish to make a super-emphatic comparison, they often resort to **padre: no presto dinero a nadie, ni a mi padre – I don't lend money to anyone, not even my father**. The exclamation ¡**tu padre!** is an irritated reaction to an action or statement that doesn't meet with the exclaimer's approval. In contrast, to describe anything as **de padre y muy señor mío** underlines its intensity or magnitude. It's not easy to provide a word-for-word translation of **le echó una bronca de padre y muy señor mío** but **he gave him a hell of a telling-off** gives an intimation of what went on during the exchange. An unaccompanied **padre** also indicates ructions: **me echó una bronca padre – he gave me an awful telling-off.**

Mentar a la madre de uno – to name someone's mother might not sound too contentious to an English-speakers' ears but is part of that very Latin custom of insulting a person through his or her mother. This is why **hijo de puta/hija de puta – son/daughter of a whore** is even now a very nasty thing to call someone. On the other hand, the proclamation that something **es de la puta madre** is a compliment meaning it is very special indeed, although again the phrase is hard to convey despite the fact that each word is easy enough to translate.

¡Tu madre! is found in identical circumstances to **¡tu padre!** but **¡mi madre!** suggests more surprise than ire and this, together with **¡madre mía!** contains its quota of exasperation, too. **¡La madre que te parió – the mother who bore you** can be another insult, but in the elliptical way of Spanish sayings, **¡viva la madre que te parió!** twists back on itself to become a lavish compliment when addressed by a male to an attractive female.

After generations of huge, not always desired or required families, Spain's birthrate is now the lowest in the European Union but verbal tradition still lays emphasis on the importance of a mother's role. So much so, that **desmadrarse**, despite its original meaning of **to wean, separate livestock from the mother** – or because of it, perhaps? – now means **to rebel**. Similarly, the noun **desmadre**, originally **the act of weaning**, is **excess, an out-of-hand situation** although no-one seems to have asked stockbreeders or nursing mothers for their thoughts on the juxtaposition.

BARRACK ROOM BALLADS

It looks as though it's going to be **a barracks**, but **una barraca** is **a hut** or **cabin**, while in the Valencia region it is much the same thing but finished with a steeply pitched (and often thatched) roof.

The more complicated kind of dictionary muddles matters by giving **a barracks** as one meaning for **barraca** while having the decency to explain that it is a Latin American military term. You often find that familiar-looking words turn out to be unhelpfully different in European Spanish but reacquire their suspected translations in Latin American Spanish. Thus you get **una parada** for **a parade** although there is no valid reason for not calling it **un desfile,** because **una parada** is the **stop** where you wait for a bus or taxi, or the **stop** made by a bus or train. As a noun, **una parada** could also denote **an unemployed woman** or, more popularly, **a too-meek, too-lethargic, not sufficiently pushy female.**

Many are beginning to prefer **presente** for what you receive on your birthday, although **un regalo** is more traditional and **presente** should continue to describe the sort that there's no time like.

Paradoxically, non-Spanish Spanish-speakers can get more het up about these modern modifications than the Spanish themselves, who often fail to see what the fuss is about. Occasionally they get mildly resentful at foreign intervention and policing of what is, after all, their own language. Because of this, the apparent relationship, actual estrangement and occasional ambiguity of some translations provoke surprisingly little friction and more raised eyebrows than tempers.

A compromise is **una transigencia, una concesión** but not the tempting **compromiso** that corresponds to an English **obligation** or **commitment**. The two only overlap when translating an embarrassing, endangering **to compromise**, expressed as **comprometer,** although you're increasingly likely to encounter **compromiso** where in the past you would have found **transigencia, concesión.**

La Peste is not a female nuisance but **the Plague** while the verb **apestar** can mean **to infect with the plague.** It has a secondary definition of **to stink** and is appropriate for many stinking English situations, too: **apestas a colonia – you reek of cologne.**

Another verb, **airar** has little to do with the **airing** my grandmother insisted upon to the extent that even handkerchiefs went onto the clothes' horse. The correct translation for **airar** is **to anger,** while the reflexive **airarse** means **to get angry.** However, if you too would like to air your handkerchiefs, insert an **-e** and stick to **airear** instead, although more opinions and grievances get aired in the Mediterranean than clothes. It is tempting to translate **un caballete** as **a clothes horse,** due to its apparently equine associations, but this is **an easel** and the closest you get to **a clothes horse** is the collapsible **tendedero** seen on many Spanish balconies or in the **utility room** which is still described as **un lavadero.**

Although **ir de etiqueta** is **to wear formal evening dress** you will find that **una etiqueta** is **a label, ticket, tag** while our **etiquette** becomes **protocolo.** Meanwhile the **ticket** spat out by scales and weighing machines is universally accepted as a phonetic **tiqué** which has spawned the commercially indispensable verb, **ticar,** as in a shop assistant's **espere un momento, que no he ticado el jamón – hold on a moment, I haven't rung up the ham.**

Neither will you find **un sauce** in your gravy boat, as this is **a willow tree. Remover** means **to stir** but not **remove** which is **quitar** and the verb **acomodar** means **to make comfortable** while **una cómoda** is a **chest of drawers. Ajustar** means **to tighten, fit** or **fasten** more often than it means **to adjust**, an activity expressed as **modificar** or, when adjusting to situations or people's plans, **adaptar.**

As for **a barrackroom ballad,** soldiers would call it **una canción cuartelera** although **una balada** obliges by being **a ballad.** Continents away, however, you find the almost identical **baladí** whose original Arabic meaning was **of national, not foreign, origin.** That's because the grass is generally greener elsewhere so it is not remarkable that it should have come to mean **worthless, trashy, paltry** or **trifling** – rather like those imported mutants that are so much more appealing than familiar, homegrown words.

VETTING PROCESS

Owning an animal, however healthy, entails visits to a **veterinary surgeon**, a term most of us shorten to **vet**, although the Spanish prefer **el veterinario** or **la veterinaria**. The **vet's surgery** is **la consulta del veterinario/de la veterinaria** and a veterinary clinic is **una clínica veterinaria**. Take care, though, because **veterinaria** can easily be confused with the accented **veteranería** meaning **seniority, long service** and **wide experience**.

Routine visits usually involve an **inoculation** and/or **a vaccination** – the easy-to-guess **inoculación** and **vacuna** but, as in English, they are often lumped together and referred to as **inyecciones - injections**. Some ailments such as **distemper – moquillo, mange – sarna, ringworm – tiña** and **worms – lombrices/parásitos internos** are exclusive to animals, but terms for an off-colour human also describe a poorly pet: **he/she isn't well – él/ella/ no está bien; isn't eating – no come; tiene fiebre – has a temperature; moquea mucho – has a runny nose; tiene legañas – has weepy eyes**. Or an owner might simply want to say **I'm worried about Caesar, Fido** or **Jock** in which case you'd say **me preocupa Caesar, Fido** or **Jock**.

However much you like your animal and however anthropomorphic you might feel about he, she or it, some portions of their anatomies don't coincide with ours and on visits to the vet you will almost certainly need to refer to, or identify, them. **A tail** is **un rabo** or **una cola; a snout** is **un hocico** or **un morro**, and a **cat's** or **dog's leg** is **una pata**. Confusingly, **a paw** can also be translated as **una pata**, since **una zarpa** applies only to **a paw equipped with claws**. **Whiskers** are **bigotes**, an animal's **fur** is **pelo** or **pelaje**, and its **coat** is an **abrigo**, literally **an overcoat**.

Translations for **claw** depend on the animal in question, so a bird or a lion has **garras** but those belonging to a **dog, guinea-pig, mouse** or **cat** – as well as our own **fingernails** – are **uñas**. The **pad** on a paw, as well as the pad on a human fingertip is **una yema**, a word you may have previously associated with an **egg yolk**.

Although it is a tragedy that diminishes beside war, earthquake and famine, the fate of an incurable or untreatable

I´m worried about Caesar, Fido...

animal still clouds a sunny day and saddens a normally happy heart. **To put down** is hard to express in Spanish, as the compassionate-sounding **sacrificar** is more appropriate to the **putting down** of **horses** or **cattle** as well as large-scale killing in a slaughterhouse. Vets tend to resort to comforting phrases like **euthanasia – eutanasia, una inyección para dormirlo/dormirla – an injection to put him/her to sleep** or **una inyección para poner fin a su sufrimiento – an injection to put an end to his/her suffering**. Only the hardest-hitting and toughest-speaking would use a stark **inyección letal**.

Many Spaniards dislike using a euphemism when a good, plain word will do, so our genteel verb **to doctor** is substituted by good, plain **castrar**. Countrymen or farmers often use the less articulate **capar** and both continue to use **capar** as well as **castrar** for **sterilising** or **spaying** a female animal, although a

265

vet would be more likely to say **esterilizar** or **practicar una histerectomía.**

Foreign cat-owners will probably be unsporting enough to curtail a male's idyllic countryside prowls and orgiastic nights out on the tiles, but Spanish men are still appalled at the callousness of doctoring a tom. This squeamishness may be due to the way that an unanaesthetised tomcat used to be bundled into a box with a strategically situated opening that allowed the vet to wield his knife without meeting violent opposition. In a country where domestic animals were required to earn their keep, it is understandable that male Spaniards were not renowned for their devotion to house pets – but when it came to carving up a tom-cat's love-life, they were as anthropomorphic as anyone else.

LETTERING

If, like Fats Waller, you sit right down and write yourself **una letra**, don't expect much of a reply because **una letra** is merely one letter of the alphabet, not something your postman delivers.

Letra often turns up in Spanish as a translation for script or type: **letra negrita** – bold type; **letra gótica** – gothic script; **letra cursiva** – italic script. Italics are **letra bastardilla** and this must be because printers regard them as less legitimate than good, upstanding script. The **letters** of an acronym or abbreviation are called **siglas** while **block letters** are **letra de molde,** but **capital, upper case letters** are **mayúsculas,** and lower case letters are **minúsculas.**

Good handwriting is **buena letra** and **bad handwriting** is **mala letra. Puño y letra,** literally **fist and letter,** sounds threatening, but **la reina firmó la carta de su puño y letra** is an unagressive **the queen signed the letter in her own hand. La letra** is also the Spanish equivalent of a song lyric and the person who writes it is **el letrista.** At the other end of the scale, the Spanish liking for diminutives can turn **letra** into **letrita** but you will soon discover that **una letrina** is **a latrine,** not **a little letter.**

Your dictionary might confirm the use of **letra** in **letter of** credit – **letra de crédito,** but this is more usually described as **una carta de crédito**. In financial circumstances **letras** or **letras de cambio** are similar to **promissory notes** and invariably turn out to be the financial version of having one's sins come home to roost.

The plural, capitalised **Letras** has no exact English equivalent and to translate it many English-speakers would choose the French **Belles Lettres**, rather than the obvious **Letters** although both sound rather archaic for the beginning of the 21st century. **Literature** provides another option, as well as a correspondingly plural **Arts: un estudiante de Letras – an Arts Student.** Watch out though, as your paint-stained **art student** is **un estudiante de Bellas Artes**.

Hacer a la letra, obedecer a la letra or **al pie de la letra** all translate **to do something** or **obey instructions to the letter. To letter** is **rotular** or a dictionary's unwieldy and virtually unused suggestion, **estampar con letras** but **deletrear** means **to spell out in letters.**

Un letrero is a **sign, placard, poster, notice** but although **un letrado/una letrada** could refer to anyone with letters after his or her name, this usually implies a **lawyer – abogado.** As in English-speaking countries, some **letrados** do most of their business from **a law office – un bufete** while others correspond to the **counsel** who makes court appearances.

A letter that is sealed into an envelope, stamped and eventually delivered by the **postman – cartero** is **una carta,** although **una carta postal** is **a postcard.** Older Spaniards still refer to **one sheet of writing paper** as **una carta,** a relic from the days when not everyone could read or write with ease and letters rarely ran to a second page. Spanish front doors do not always have provision for the kind of **letter-box** that we are familiar with, so **un buzón** generally bears more resemblance to a **private mail box** and also describes a **pillar-box**.

As well as letter, chart and charter, la carta is what a Spaniard asks for in a restaurant when he wants the menu. Most English-speakers will have discovered long ago that a request for un menú gets you un menú del día – and that can turn out to be an entirely different mess of pottage.

IN THE DRINK

The belief that you rarely see a drunken Spaniard figures prominently in expat folklore and is partly true, because Spanish and the drinking patterns of English-speakers differ radically. For the majority of Spaniards, to **drink – beber** is concomitant to food or, in the case of brandy and liqueurs, the **period following meals – la sobremesa**. Even the **glass of beer – caña de cerveza** or **glass of wine – chato de vino** ordered in an inland or city bar will be accompanied by an unordered **tapa**.

In resorts, the practice is not always observed, as many foreigners are content merely to **drink without food – beber a palo seco**. The Spanish regard this as unhealthy, so when ordering drinks they ask for **una tapa** or at least **aceitunas – olives** or possibly **peanuts – cacahuetes**, known to the jocular as **jamón de mono – monkey's ham** because they are cheap but no substitute for a plate of **jamón serrano**. They might request **algo para picar** or, depending on the time of the day, **el aperitivo**. We tend to regard an **aperitif** as a **pre-meal drink** but in Spanish it can include what accompanies it. Spanish also saves you time and trouble by allowing **aperitivo** to cover a medical **aperitive** and the non-medical but occasionally medicinal **aperitif**.

Spain drinks **wine – vino** in large amounts and until Coca Cola muscled its way onto every table, wine-drinking started early. It would be suitably diluted with water or **gaseosa**, a **carbonated soft drink** invariably referred to by the best-known brand, **Casera**. Beer is drunk with meals too, although connoisseur beer-drinkers claim that the national brew no longer tastes of anything in particular. Each region had its own **breweries – cervecerías** and although those remaining now trickle into each other's territories, **madrileños** still prefer **Mahou**, those from the South like **Cruzcampo** and in Levante they go – predictably – for **Estrella de Levante**. A weakness for drinking beer with meals like **paella** is largely to blame for Spanish indigestion, which is intermittently ignored or pandered to with hefty doses of post-meal bicarbonate of soda. Spain must be one of the few places where a waiter will, if requested, present **el bicarbonato** at the end of a meal as ceremoniously as the preceding courses.

There's more to Spain's drinking habits than wine, beer and brandy as they also put away large amounts of what used to be called champagne. This must now be referred to as **cava** to placate the French although older Spaniards invariably forget and ask for **champán**. For the same Gallic reason, **brandy** should not be – but still is – described as **coñac**. Since a Spaniard tends to swallow a consonant at the end of a word, this often emerges as **coñá** but they make a better job of **whisky**, which is spelt **güisqui**.

The Spanish don't use the term **spirits** as we do and **alcohol** – from the Arabic **al-Kuhul** – is often synonymous with **drink** itself: **el alcohol es la maldición de la clase trabajadora – drink is the curse of the working class.** Rather than **liquor, licor** mostly describes a sweet sticky **liqueur** like **anís** or **chinchón** although both are available in dry versions, too.

You rarely see a Spaniard the worse for drink but this does not infer that they don´t get drunk, merely that you don't always realise when they are. There are various ways to describe **inebriety** in Spanish: the illogical-looking **ebrio**, together with **embriagado, borracho** and the logical **bebido,** the past participle of **beber – to drink.** You can use **intoxicado** but this, together with the verb **intoxicar**, is also used in connection with eating, drinking or inhaling something that is **contaminated.** To **become drunk** is often expressed as **coger una trompa. Una trompa** means **a horn** (on a musical instrument, not a cow) and also **a trunk** (an elephant's, not luggage) but it is anyone's guess as to which is grasped when drinking too much. Much more vulgar is **coger una moñiga,** a bowdlerisation of **una boñiga – cowpat** or good old **dung.** More vulgar still is **coger un pedo,** a flatulently quaint saying that involves **breaking wind.**

On the whole, Spanish society is less self-conscious than ours about drink and alcohol – for where else would you hear a Christmas carol with **beben y beben y vuelven a beber – they drink and drink and drink again** for a chorus? Admitted, it refers to **los peces en el río – the fish in the river** and not people – but it's easier to sing this sort of thing if you've had wine and Casera with your meals since childhood.

269

WEATHER OR NOT

Spanish weather **does** but English weather **is** and anyone who was so inclined might detect something faintly philosophical or mildly metaphysical about the way Juan García says **hace frío – it makes cold** and John Smith says **it is cold.**

In English we **feel cold** or **warm** but in the same circumstances a Spaniard has no feelings to speak of and regards himself as being less of a victim and more in control of the situation. He *has* **cold** or **warmth** instead of enduring them: **tengo frío, tengo calor.** Poor old John says **I am cold, I am warm** and it's obvious that a Spanish relationship with the weather is conducted on a different plane.

The word **weather – tiempo** can also be translated as time: **¿qué tiempo hace? – what's the weather like?** and **hace tiempo que no te veo – it's some time since I've seen you.**

Then there is **temporal**, a word that means **storm, tempest, squall** depending on what it's doing when you're caught with your umbrella down, not forgetting **un temporal de nieve – a blizzard**. However, **temporal** also means **temporary, not enduring** which is usually true of Spanish storms, squalls and blizzards.

A Spanish-English dictionary tells you **wind** is **viento** but you hear it described as **aire** whether it's blowing a gale or gently ruffling your hair: **¡qué aire hace hoy! – how windy it is today!** as well as **¡que aire más agradable! – what a pleasant breeze!** On the other hand, when J. García complains **tengo aire** he is in the same bloated boat as J. Smith who moans **I've got wind.**

A gale, when not translated as **un temporal** or **aire** is **un vendaval**. **A shower** can be **un chubasco** or **un chaparrón** while **a storm** is variously described as **una tempestad, una borrasca** or **una tormenta**. This should not be confused with the masculine noun **tormento** meaning **torment** or **torture.**

Good weather is uneventful and undramatic so it is dismissed as **buen tiempo. A nice day** is **un buen día** and on a fine day in the depths of winter you are likely to say or hear **hace un día de primavera – it's** (like) **a spring day.**

The Spanish enjoy complaining when it's hot and protest

270

¡vaya calor que hace! – how hot it is! or estoy asando – I'm roasting. Some will sit indoors all summer long with the blinds drawn, only peering through the slats every now and again to exclaim ¡mira como la gente se está achicharrando en la calle/playa – look how the people in the street/on the beach are frying themselves!

A heat wave is an unchanged ola de calor but you will now have the privilege of experiencing a cold wave, too: una ola de frío. When this happens as it does most winters, everyone shivers and says heroically yet masochistically estoy helado – I'm frozen and hace un frío que pela – it's cold enough to peel you.

SHOPPING LIST

A shop is una tienda but many Spaniards still call it un comercio especially when generalising instead of naming one type in particular. It is a self-explanatory name which sounds less enticing to the young who often prefer to spend their money in a similarly self-explanatory boutique. Nevertheless, all generations enjoy whipping out a credit card – tarjeta de crédito in department stores – grandes almacenes.

Shopping in Spain used to be a frustrating experience because an orderly queue – cola was not deemed essential. Fish and meat were mainly sold from market stalls – puestos de mercado which opened only in the morning. Acquiring food required fortitude and such a thick skin that tongue-tied foreigners often went hungry or shopped at the last moment when earlier, pushier customers were at home preparing lunch.

The Spanish now queue because supermarkets as well as the busier market stalls oblige a customer – un cliente to tear off a numbered ticket. This English word has the crossbred translation of tiqué and once acquired it is necessary to wait with docility until the corresponding number appears on a small screen.

This has eradicated randomness and peril from food shopping but doesn't mean you can relax entirely. It is advisable to learn to count up to a hundred as the assistant -

dependiente/dependienta will also bellow out the displayed number. On seeing and/or hearing your **number – número** it's up to you to respond with a corresponding bellow of **¡aquí! ¡yo! ¡soy yo!** or a calmer **me toca a mí.** If you opt for the last, you are using the verb **tocar – to touch, feel, handle** in a situation where you wouldn't in English.

When business is slack and customers sparse, people don't bother to take a ticket and the assistant won't demand it. If you encounter only one or two people palely loitering, it is prudent to ask if the numbering system is operating with **¿esto va por número?** When the answer is **no,** ask **¿quién es la última?** or if there is a token male, **¿quién es el último?** Someone will answer **yo** and once he or she has been served, it's your turn.

When your turn arrives steel yourself for the question **¿qué quiere?** or **¿qué le pongo?** Don't panic if you hear **¿qué desea?** – and don't get thrown by the curter type of assistant who merely raises an eyebrow and asks **¿sí?**

An **order** when shopping is **un pedido** but when you want **to order** something, the word to use is **encargar,** whether you're after a suit, a three-piece suite or a birthday cake. The object you **buy** is **una compra,** which, once acquired, is accompanied by the **bill – la factura, la cuenta** or the unlovable **tiqué.**

In Spanish **food shopping** is generally singular: **hacer la compra,** but **to *go* shopping,** especially for non-essentials, is a promisingly plural **ir de compras.** Whatever you need, you can save time, sweat, blood, tears and language lessons by going to **supermarkets – supermercados, hypermarkets – hipermercados** or **shopping centres – centros comerciales,** all of which are sometimes described as **grandes superficies.** There, it is possible to acquire all you need without uttering a word by slinging everything into **a trolley - un carro** and paying at the **checkout – la caja** in similarly dumb fashion, thanks to pre-packaging and the invention of the **bar code – código de barras.**

It is easy to be unnerved by the infinitely different ways the Spanish ask for what they want when shopping. For instance **me va a poner dos calabazas** sounds brusque and menacing: **you are going to serve me two pumpkins** but this is an extreme example. You usually find that **dar – to give,**

poner – to put and **querer – to want** (not **to love** in this case), are more frequently used although they, too, can sound demanding.

All matters are conducted with courtesy in Spain, but the Spanish say **please** and **thank you** less often than we do. Consequently no-one is offended by bald-sounding requests like **déme salmón ahumado – give me smoked salmon; póngame tres cuartos de percebes – give me three quarters of goose barnacles** or **quiero seis botellas de cava – I want six bottles of cava**.

An easy way to get what you want is to state the **weight – peso, amount** or **number – cantidad** of whatever you want, followed, if it makes you happier, by the not-entirely obligatory **please – por favor**. Thus **doscientos gramos de queso manchego, por favor** gives you a fair chance of getting **two hundred grammes of Manchego cheese**.

I 'll have six bottles of cava

A nice feature of shopping in Spain is that you can ask for a lot or a little, so you can buy **fifty grammes – cincuenta gramos** if that's all you want, although trifling requests are best preceded by a deprecating **sólo – only** and followed by an apologetic smile. It's also possible to buy just one **chop – chuleta**, and if you don't want to buy a whole **leg** or **shoulder of lamb – pierna de cordero** and **paletilla de cordero,** butchers are prepared to cut chops off these, too.

The habitual word for a slice of ham or cheese or the more solid kind of paté is **una loncha** but when you want **the butcher – el carnicero** to **cut off slices of raw meat**, you ask him to **cortar filetes.** These sound like fillet steaks but are less luxurious and not necessarily **beef – carne de vaca/ternera** and can be cut from **pork – cerdo** and **chicken** or **turkey breast – pechuga de pollo/pechuga de pavo**. When there's cash in the kitty and you splash out for **fillet steak,** ask for **solomillo**.

When you can only run to **stewing steak**, ask for **carne para guisar** instead. Sometimes this is already cut into **pieces – trocitos,** but if you want **roasting meat – carne para asar** in a **lump/one piece**, say **lo quiero en un trozo, lo quiero entero** or **lo quiero en un pedazo.** Words tend to be a matter of taste anyway, so some people favour **cachitos** for little bits or **un pedazo** for the Sunday joint and/or feeding multitudes. Another way of expressing **a big lump** or **a thick slice** is **una tajada** while **taquitos** makes it clear that you have **neat, small pieces** in mind. If it's **minced meat** you're after, ask for **carne picada** or if you prefer to witness the process, say **píqueme medio kilo de ternera/cerdo – mince me half a kilo of beef/pork.**

The preceding terms are not restricted to meat, so you can ask for **un pedazo de queso – a lump of cheese, taquitos de jamón – cubed ham; un cacho de pastel – a piece of cake, una tajada de sandía – a slice of watermelon.**

Filetes turn up again at the **fishmonger – la pescadería,** where they correspond to **fish fillets.** If you can't face gutting fish, ask **¿me lo puede limpiar? – can you clean it for me?** although some prefer the rather graphic **vaciar – to empty.** If you want the fish boned, ask **¿me puede quitar la espina?** and if you want **fillets**, say **¿me lo puede hacer filetes?**

Sometimes huge fish are sold piecemeal, in which case you usually ask for **una rodaja,** a word understood to mean a slice, but in fact **a small disc**. If you want to buy a large-ish section of it, revert to **trozo/cacho: quiero un trozo grande de merluza - I want a big piece of hake.**

When food shopping, you will be asked **¿qué más?** or **¿algo más?** after each item. This is your cue to ask for the next thing on your list or, if you've got everything you want, answer **eso es todo – that's all** or **nada más – nothing more.**

On being offered something you don't like the look of, it is easy to explain why, because the Spanish are terse when shopping and it is permissible to dispense with verbs. You can resort to an unadorned **demasiado – too much; demasiados/demasiadas – too many; demasiado grande – too big; demasiado pequeño/pequeña; demasiado grueso – too thick, demasiado fino – too thin**. **Demasiado** is handy to have around whether shopping in a boutique or an ironmonger's as you can use it whenever something fails to meet your requirements: **demasiado ancho – too wide; demasiado estrecho – too narrow; demasiado corto – too short; demasiado largo – too long.**

Don't forget the depressingly important **demasiado caro – too dear.** It's doubtful that anyone will have an overwhelming need to say **too cheap** – but in case you're wondering, it's **demasiado barato...**

A QUIET REMINDER

There are some dark shadows cast by the Spanish sun and a Spaniard can take masochistic pleasure in wallowing in the depths of glumness by maintaining an unbroachable **silence – silencio**. Despite this, keeping **quiet** is not significantly Spanish so perhaps it is inevitable that an English **quiet** will not be an automatic translation for **quieto**. Neither does **quiet** possess an all-purpose, comprehensive equivalent.

You have the **quiet** that a Spaniard regards as **tranquilo,** a soothing adjective meaning **still, calm** and **peaceful** as well as **tranquil,** so those who live in **a quiet neighbourhood** refer to it as **un barrio tranquilo.** When applied to a person, **tranquilo** continues to imply **still, calm, peaceful or tranquil.** This enviable person needn't be **a person of few words** – **una persona de pocas palabras,** but on the other hand, he or she probably won't be a **chatterbox** – **un parlanchín/ una parlanchina** or the unexpected **charlatán/charlatana.** Translation divests this of the untrustworthy, wide-boy or *poseur* image we associate with the word in English, although it's not particularly complimentary.

When a machine or motor is **quiet** it is described as **silencioso** as well as **sin ruido,** literally **noiseless** and you're as likely to say **quiero un secador que no haga ruido** as **quiero un secador silencioso** when you want **a quiet hairdryer.** The usual term for **a car's silencer is un silenciador,** although mechanics sometimes refer to it as **el silencioso;** as an adjective, **silencioso** describes a person who **moves silently** rather than someone who keeps his lip buttoned. **Sin ruido** is also more suitable for objects than silent individuals who would be better summed up as **callado, reservado** or even **aburrido** – **boring,** which is patently unfair since being quiet isn't unavoidably synonymous with being a bore.

Callado is the past participle of **callar,** a verb whose most usual translations are **to say nothing, not to mention something, to keep back information, to keep secret** and also **to hush up.** None of these definitions corresponds exactly to the nice, peaceful English-speaker's notion of **quiet** although someone who is **thoughtful** or **sulky** will be told **estás muy callado** – **you're very quiet.** ¡**Que niño mas callado!** conveys the same element of wonder combined with mild anxiety that the phrase conjures up in English: **what a quiet child!**

¿**Quieres callar?** looks and sounds like a question but is actually an order to **be quiet/shut up.** It is also a verbal kick under the table when you want to nip the blabbing of blabbermouths in the bud but **calla, calla,** or the polite third person **calle, calle,** is the plea you hear when tears are running down a Spaniard's cheeks and he is doubled up, not with indigestion, but laughter.

Many years ago, "**come y calla**" used to be embroidered on babies' bibs, a no-nonsense injunction to "**eat up and be quiet.**" **Callar** figures in two very Spanish sayings: **quien**

calla, otorga – who says nothing, gives tacit permission while **dar la callada por respuesta** sounds like ventriloquism but allows you to pass the buck, wash your hands and keep your nose metaphorically clean all at the same time: **to respond with silence.**

Options for the reflexive **callarse** include **to keep quiet, to be silent, to remain silent** or **to become silent. Cállate** – **be quiet** is the inevitable admonition to an unquiet child who insists on being heard and seen, as well as a barking dog, a noisy canary or grumbling spouse. The apparent courtesy of the **usted** version, **cállese**, is not guaranteed to impress and although **cállate la boca** and **cállese la boca** are often heard and often said, they are a virtually unforgivable **shut your mouth.** Neither will ¡a callar! go down well within the family or with close friends, but it is indispensable for teachers and anyone obliged to call for large-scale silence.

If words fail to procure the tranquillity, silence and above all, the **quiet** that you seek, there is always the inarticulate but expressive **sshh.** With **CHSSSS** the Spanish produce a much louder **sshh** than we do, but it is inevitable that the inhabitants of one of the world's noisiest countries should feel duty-bound to live up to their reputation even when calling for silence.

BEAUTY IS AS BEAUTY DOES

As we all are, the Spanish are susceptible to **beauty – belleza,** and possibly even more so because both this noun and the adjective, **bello/bella** are applied to objects or people considered to border on perfection. Although they are habitually used in Latin America, these words occur less often in everyday European Spanish and tend to appear in polished prose, verse or speech-making. Because **belleza** is so special a concept, in some parts of Spain, and particularly in the Southeast, it is often the official title of the young woman and her attendants who are chosen for their good looks to preside over local fiestas.

Hermoso/hermosa and **hermosura** are other variations

on the beautiful theme, but although they, too, are rather consciously articulate you can expect to encounter them more often. Obviously they are used to describe good-looking men, women, children and animals but you also meet them in un-English surroundings. In the fruit and vegetable market, for instance, it is quite customary to hear stallholders using **hermoso/hermosura** to describe their wares: **¡mire que geranios más hermosos! – look at the lovely geraniums!** or **tengo unas berenjenas que son una hermosura – I've got aubergines that are real beauties.** And yes, even when talking about more than one **berenjena, hermosura** remains singular.

By and large, however, and outside the market or literature, the adjective you use and hear is **guapo** for **a handsome man, boy** or **child** and **guapa** for **a beautiful woman, girl** or **child.** Thus you would say, **that checkout girl/boy is very beautiful/handsome – esa cajera es muy guapa/ese cajero es muy guapo.** These are adjectives and, much as you try, you won't find a noun with the same root. On second thoughts, that's not strictly true, but after more than three decades in Spain I have yet to come across anyone actually using the totally legitimate but totally ignored **guapeza.** If you feel that an unadorned **guapo** or **guapa** does not convey your desired degree of beauty, this can be turned into a superlative in the usual way by lopping off the final **–o** or **–a**, and tacking on **-ísimo** or **–ísima** to form **guapísimo/guapísima.**

Adding the suffixes **–azo** or **–aza** transform **guapo** and **guapa** into **extravagant compliments – piropos** exclaimed by dazzled men (and women, these days): **¡guapaza!** or **¡guapazo!** To describe a man as **un guaperas** is less of a compliment, though, and implies that he is somewhat too good-looking for his own good and rather too aware of it.

For the downside, **ugly,** the Spanish use **feo** or **fea.** Iinterestingly, this describes not only what is physically **unsightly** but also what is deemed to be **unseemly** so that discourtesy, uncouthness, insensitivity or indiscretion can also be **feo** or **fea.**

Not everyone is blessed with beauty, but some are still lucky enough to be considered **bonito/bonita – pretty** or **atractivo/atractiva.** Then, of course, there is **glamour.** This elusive quality is not easy to define, and although the Spanish have no difficulty in recognising it, translating it is harder. A Spanish-English dictionary suggests **encanto** which, despite its literal **charm**, does not convey **allure, magnetism, charisma** and all the other attributes we associate with **glamorous – encantador/encantadora. Hechizo** or **embrujo** – which both mean **spell** – together with the adjectives **hechicero** is another possibility. Knowing itself to be at an uncharacteristic loss for once, Spanish is beginning to use **glamour** and resorts to the South Americanism, **glamoroso/glamorosa** for **glamorous** – reprehensible, no doubt, but what else to do when faced with this intangible but unmistakeable trait?

A **glamorous** person tends to possess star quality and, as in English, it is usual to describe him or her as **a star – una estrella,** someone who knows how **to succeed – tener éxito** in a particular field. This satisfactory condition falls back on **tener – to have**, added to **éxito – success.** Don't confuse this with an English **exit**, as **those who are successful – los que tienen éxito** seldom find themselves on the **way out.**

THE SPANISH MAIN

Most Spanish towns and villages have **a Main Street – una Calle Mayor** and **a Main Square – una Plaza Mayor** but apart from these convenient parallels and that of **mainsail – vela mayor,** most of the time **mayor** does its own thing. Neither can you translate **mayor** as **major** except in music: **tono mayor – major key**.

Very often **mayor** corresponds to **old: ese hombre es muy mayor – that man is very old** although mayor can also mean **older: tu hijo es mayor que mi hija – your son is older than my daughter.** Unlike many Spanish adjectives, **mayor** is appropriate for masculine and feminine nouns alike, whether singular or plural: **obras mayores – major works**.

Mayor also means **bigger: este aljibe es mayor que aquel – this water deposit is bigger than that one.** Mayor continues to confuse as it is also the superlative **biggest, oldest, greatest** and (nice and near to English) **main: mi mayor preocupación es evitar que se metan los gatos en la huertecita de Fausto –**

my main worry is stopping the cats from getting into Fausto's vegetable plot. How to decide which is what? As a rule, if it's immediately followed by **que,** then **mayor** is the comparative **bigger, older, greater;** if **que** is absent and **mayor** is preceded by **el, la, mi, tu** or another possessive adjective, it's almost certainly going to be **biggest, oldest, greatest, main**.

Que can sometimes be zapped though, so **ese patio es mayor** implies **that patio is bigger. Ese patio es el mayor** means **that patio is the biggest** and in constructions like these the preceding definite article reveals that you're dealing with a superlative.

A parent refers to **el mayor** or **la mayor** when referring to the **elder/eldest child** and Elena says of Nieves: **mi mayor estudió inglés – my oldest studied English** and charming as Nieves is, this has no bearing on comparative or superlative kids. She would also say **Nieves la mayor de mis hijos – Nieves is the eldest of my children**.

The rank corresponding to **major** in Spain and Spanish-speaking countries is **comandante,** but **un mayor de edad** is a person who is **of age** but an English **mayor** who presides a town hall is **un alcalde.**

As a plural, **los mayores** are **adults** or **elders** but an ominous **no queremos que esto llegue a mayores** alludes not to children or their elders but to **a difference** or **quarrel: we don't want this to get out of hand**. Situations of this type often lead to **palabras mayores – insults** and in less outspoken times, five were listed as intolerable: **gafo – leprous**, the no-need-for-translation **sodomético, cornudo – cuckold,** traidor – traitor and **hereje – heretic**. There was also **"la de cuatro letras, que se decía a mujer casada" – the word of four letters addressed to a married woman,** which was **puta – whore**.

Caza mayor is **big game** (jumbo-sized animals, not an important football match). **Un colegio mayor** sounds as though it could be a high school but is **a hall of residence** while **un mayorista** is a **wholesaler** and **venta al por mayor** is the equivalent of **wholesale.** A Spanish **butler** is **un mayordomo** while **un mayoral** was **an overseer** or **foreman** but these days is more likely to be a **member of a fiestas committee.**

Translations for **main** include **principal, fuerte, importante:**

main course – plato principal although **plato fuerte** could be more apt for a meal like paella or cocido. Not many people use the ready-made **mayormente** for **mainly,** preferring **principalmente,** but **en su mayor parte** does correspond to **in the main: en su mayor parte, la política es un rollo – in the main, politics are a bore.** The **main thing** is an interchangeable **lo importante, lo fundamental, lo principal.**

When spoken of by the untechnical, electricity or water **mains** are generally expressed as a vague **la general** but a poetic or nautical **main** is **la mar** rather than a geographic **el mar.** Surprisingly, neither **el Mar de las Antillas** nor **el Caribe** makes reference to the first Europeans who sailed them, and are customary translations for what privateers, pirates, freebooters and other assorted swashbucklers from our anti-Iberian past did not object to calling the **Spanish Main.**

ANIMAL CRACKERS

As they do in most languages, animals wriggle their metaphoric way into Spanish although different creatures can be involved, so **a bookworm** is **un ratón de biblioteca – library mouse.** A counterpart to an English-speaker's **church mouse** which portrays **someone who is genteelly poor** does not exist in Spain, but a person who is both **hard-up and frugal** is dismissed as **rata – rat.** The offending noun also transposes into an adjective: **él es muy rata y compra todo de segunda mano – he's very careful and buys everything second hand.**

On those occasions when you would exclaim **rats!** in English you now say **¡caracoles! – snails!** or **¡ostras! – oysters!** although these words are potentially ruder than rodents as the former substitutes a similar-sounding Spanish swear-word and the latter replaces a blasphemous **hostias** or **hosts.**

Another's selfishness, eating habits, political beliefs or even occupation can prompt a reaction of **pig!** in English, pronounced with differing degrees of vehemence and virulence. The Spanish match, and easily overtake, English-speakers for vehemence and virulence but leave pigs out of it and prefer the more generic **¡animal!**

If and when the Spanish throw the odd ¡cerdo! or ¡cochino! (which still means **pig**) at each other, it's usually in connection with the amount of food consumed and the way it has been shovelled into an ill-mannered mouth. **Una cerda** might be a label for a woman no-one wants to invite to lunch, but is more often **the bristle** (originally a pig's) of a tooth- or paint-brush. English-speakers **throw pearls before the swine** but what the Spanish waste on the philistine and unappreciative are **daisies: tirar margaritas a cerdos.**

Little piggies don't go to market in Spain and infant toes are tweaked to a rhyme beginning **diez lobitos tiene la loba – mother wolf has ten little wolf-cubs** although outside the nursery you meet the more adult **lobezno** for **wolf-cub.** A male **wolf** or seducer has no animal counterpart, apart from the unsavoury Don Juan, the nearest being the very idiomatic **ligón** whose activities are eminently wolf-like. Be prepared also to meet **una ligona,** who will neither look nor act like Mother Wolf.

Ver las orejas al lobo is what **Caperucita – Little Red Riding** did: she was finally able to **see the wolf's ears** or, in other words, she saw through the subterfuge. On a more horticultural note, **garganta de lobo – wolf's throat** is the flower we recognise as a **snapdragon, antirrhinum.**

Although **jabato** doesn't look porky it is the **young of a wild boar (jabalí)** and, like **rata**, is a noun sometimes used as an adjective: **¡que jabato era, matar la araña así! – how brave he was, to kill the spider like that!**

It is no compliment to be compared to **a goat** in English but in Spanish, the term has no lecherous associations and **estás como una cabra** means **you're crazy.** Many animals' names end in **–a** in Spanish but do not exclusively denote female gender; however, tacking on a masculine suffix will not always produce the desired result. Therefore **un cabrón** is neither inane nor insane but wears the horns of **a cuckold** and even in these outspoken days it's wise to think twice before using it.

Not all animal names get you into hot water, though, and **un gato – cat** is a **jack** for a car as well as a nickname for **un madrileño,** so a woman referred to as **una gata** is more likely to come from Madrid than to be **catty.** When she's catty, however, she is described as **maliciosa** but if you still want a name from the animal kingdom, call her **una bicha.** This isn't a bitch but covers everything from **a small animal, vermin** down to **a worm** or **insect**.

Estar mosca is one of those phrases whose meaning has shifted over the years. Formerly it meant **to be suspicious** but is now also accepted as **to be annoyed** and **mosqueado** is the adjective for someone who is **cheesed-off.** Another insect, **hormiguita** – the diminutive of **hormiga** or **ant** – is less irritated and is **b.**

The literal meaning of **matar al gusanillo** is **to kill the little worm** and can describe **having a bite to eat** – something that used to be described in English as **keeping the worms away. Matar el gusanillo** also exists in the sense of **doing or getting something out of your system that has been bothering, irking or nagging at you.**

Gallina – **hen** is slightly out-dated slang for **money** but the damning **es más puta que las gallinas** implies a woman **is**

A library mouse

as amoral as a hen. **Un loro - a parrot** is again slang, this time for **a transistor radio,** but **estar al loro** means **to be up-to-date, to be on the ball.** Someone who sighs **supongo que yo pagaré el pato** isn't moaning about having **to pay for the duck** but complaining **I suppose I shall carry the can back. Coming out in goose-pimples** is illustrated by the verb **erizarse – to bristle, to stand on end** as this is what happens to the spines of **un erizo – a hedgehog.**

When a Spaniard wishes to convey the clumsiness of **a bull in a china shop** he has recourse to **un elefante en una cacharrería – an elephant in a china shop** or to **un burro en un garage – a donkey in a garage.** Finally, because human nature doesn't change all that radically from one country to another, **a dog in the manger** is easily found in Spain where it is called **el perro del hortelano – the gardern's dog.**

REAL WRITING

As well as being an adjective synonymous with **very, really** keeps chat flowing without having to say anything in particular and can be followed by an unspoken exclamation or question mark. Thus **I'm going home** can be followed by an incredulous **really!** or an interrogatory **really?** The same statement might provoke similar reactions in Spanish but reality won't come into it, and if **me voy a casa** comes as bad news it will be met with an incredulous **¡no!** or **¡toma! – take (that)!** It could also provoke the longer but equally exasperated **¡no me digas! – you don't say!** and **¡no puede ser! – it can't be!**

There is less choice for a questioning **really?** which usually becomes a simple **¿no?** or a less simple **¿es verdad? ¿de verdad?** and **¿de veras? –** all variations on **is it true?**

A Spanish-English dictionary maintains that **¡ca!** will do for a contradictory **really!** But although this crops up in crosswords as a two-letter word meaning **no!** even the sharpest-eared of Spanish-speaking residents will probably agree that they have never heard it, for the simple reason that no-one uses it anymore.

As for the **really...** that stands for nothing in particular but keeps conversation afloat, you hear a Teutonic or Sloaney **ya, ya...** Its literal meaning is **now, now...** but bears no resemblance to the English remonstration, which is better translated as **¡vamos!** Other options for **really... es verdad... (it's true...)** and the ever-ready **claro...**

The obvious **realmente** doesn't fit the bill unless **really** implies **very: this book is really interesting – este libro es realmente interesante. Realmente** is valid Spanish but on a par with an English-speaker's **seriously:** still correct but with early 21ˢᵗ century overtones. Other translations for **realmente** are nearer to **in fact** and **in effect** as well as **actually**, which can also be translated as **en realidad: en realidad el libro no era tan interesante – actually the book wasn't so interesting**.

In English we use **real** for people, places or things whose reality is not in doubt but who deserve special emphasis for being **genuine: a real lady** or **a real surprise**, for instance. In each instance this is translated as **verdadero** or **auténtico** and as a rule they precede the accompanying noun when they mean **real** but follow when conveying **not false: Una auténtica señora** or **una verdadera sorpresa** but **oro auténtico – real gold**.

The verb **realizar** only conforms to the English **realise** in the financial sense of **to bring in, produce**. To translate **I didn't realise he'd written other books** you'd use **darse cuenta: no me había dado cuenta de que había escrito otros libros.**

You meet **real** as the adjective **royal** while **realeza** is our **royalty** but the **royalties** that writers are anxious to receive are **derechos de autor**. To **live like royalty** is **vivir a cuerpo de rey** and **to treat royally** is **tratar como un rey – to treat like a king** or **tratar como una reina – treat like a queen** depending on who is getting the VIP treatment.

Reina is also a casual endearment bestowed on a woman by market stallholders, waitresses (but not waiters), shop assistants and other sundry people of both sexes; a man can likewise be addressed as **rey** – but only by women.

Reyes is another of the enigmatic names bestowed on Spanish females, a mystery that can be cleared up by explaining that the full name is **María de los Reyes – María of the Kings**. It is because of **los Tres Reyes Magos – the Three Kings/Three Wise Men** that a Spanish Christmas lasts so long and over-eating and over-drinking continue until **6ᵗʰ January –**

the Epiphany. This is because there are still **los regalos de Reyes – Twelfth Night presents** to look forward to when all that remains of an English-speaker's Christmas are pine needles on the carpet and a dustbin full of wrapping paper and ribbon.

COMMON KNOWLEDGE

Unbelievably for the beginning of the 21st century, a certain type of English-speaking female is still capable of labelling another English-speaking female as **common**. Not to be outdone in pseudo-gentility, a certain type of young Spanish-speaking female dismisses less-advantaged contemporaries as **macarra, hortera.** Neither the English nor the Spanish terms have any connection with **común** but the sentiment is the same, especially when coming from someone who regards herself as **una pija,** a preppy sort of yuppy. Careful with this one, though, not only because it is an adjective that doubles as a noun but because this word is also slang for something male and anatomically private.

Macarra and **hortera** are noun-adjectives whose unfaltering ending in **-a** does not prevent their being applied to men. The literal meaning of **macarra** is **pimp**, while **hortera** initially described anything or anyone originating from **la huerta** – areas producing fruit and vegetables.

Transatlantic Spanish often equates **ordinario/ordinaria** with **ordinary** but older, European Spanish-speakers still settle for **ordinario** rather than the younger **macarra, hortera** for **common, vulgar, coarse.** If you want to translate **ordinary**, use **corriente: siempre compran vino corriente – they always buy ordinary wine;** nevertheless, as often happens in Spanish you loop the loop to find that **ordinary salt** is **sal común** and **out of the ordinary** is **fuera de lo común.**

Común is a labour saving adjective which accompanies masculine or feminine nouns, as does its plural, **comunes.** Despite not fitting the bill for **vulgar** or **coarse, común** does have other uses, so you continue to possess or lack **sentido común – common sense.** A **common purpose** would be regarded as **una meta en común** but **a common end** is **un mismo fin.**

It is not uncommon to encounter **costumbre** joining **común** in **era costumbre común veranear en la costa – it was common custom to spend the summer at the coast. Habitual** will also translate **common: era habitual veranear en la costa.** Common knowledge is neither common nor knowledge but an unexpected **del dominio público.** Minus the preposition **del,** this also means public property although when **a Common** or **common, uncultivated land** is found in Spain its formal (but little-used and little-heard) name is **un ejido.**

Common interests are **intereses comunes** and **in common** remains common too: **Fuensanta y Esperanza tienen poco en común – Fuensanta and Esperanza have little in common.** The **common ground** of coinciding opinions rather than shared acreage are **puntos en común** but when referring to Britain's House of Commons, the Spanish always say **Los Comunes.** They describe their own parliament as **Las Cortes, la Cámara Baja** or **el Congreso de los Diputados** as the fancy takes them.

That common ailment, the **common cold** is **un resfriado común** although a doctor might refer to it as **un resfriado banal** (and yes, that's the same as our banal). However, Spanish men are like men everywhere in that they are prone to the oxymoronic **gripe común – common flu. A common soldier** is **un soldado raso** but a **common** (not a political) **prisoner** is **un preso común. Common courtesy** is as easy (or easier) to find in Spain as it is elsewhere, but is known as **simple cortesía.**

Our **common or garden** is reduced to a terse **común** and the adjective **commonplace** reverts to **corriente** although **a commonplace** or **a trite remark** has the convenient translation of **un lugar común. Common law** is a very specific **ley consuetudinario** but **a common law wife,** common enough in English-speaking communities, was less in evidence in Spain. In the past she might be explained away as **la mujercita de Pepe – Pepe's little wife,** as though the diminutive would convey the lack of marriage lines in the days when **una pareja de hecho – a cohabitating couple** was still **uncommon – poco común.**

FOREIGN BODIES

China figures largely in Spanish figures of speech, so **un cuento chino – a Chinese story** is **a tall** story, while in the past someone whose finances were precarious used to say **tengo más trampas que una película china.** This simile is still used by the middle-aged and over but loses much of its jaunty desperation in translation and sounds nearer to farce than tragedy: **I've more pitfalls than a Chinese film.**

All cities and large towns in Spain possess **un barrio chino – Chinatown** although it is closer to a red light district than a neighbourhood where restaurants serve Peking Duck. Less specialised on both counts is **tinta china,** which goes under the name of **Indian ink** at an English-speaking stationer's, while any type of **work – trabajo** involving considerable time and patience is described as the now politically-incorrect **trabajo de chinos**.

The phrase **¡naranjas de la China! – Chinese oranges!** (do they mean mandarines?) conveys scepticism, so a statement like: **dice Esperanza que va a hacer régimen – Esperanza says she is going to diet** could provoke a reaction of **¡naranjas de la China! – I don't believe it!** You sometimes hear **la quinta china** for **the back of beyond,** although no-one can confirm whether this means **the Chinese estate, a group of recruits called up to go to China** or a scrambled version of **el quinto pino – the fifth pine** which is yet another term for **the back of beyond.**

China does have the Spanish meaning of **fine china, porcelain,** but the type of **china** produced in Staffordshire is **loza.** This is probably the right moment to point out that **China** with a capital letter refers to the country itself but because adjectives of nationality are written without capital letters in Spanish, **una china** means **a small pebble** as well as **a Chinese woman.**

Un chino is a slightly more rustic word for a similarly small pebble, and **jugar a los chinos** refers to the game often played by carousing adults to determine who pays for a meal or the next round of drinks. It consists of guessing the combined number of small objects concealed in a fellow-player's closed fist, and whoever guesses least consistently foots the bill.

A **Venetian blind** changes nationality to become an Iranian-sounding **persiana** and a **bed that folds away into a cupboard** was a common feature in large families and was called **una cama turca – a Turkish bed.** **Leatherwork** is known as **marroquinaría – Morocco-work,** but **Morocco leather** is **tafilete.**

The much-embroidered and fringed shawl that was an important part of a Spanish woman's wardrobe until not so long ago is **un mantón de Manila – a Manila shawl.** Somewhere along the line **a monkey wrench** became **una llave inglesa** or **English spanner** but **cuadros escoceses – Scottish checks** are easy to identify as **plaid** although it might take you longer to guess that **un chotis**, a thoroughbred dance inseparable from Madrid, is really **a Schottische. A man's jacket** is **una chaqueta americana** or simply **una americana – an American jacket** but **un americano** is **coffee diluted with water** instead of milk.

A vegetable **swede** is **un nabo sueco** but when said of a Spanish person, **hacerse el sueco – to behave like a Swede** means **to pretend not to understand what is going on or being said. Holanda** means the country, **Holland,** but **holanda** is **very fine cotton material** and what we know as a **Great Dane** is a doggy-sounding **dogo.**

If you were under the impression that **una montaña rusa – a Russian mountain** would be located in the Urals, you'd be wide of the mark because it is **a big dipper, roller coaster. Tener más mocos que un pavo ruso** conveys having **a runnier nose** (to put it as pleasantly as possible) **than a Russian turkey.**

Due to anti-Communist fervour in the aftermath of the Civil War, **Russian salad** was renamed **ensaladilla nacional,** but the substitution didn't prosper and people continued to ask for **ensaladilla rusa. Un suizo,** literally **a Swiss,** is a kind of **bun** and everyone knows that the world's best **omelette** is called **tortilla española,** so one-upmanship may be responsible for identifying the world's least interesting **plain omelette** as **una tortilla francesa. Patatas inglesas – crisps** are England's only contri-bution to Spanish cuisine – but who's prepared to say whether this is an indictment of English cooking or Spanish taste?

BITS AND PIECES

Vague, plural **bits and pieces** can be a vague **cachivaches,** a vaguer **cosas** or the inevitably diminutive **cositas.** The equally vague but similar **bit, a little** is usually translated as **un poco.** **I'd like a bit of cake** is a potentially risky request if it has been baked by Elena, who is erratic where baking is concerned, but it does promise trouble-free translating: **me gustaría un poco de tarta.**

Un poco turns up in **a bit more, some more: me gustaría un poco más de tarta – I'd like a little more cake.** And at awkward moments when you are asked if you like something or someone but are unable to give a favourable opinion, you can always mutter **un poco...**

Where we use **bit,** the Spanish often choose **algo – some: me gustaría algo de tarta – I'd like some cake/a little (of the) cake. Algo más,** logically enough, corresponds to **a bit more: me gustaría algo más de pastel – I'd like a little more cake.**

This can also be an unenthusiastic response and **¿te gustó la tarta que hizo Elena? – did you like the cake that Elena made?** might elicit a non-committal and non-specific **algo...** or, again, **un poco.**

If **a bit** is an understatement, it continues to be translated either as **algo** or **un poco: this is a bit worrying – esto es algo preocupante** as well as **esto es un poco preocupante**. The sharp-eyed will have eyed up the preceding phrases and seen that **poco** is preceded by the indefinite article **un** but **algo** is not. If the **un** in **un poco** were omitted, you'd be saying something rather different, since **esto es poco preocupante** implies **this is hardly worrying.**

A pinch of salt is **una pizca de sal** but **the crumbs** left over from Elena's cake are **migas** and **a bit of bread** is **un mendrugo de pan, un cacho de pan, un trozo de pan** or **un pedacito de pan. Un mendrugo** is a term exclusive to bread and bread alone, but **un cacho** and **un trozo** are relevant to anything that can be cut or sliced into **pieces** or **chunks.** A sandwich-friendly **slice of bread** is **una rebanada de pan** but a **slice** of meat, salami or smoked salmon is always **una loncha.**

The word **pieza** in Spanish does not correspond to an

English **piece** of cake or ham for instance, because **a cake** or **a ham** is considered **una pieza** in Spanish only before it's been cut or divided into portions. **Una pieza is an object, item: una pieza de tela – a piece of cloth; una pieza de música – a piece of music.** If something is described as **de una pieza** it is **all of a piece, all-in-one** although **una pieza,** or **una pieza de recambio,** is the **spare part** a mechanic needs to repair a car.

A drop of something can be literally translated into **una gota: sólo me gusta una gota de leche en el café – I only like a drop of milk in coffee.**

You don't always want just a bit or a little of something and there are occasions when you want **a couple** of something: **a couple of bottles of cava,** for instance: **un par de botellas de cava. Un par** is appropriate for most things that comes in twos: **un par de libros** is **a couple of books** but **a couple of children** are **dos niños.** If the two kids are a nice pigeon pair or a couple is composed of a man and a woman (or even two men or two women, these days) you say **una pareja.** A **married couple** are invariably called **un matrimonio** in a rock-solid show of inseparable unity.

A pair is sometimes translated as **un par** and since **a pair of socks** or **a pair of gloves** is composed of two elements, there is no reason not to translate them as **un par de calcetines, un par de guantes.** Our habit of referring to **a pair of scissors, a pair of trousers, a pair of spectacles** sounds to Spanish ears like **two** pairs of scissors, trousers or spectacles if translated as **un par de tijeras, un par de pantalones, un par de gafas.**

As far as Spanish is concerned, **un par** has to represent two separate items so **a pair of scissors** is **unas tijeras, a pair of trousers** narrows down to **un pantalón** and **a pair of spectacles** becomes **unas gafas.** The same goes for **a pair of (men's) braces – unos tirantes** and those double-sounding undergarments, **a pair of knickers – bragas** and a **pair of underpants – calzon-cillos.** In fact, it's not unknown to encounter **underpants** referred to as **un calzoncillo** – an unexpectedly singular term in a language that generally encourages plurality and which also provides a misleading insight into the anatomy of the Spanish male.

NEWSPEAK

Newspeak infiltrates language the world over and Spain is no exception. The Spanish version is known as **neolengua,** literally **new tongue**, while a snappy **new word** is **un neologismo**.

Some are serviceable, and there can be few valid objections to **transfocador – a device allowing a film or video camera to effect the rapid advance or retreat of an image.** Following this mouthful, my kindly **Diccionario de neologismos** thoughtfully adds **zoom**. Or there's **esteatopigia**, a feminine (it would have to be) noun meaning **an adipose mass on the hips and buttocks**. Not much to complain about there, unless you suffer from it.

Other words grate, though, because they trade old terms for new and borrow unnecessarily from English. Why prefer a mispronounced **performance** to **actuación,** why refer to **los homeless** instead of **los sin techo** or substitute **un manager** for **un gerente?**

Newspeak is one thing, but **new** is another and it possesses a variety of old translations, the most usual being **nuevo, reciente** or **fresco** depending on the nature of the object described. Predictably, **reciente** and **fresco** are found in connection with something that is either **recent** or **fresh: pan reciente – new bread; huevos frescos – fresh eggs.**

By chopping off the –te of **reciente,** adding an accent and tacking on a past participle plus an accent, you turn it into something more descriptive: **pan recién hecho – newly-made bread; huevos recién puestos – newlaid eggs; una pared recién pintada – a newly-painted wall**. The **recién** formula also provides some English nouns incorporating **new: un recién nacido – a newborn; un recién llegado – a newcomer** (and often parvenu to boot).

According to the Diccionario de la Lengua Española, **nuevo** means not only **newly-made, newly manufactured** but also **what is seen or heard for the first time**. This means **nuevo** can be used in the same situations as an English **new: un punto de vista nuevo – a new point of view; una nueva era – a new age** as well as the less abstract **un abrigo nuevo – a new coat** or **una casa nueva – a new house.**

There are other words connected with **nuevo,** with

recognisable connections that do not necessarily correspond to their English versions. **Novel** is one of these. It is an adjective describing someone who **begins to practise an art or profession or has little experience in it** – in other words, **a novice**. An English **novel** is an uncomplicated **novela** but **una novedad** isn't confined to **a novelty** or any **new line of merchandise** but also means **a change produced in an object or situation, an alteration in health** as well as **a recent happening, recent news**.

A routine commentary by a watchman or indeed anyone watching for a change in a given situation is **sin novedad** – **nothing new,** although the greeting-question **what's new?** is **¿qué hay de nuevo?** often shortened to **¿qué hay?**

You see less of them in these supermarket-dominated times, but shop signs often proclaimed **novedades** which meant customers could expect to find all types of **novelties** from knick-knacks to haberdashery.

Una novatada can be the gentle **ragging** or savage **initiation** inflicted by old hands on newcomers, usually on changing from primary to secondary school or when starting University. A less intimidating aspect of **una novatada** is its complementary meaning of **a mistake made through inexperience,** while **un novato** or **una novata** is a **beginner, tyro, novice.** When you do meet **un novicio** or **una novicia** he or she will be a person who has just entered a religious order.

New is not visible in all translations, one of the most notable being **news** which is **las noticias** whether you read them in a paper, see them on television or listen to them on the radio. The **news** on the radio used to be known as **el parte**, a word meaning **message, report** and this evolved into **el diario hablado – the spoken newspaper**. The television news is still programmed as **el telediario** although viewers persist in calling it **las noticias – the news,** and **a newsreader** on either radio or television is **un locutor** or **locutora**.

A newspaper can be **un diario** or **un periódico** although the latter is now the more-used term. **A newsagent's shop** is **una librería,** but **a library** is **una biblioteca**.

Spanish habitually comes up with nice verbal surprises and **estrenar** is one of them. It has no English equivalent and its various meanings include **to use something new for the first time, to put on a new show or film, to start a new occupation.**

293

Amongst salesmen or shopkeepers, **estrenarse** signifies **to make the first sale of the day; un estreno** is the **first night** or **premiere of a play, film, show** while anything that is **new, used for the first time** can be described as **estrenado**. Take note of that very Spanish letter – **ñ** – in the similar-sounding **estreñido** and do your best not to confuse them, since **estreñido** means **constipated** – and there's nothing very new about that.

THE CHEERS AND THE JEERS...

Many remember Hilaire Belloch's "Tarantella", because of the syncopated **fleas that tease in the high Pyrenees and the wine that tasted of the jar.** That's the bit everyone recites although **the cheers and the jeers of the young muleteers** is much-quoted too, even if it sometimes emerges as **the sneers and jeers** instead.

More motor homes, motorbikes and Mercedes cross the Pyrenees these days than young muleteers making their way to or from Spain. You find **cheers, jeers** and the misquoted **sneers** in low-lying regions as well but generally speaking the Spanish are not a consistently **cheery** race, even when divided ethnically but inaccurately into Celts and Iberians. Similarly, the nearest Spanish gets to round-cheeked **jollity** are the adjectives **jovial, divertido and alegre.**

Things change at football matches, however, because Spain is now essentially a footballing, not a bullfighting, country and it's on the football ground where Spaniards are seen and heard to **cheer** with such enthusiasm it's a pity they don't have a specific verb for it.

Your dictionary will suggest **vitorear**, which is adequate enough but also means to acclaim, and although a footballer can enjoy as much acclaim – or more – than a Nobel prize-winner, **rugir – roar** or **gritar** do a better job at conveying the hearty, partisan cheering of football fans.

Aplaudir is more sedate and closer to the **cheer** that goes up after a play or concert while **aclamar** suggests an even greater degree of appreciation. Although a **cheer** can be **un grito** or **un vitor**, instead of calling for **three cheers for Blas!** you shout ¡**viva Blas!** – **long live Blas!** and those present respond with ¡viva!.

Cheering isn't confined to sport or the theatre, as the Spanish **cheer on** – **animar** as well as **cheer up** – also **animar** – although not every English-speaker would regard these two as interchangeable. For **cheering up** there is also **alegrar** and the reflexive **alegrarse**, meaning **to gladden, to make happy** and **to make merry**. Few would argue with the first two translations but the third can also hint that drink has been taken at some stage, since the adjective **alegre** is a Spanish euphemism close to **tipsy** as well as a stone-cold sober **cheery**. Another description for those who are **cheery** is **jovial**, but **acogedor** is more apt for furnishings, rooms or dwellings that are **cheery** because they are **cosy**.

Cheers one day, **jeers** the next – most of us are sufficiently world-weary not to expect life to be otherwise. Every nation has its own particular way **to jeer** but you will not find it easy to pin down the Spanish version. Even a dictionary appears to scratch its metaphoric head and is reduced to suggesting **mofa** for a **jeer**, together with the reflexive mofarse for actively **jeering**.

Mofarse is certainly a verb you'll read but you won't hear it or say it every two minutes. As for the alternatives, the noun **befa** and the verb **befar** – I can sincerely lay my hand on my heart and swear that I have never heard either in the thirty-five years I have lived in Spain. **Insulta** and **insultar** are closer but what most people use in these circumstances are the noun **burla** and the verb **burlarse** or **hacer burla**, together with **abucheo** and **abuchear**.

Abuchear is multi-purpose because it also means to **boo, hoot, hiss, give the bird** and **to howl down** as well as **to jeer**. A **jeer** need not be the same as a **sneer** but nevertheless you are likely to come across **to sneer** translated as **mofarse, burlarse** or **hacer burla**. A **sneer** can be **una mirada de burla, una mirada de desdén** or **una mirada de desprecio**, all of which are guaranteed to make you want to slink round the nearest corner or sink into the ground.

All this talk about **jeers** and **sneers** threatens to obscure one of the nicest aspects of cheers, the ritual murmur on clinking your glass against someone else's. In Spanish you can choose between a brief **salud – health** or if you are in a more expansive mood you may repeat **salud, pesetas y amor**. This traditional phrase will have to be amended to **salud, euros y amor** but whichever currency is chosen, the order of Spanish priorities remains clear: **health, money and love...**

YAA BOO SUCKS!

The Spanish have a reputation for dignity but this does not prevent outraged dignity from provoking an undignified response of ¡**chínchate!** which amounts to a derisive **yaa! boo! sucks!** This is more generally heard in the familiar, second person of the reflexive verb **chincharse** because it should be restricted to someone you are able to mock.

Translations for the non-reflexive **chinchar** are to **irritate, annoy, pester, bother** although in these particular circumstances a European Spanish-speaker is more likely to use **picar – to prick** or **crispar – annoy, irritate: me crispa no acordarme del nombre de ese libro – it bothers me that I can't remember the name of that book.**

Picar is a prince among Spanish verbs because it also means **to prick, puncture, pierce, pit, pock, punch, clip, sting, bite, peck, goad, stimulate** – but why continue? The object of this particular exercise isn't **picar** nor is it **chinchar/chincharse** but the functions of that plebeian amongst English verbs, **to suck.**

Generally, **to suck** is **chupar**, as English-speaking parents of Spanish-born children soon discover. Babies start off with **un chupete – a dummy** and progress to **un Chupa-Chups, a lollipop** (not an ice-lolly) which, like a Hoover, is referred to by this brand-name, whatever the make.

As well as **dummies** or **lollipops, chupar** translates pursed-lipped **sucking** but **to suck under** or **to suck down** are conveyed by the reflexive **tragarse: se lo tragaron unas arenas movedizas – he was sucked under by quicksands.** This is not a risk run by the majority of us, although a Spanish-speaker will, in embarrassing moments, revert to **tragar** and intone ¡**tierra, trágame!** This consistently-ignored entreaty means **swallow me, ground!**

Chupar crops up again to describe **sucking/soaking: las berenjenas chupan mucha aceite al freírlas – aubergines soak**

up a lot of oil when they are fried. If the aubergines are particularly tasty, the Spanish might say **son para chuparse los dedos** – and they were saying it decades before morsels of fried chicken were proclaimed to be **finger-lickin' good**.

The past participle of **chupar** – **chupado** is a not-over-articulate adjective describing anything **easy to carry out or understand**, so **eso está chupado** implies **that's a piece of cake**. On the other hand, someone thin and hollow-faced who looks as though he or she hasn't had a square meal in weeks is described as **chupado/chupada**.

Un chupito now means a small, shot-sized drink while **una chupa** is a **leather bomber jacket/windcheater** and although the garment is acceptable enough, the strait-laced regard the term as too racy and prefer **cazadora**. Infinitely more respectable is **un chupatintas,** literally **an ink-sucker** but equivalent to a **penpusher,** an enduring term that these days also applies to someone who picks away at a computer keyboard.

No me chupo el dedo is a figure of speech with the superficial meaning of **I don't suck my finger** which implies: **you can't fool me**. Of course, a classic way to flatter or to please is **to suck up to** someone, as expedient in Span as elsewhere and known as **hacer la pelota**, literally **to make like a ball**. Another way of making yourself indispensable or popular is to **dar coba,** implying **to soft soap** although **coba** actually means **an amusing fib, flattery**, which shows just how much sincerity to expect when being **sucked-up to**.

The **sucker** that helps a squid get around is **una ventosa**, not to be confused with **una ventosidad** which is produced on breaking wind. The uncultivated **sucker** or **off-shoot** of a cultivated plant is **un borde** which in turn has become slang for **a person who takes liberties**.

That ingenuous individual, **a sucker** who is easily taken in, is **un primo – a cousin**; alternatively there is the less scornful, more indulgent **bobo** or the patronising **tonto – silly**. There is also another type of person who, far from being ingenuous, is **a grasper**, and the Spanish have just the right way of putting this because they call him or her **un chupón** or **una chupona – someone who sucks a lot**. Enough said.

NAME-DROPPING

Despite the seductive and near-to-hand translation of **number**, the noun **nombre** means **name: el nombre de mi tío es Federico – my uncle's name is Frederick**. Names have different names in Spanish, so a **Christian name** is **nombre de pila**, literally name **given at the** (baptismal) **font**. The **full name** you put on a dotted line can be translated as **nombre completo** but a Spanish form will probably ask for **nombre y apellidos – name and surnames** or possibly **datos personales**. Every Spanish person possesses two surnames, the first of which is the father's and the second the mother's. The law has now been changed so that the mother's surname can come first – but only if both she and the father are in agreement over this.

The noble and the would-be noble like to link their surnames with **y – and: Arturo Giménez y Gómez**. The aristocratic are also fond of making references to earlier alliances, giving rise to Uncle Tom Cobley situations: **Arturo Giménez de García-Pérez y Jiménez de la Tira**.

In a society where females did not enjoy a noticeable amount of civic privilege, a Spanish woman was not only allowed, but expected, to retain her **maiden name – nombre de soltera**. Arturo's wife continues to regard herself as **Genoveva Pérez** although she might give her name as **Genoveva Pérez de Giménez** and should her photograph appear in the society pages, the caption would read **Señora de Giménez (don Arturo)**.

When wanting to know a person's name you ask **¿cómo te llamas?** literally **how do you call yourself?** and Arturo would answer **me llamo Arturo – I call myself Arturo**. In contrast, if someone calls Arturo on the telephone and asks to talk to **Sr. Giménez** his secretary will ask **¿de parte de quién?** rather than **who's calling?**

Nombrar means **to name** although this is less suitable for labelling infants, so it is more Spanish to translate **they are going to name their son José as a su hijo le van a llamar José**. An alternative involves the verb **poner: a su hijo le van a poner de nombre José** but you do find **nombrar** in situations like **a Arturo le van a nombrar ministro – Arturo is going to**

be appointed minister. His **appointment** would be translated as **nombramiento** but **an appointment** with a hairdresser or doctor is **una cita**.

As in English, **nombre** also implies **reputation: Arturo tiene buen nombre como abogado** – **Arturo has a good name/reputation as a lawyer.** The past participle **nombrado** when used as an adjective is a predictable **named: Arturo no quería ser nombrado como implicado en el proceso** – **Arturo didn't want to be named as being involved in the case.** In other circumstances and with or without the suffix **re-,** it becomes **renowned: Arturo es un nombrado** (or **renombrado**) **abogado** – **Arturo is a renowned lawyer.**

Sin nombre and **nameless** can be translated superficially as **nameless** but both possess the further definition of **unspeakable: había cometido crimenes sin nombre** – **he had committed unspeakable crimes** as well as **no tiene nombre lo que ha hecho** – **what he has done is unspeakable.**

A Spanish **nickname** is **un apodo** or **un mote,** while a **name day** or **saint's day** – which may or may not coincide with a birthday – is **la onomástica. Un tocayo** is **a namesake** and **Arturo** takes pleasure in announcing **soy tocayo tuyo** when meeting other Arthurs. Some terms bear more resemblance to English and can be translated almost word-for-word: **a marriage in name only** is **un matrimonio sólo de nombre** while **open up in the name of the law!** would be **¡abra en nombre de la ley!**

Once in a while you can give in to temptation and translate **nombrar** as **to number** although it continues to involve names, not numbers: **siempre te nombraré entre mis amigos, y cuando sea ministro, también** – **I'll always number you among my friends, and when I'm a minister, too.**

A certain type of Spanish person is as addicted to **name-dropping** as a certain type of English-speaker but the only translation for this social affliction is the long-winded **siempre estar dejando caer los nombres de gente importante**. My dictionary comes up with an appalling suggestion: **una persona dada al name-dropping** – just the kind of unspeakable linguistic crime that should remain nameless.

HALLO AND GOODBYE

English-speakers are aware of their international reputation for saying **please** and **thank you** too often and too meaninglessly, but the Spanish are similarly heavy-handed with greetings. What is more they are ambiguous about them, too.

If I meet someone I know in the street and we are in a hurry, or not in the mood to chat, we'll probably nod pleasantly, murmur **adiós** in unison and continue on our way. But it's illogical to say goodbye to someone you've not yet greeted, especially as I could complicate matters still further by saying **hola** while my acquaintance calls out **adiós**.

An alternative to **adiós** is **hasta luego – until later**, implying subsequent meeting to be held some time in the future. There is also **¿qué tal?** which amounts to saying **how's things?** There are occasions when we would enjoy explaining at considerable length just how things are, enumerating woes, cataloguing joys and trotting out a complaint or two. However, anyone enquiring **¿qué tal?** does not expect a detailed reply and the correct response is **muy bien, gracias ¿y usted? – very well, thanks – and you?** This gives others the chance to wedge a toe in the conversational door by enumerating woes, cataloguing joys and trotting out the odd complaint.

¿Qué hay? is tricky. It means **what is there?** but implies **what's new?** You won't get out of this one with **muy bien, gracias ¿y usted?** because it doesn't make sense and the best you can do is cover every option by simultaneously smiling, shaking your head and nodding.

The Spanish claim to be irritated by our abuse and over-use of **please** and **thank you** but I can't be the only person who has had a tentative **por favor** shot down in flames with a stern **SIN favor**. It is no doubt meant with kindness and is obsequious in its own way, but I am not grateful for being exempted from saying **please** and **thank you**.

On the other hand, a Spanish person would be mortified not to make a proper greeting. This practice is less widespread in tourist-dominated areas, but on entering any non-self service shop, office or waiting room in Madrid, Murcia or Medina del Campo good manners require you to look round

Dog walkers greeted those who crossed their paths
with buenas noches

the assembled company and verbally embrace them with a collective **buenos días, buenas tardes** or **buenas noches** as the case may be. Some will answer, some will only nod but no-one will ignore you. It doesn't matter terribly if you say nothing at all, but greetings are appreciated and, naturally, you should also make your farewells.

This also applies to entering and leaving lifts where reserved, uncommunicative English-speakers can earn themselves a reputation for surliness. Sometimes the ritual appears to be too much effort even for the Spanish and they limit themselves to a truncated **buenas...** on entering and another **buenas...** on exiting.

Before everybody had cars, televisions, videos and computers, pavements weren't as deserted late at night as they are now. People out on the town, dog-walkers and men returning from a game of dominoes or cards at their local bar or **el casino** when this was still basically a men's – gentlemen's – club, greeted those who crossed their paths whether they knew them or not with **buenas noches** or simply **adiós.** Some dog-walkers continue to observe the niceties but the most you can expect from a dog-less pedestrian is a sideways glance and a hastening of the step.

Notwithstanding a growing lack of faith in the outcome of late-night encounters, the Spanish continue to regard greetings and leave-takings as an important aspect of social intercourse. Consequently, there are days when I seem to say **buenos días, buenas tardes** and **buenas noches** all day and all night long to people I have never seen before and may never see again. What's more, if we both choose to say **adiós** I can't make up my mind whether I'm coming or going, either.

For a free catalogue
of all our books on Spain
contact:

Santana Books,
Apartado 422,
29640 Fuengirola (Málaga).
Tel: 952 485 838.
Fax: 952 485 367.
E-mail: sales@santanabooks.com
www.santanabooks.com

UK Representatives,
Aldington Books Ltd.,
Unit 3(b) Frith Business Centre,
Frith Road, Aldington,
Ashford,Kent TN25 7HJ.
Tel: 01233 720 123.
Fax: 01233 721 272
E-mail: sales@aldingtonbooks.co.uk
www.aldingtonbooks.co.uk